IL DUCE'S EXPLORER

THE ADVENTURES OF GIUSEPPE TUCCI AND ITALIAN POLICY IN THE ORIENT FROM MUSSOLINI TO ANDREOTTI

WITH THE CORRESPONDENCE OF GIULIO ANDREOTTI

ENRICA GARZILLI

TRANSLATED BY
TODD PORTNOWITZ

VOLUME 1

ASIATICA ASSOCIATION

Typesetting by Ludovico Magnocavallo.
Cover images from *L'Illustrazione italiana*.

Asiatica Association, via Vincenzo Bellini, 4 - 20122 Milano

First edition: November 20, 2015

19 18 17 16 15   5 4 3 2 1

ISBN 978-88-900226-8-5

Enrica Garzilli's compelling biography of Giuseppe Tucci reconstructs the life of Fascism in Asia and of a preeminent explorer-scholar who traveled widely in India, Tibet, Nepal, Afghanistan, Japan, Pakistan and Iran. Few scholars today have Garzilli's enormous breadth to weave together Tucci's contributions in history, linguistics, archeology, philosophy and anthropology under Fascist Italy and the Italian Republic.

—Paul Arpaia, Indiana University of Pennsylvania

The first book dedicated to one of the most important and mysterious men of Italian culture. Explorer, archaeologist, scholar, spy: Giuseppe Tucci is "x-rayed" by this strictly scientific work that reads like an adventure novel.

—Guglielmo Duccoli, Director of "L'Illustrazione Italiana"

Giuseppe Tucci has long been known as a foundational figure in the European discovery of India and Tibet as well as founder of IsMEO. This exhaustive new biographical study tells us much more about the academic side of his achievements, but also about his little-known collaborations with Mussolini and his sponsorship of Indian luminaries' visits to Fascist Italy. It will be indispensable for anyone seeking a complete understanding of Orientalist enterprises in the early twentieth century.

—Sumit Guha, The University of Texas at Austin

As Italy takes up arms and Mussolini sets his eye on supplanting the British Crown – a fact elegantly and rigorously uncovered by Garzilli in these pages – Giuseppe Tucci manages to maneuver his way through the treacherous landscapes of the Himalayas and of Fascist politics to emerge as the country's foremost scholar and archaeologist of the Orient. His achievement is monumental, and Garzilli's monumental biography brings him joyously to life, through archival documents, personal letters, travelogues, lectures, interviews, articles, photographs, films, and her own tireless travels. Here is a hunt in search of a hunter.

—Michael Witzel, Harvard University

[...] because many are called, but few are chosen.

I know your works, that you are neither cold nor hot. I wish you were cold or hot. So, because you are lukewarm, and neither hot nor cold, I will vomit you out of my mouth.

Revelation 3:15–16

Figure 1: Giuseppe Tucci in Gu-ge, sPu-rang-rdzong (Taklakot), July 3, 1935.
Photo Eugenio Ghersi, courtesy of Arte Nomade

SERIES VOLUMES

CONTENTS OF VOLUME 1

INDEX OF MAPS IN VOLUME 1

INDEX OF FIGURES IN VOLUME 1

PREFACE TO THE ENGLISH EDITION

When the capital of Tibet was still the mythical, "Forbidden City", a destination for the most daring explorers, when Nepal was covered with forests and swamps, swarming with dangerous beasts and cut off to foreigners, when Italy was ruled by the Fascist regime greedily eyeing potential colonial possessions in Asia, a learned and adventurous man – a perfect embodiment of the era's virile ideals – entered a land, alone, where no Western man had before set foot: crossing glittering, snow-capped peaks, desolate deserts and the ruins of ancient cities, constantly pushing himself to his limits, he discovered archaeological treasures from past civilizations. Even today, in the East as well as in the West, the name of this intrepid Italian explorer and insatiable researcher is cloaked in an aura of legend.

One could hardly imagine a richer and more exciting life than that of Giuseppe Tucci (1894–1984), a scholar who may rightly be considered one of the fathers of modern Oriental Studies and the central protagonist of Fascist cultural policy in Asia: from his first expeditions to the valleys of the Himalayas and the plains of the Ganges, to his diplomatic activity in Japan as Il Duce's spokesman; from his encounters with scholars and leaders such as Gandhi, Tagore, the Dalai Lama, Mircea Eliade and Giovanni Gentile – his great protector, along with Giulio Andreotti – to the archaeological excavations in Pakistan, Afghanistan and Iran in his later years, his is a human and intellectual adventure tied inextricably to the history of modern Italy, which Tucci himself helped to forge. An adventure that can now be retraced in the pages of this book, where the pace of a thrilling narrative combines with the scientific rigor of reconstructing the history of

Fascist policy in Asia and of Tucci's precious creation, the powerful Italian Institute for the Middle and Far East. A history based
on eyewitness accounts and historical documents, including the
original and unedited correspondence of Tucci and Andreotti,
and the unpublished notes of Mussolini.

This volume is the first in a series of nine, which together represent a translation of the two-volume Italian book, *L'esploratore
del Duce: le avventure di Giuseppe Tucci e la politica italiana in Oriente
da Mussolini a Andreotti. Con la corrispondenza di Giulio Andreotti*
(1st ed. not for distribution, Milano: Asiatica Association, Roma:
Memori, January 29, 2012; 2nd rev. ed., Milano: Asiatica Association, Roma: Memori, August 13, 2012; 3rd rev. ed. Milano: Asiatica
Association, April 14, 2014).

The decision to publish the book in a series of nine, shorter
volumes was made for two principal reasons. The first, to get the
book in readers' hands in a timely fashion, by releasing volumes
of reduced pages at regular intervals. Between translation and
editing, to have produced the entire book at once – which stands
at 1,493 pages – would have required four years of work. The
second reason, and the most important, is to meet the reader half
way in regard to price: the cost of the entire volume in English
would be substantial, while acquiring briefer volumes over time is
far more feasible. In the table of contents, found in the previous
pages, readers may survey the various topics treated in the nine
volumes.

Readers can also follow the adventures of Tucci and of Italian
policy in the Orient during the twenty years of Fascism by visiting
the blog *Il Duce's Explorer: The Adventures of Giuseppe Tucci*[1] and its
corresponding Facebook page.

Enrica Garzilli
Milano, November 1, 2015

INTRODUCTION

The idea of writing a history of Giuseppe Tucci (1894–1984) developed initially from an exchange of Sanskrit letters between Tucci and the pandit, Hem Raj Sharma (1879–1953), the Royal Preceptor of Nepal, which I first came across in late 1998, early 1999. Tucci was an explorer in the Himalayan countries during the Fascist regime and the golden years of Christian Democracy, when foreigners were still barred entrance into those lands. He spoke and read in numerous languages, ancient and modern, and was a voracious scholar and insatiable collector of books, manuscripts, art works and archeological artifacts, whether Buddhist, Hindu, or Bon, from the vast regions of central, southern, and eastern Asia, from Iran to Japan. He served as professor of Chinese Language and Literature at the University of Naples "L'Orientale" – known at the time as the University Institute of Oriental Studies of Naples - and, subsequently, as professor of Philosophies and Religions of India at the University of Rome, and academician at the Royal Academy of Italy. He would promote, as well, the foundation of the Italian Institute for the Middle and Far East (Istituto Italiano per il Medio ed Estremo Oriente - IsMEO), of which he served as president from 1947 to 1978. In the late 1930's, Tucci stood at the fore of Mussolini's political propaganda in Asia, his persistent cultural interactions often flanking, and at times preceding, official diplomacy. He founded the National Museum of Oriental Art and, in the 1950s, organized Italy's first archeological expeditions in Asia. When he traveled to Nepal, he was the first Italian to do so since eighteenth century missionaries, eventually leading five expeditions there; another eight, he would carry out in Tibet.

To address the life of Tucci is to address, by consequence, the lives of the countless others with whom he crossed paths. Hem Raj, to start, whom in 1957 the great Buddhologist and Indologist Rahul Sankrityayan referred to as «the encyclopedia of Nepal». His immense library – the largest private library of central and southern Asia – his teachings, his advice, and his political mediation proved an indispensable aid to Tucci, as well as to many other leading scholars. Then, of course, there are Giovanni Gentile and Giulio Andreotti; along with Carlo Formichi, his professor of Sanskrit and a guiding presence in his life; Nobel laureate, Rabindranath Tagore; Sylvain Lévi, William F. Thomas, Rahul Sankrityayan and Vishnu Sukthankar, to name only a few – all of whom responsible for forging the Orientalist culture of the first half of the twentieth century.

Carlo Formichi, Giovanni Gentile, and Giulio Andreotti stood as the three, key figures in Tucci's life, without whom he would not have reached the heights of his achievement. For which reason, I have interspersed a biographical sketch of Formichi within the text, illustrating his profound effect on Tucci's studies, his ideals, and his deep love of India. I've also incorporated (and dated) the correspondence of Tucci and Gentile, who supported him in full and often served as liaison between him and Il Duce, and have reconstructed the political outlook of the Fascist regime, as well as Tucci's role in the political culture of the period. With the Fascist era come to a close, Tucci persisted in his accomplishments, even broadening his efforts, thanks to his scientific foresight and his finesse in dealing with figures of power – together with the support of one, exceptional political personage: senator Andreotti. He kindly provided me with his and Tucci's correspondence; and a chapter of this biography has been dedicated to introducing and explaining their letters.

This history, without the many characters who colored Tucci's life, who believed in him, who aided him in every way and stood behind his initiatives, would be a deficient history. To understand his life, one must understand the lives of the important figures who fostered and supported him, such as the Chancellor of the Chamber of Deputies and his father-in-law, Luigi Nuvoloni, Nobel laureate Rabindranath Tagore, and the Nepalese general, Kaiser Shamsher Rana. So too would it be incomplete without addressing his many remarkable relationships, some of which would last for decades, such as those with Gandhi, the 14th Dalai Lama, Tenzin Gyatso, Pandit Nehru, Indira Gandhi, Fosco Maraini, Subhas Chandra Bose, Aldo Capitini, Surendra Nath Dasgupta, Mircea Eliade, Julius Evola, Karl Haushofer, Prassitele Piccinini, Pio Filippani-Ronconi and others, all figures who played a notable role in the cultural debate of the age and, in many cases, acted as key religious and political protagonists. I'll speak also of well-known intellectuals, Sibilla Aleramo, Mario Carelli, Alexandra David Néel, Dilli R. Regmi, Rishikesh Shaha and others, such as the Sherpa, Tenzing – they, too, important in the unfolding of Tucci's life. And, still more, I'll speak of his wives. Among them, his last wife in particular, the most beloved, Francesca Bonardi, who was there with him through so many of his voyages and who stood tenderly, steadfastly at his side in his final days.

Through Tucci's efforts, the world has come to know with greater depth the most widely-practiced religions in Asia; with his critical editions, his original translations of invaluable texts in Sanskrit and Tibetan, and his historical depiction of dynasties and principalities, Tucci stands as a pioneer in the scientific study of the Himalayan countries. With his legendary explorations in Tibet, Nepal, Ladakh, and Sikkim, he paved the way for future geographers and travelers. And as a result of the archeological expeditions and conservation and restoration efforts he initiated and promoted in Iran, Pakistan, and Afghanistan, Italy has become a central player in the international endeavor to discover, restore and preserve ancient civilizations.

Following in the footsteps of Formichi, Tucci breathed new life into the age-old methods of studying Asian languages. By working in the field, he gained a first-hand understanding of the cultures surrounding and informing those languages, employing his formidable knowledge of Sanskrit, Tibetan, Chinese, Pāli, and several other Oriental languages, such as Hebrew, Bangla, Nepali, Urdu, Iranian, Pashto, Mongolian, and still others, to better comprehend ancient civilizations. By intersecting various disciplines, including philology, history, archeology, anthropology, epigraphy, toponymy, etc., Tucci enriched our vast heritage of human knowledge. To this day, the large majority of his works have maintained their scientific validity, and several remain essential tools for aspiring scholars of Tibetology, Indology, Sinology, and the history of the Himalayan countries.

His was a labor of discovery, of recovering and preserving ancient art works and rare manuscripts now housed in Rome at the National Museum of Oriental Art, and, until January 2012 when the institute was closed, the Tucci Collection in the Oriental library of the Italian Institute for Africa and the Orient (IsIAO, ex-IsMEO), safe from ruin in the merciless Asian climate, from worms and rats, from fire, or worse, from men: as a result of China's invasion of Tibet, and also due to the negligence or to the greed of merchants, an enormous patrimony was lost. His expeditions into the hitherto inaccessible territories of the Himalayan region marked, for those countries, the definitive entry of their cultural and environmental heritage into the course of human history and the history of modern exploration, and not only for those directly involved with the effort.

An awareness of Tucci's importance in twentieth century culture, the weight he carried in the political balance of the epoch, the sheer intrigue of his adventurous life, as well as an interest in Hem Raj – known only to very few scholars of the last century, despite his fundamental importance in the discovery, restoration, and preservation of many ancient and precious Buddhist and Hindu texts – and, more generally, in an entire epoch scarred by totalitarianism in Europe and Asia were what drove me to my research, to write of this momentous scholar from Macerata, of his age and its protagonists. Some of whom have only just departed, and already have taken their place in legend and in history.

In fact, Tucci's life and work would be incomprehensible without taking into account some of the major events of his time – the rise and fall of authoritarian and totalitarian regimes in Europe, the revolutions in China and Nepal, the liberation of India, the invasion of Tibet, the Second World War and the Anni di Piombo (Years of Lead) in Italy – all of which had a profound influence on his work. The Asian and European dictatorships served both as backdrop and financial backing for the voyages and cultural studies of many of the scholars discussed in this book: particularly in the cases of Professor Formichi, Giuseppe Tucci, his prized student, and their acknowledged teacher, Hem Raj.

Tucci was a scholar of broad and prolific scientific production. Along with Marco Polo, Matteo Ricci, Benito Mussolini and only a handful of others, he stood throughout Fascism and the golden age of Christian Democracy as the most renowned Italian in Asia. And he remains so to this day. In recent years, an aging pandit could still recall his lectures in fluent Sanskrit and the poets who came from every corner of the country to pay him homage, composing verses for him in a myriad of Asian languages. As the foremost Italian scholar on Asia for more than sixty years, it is essential that we understand his life in greater detail.

Despite his importance, no book has yet been published on his life, on his discoveries, on his brilliant insights, his relationships with the most noted cultural and political personalities in the world, responsible for drafting not only the history of Oriental studies in the age of Fascist Italy, but the history of international relations between Europe and Asia and, tangentially, their diplomatic history. As a scientist, Tucci did not limit his scope to studies and explorations, but turned his efforts also to strengthening Italy's relations with India, Nepal, Tibet, Pakistan, Iran, Afghanistan, Japan, and lastly, with China, operating first in service of the Fascist regime, and subsequently under the democratic government. In October 1936, Tucci was sent for some six months by Mussolini to the Land of the Rising Sun to spread propaganda, to forge cultural bonds and strengthen and broaden diplomatic relations, paving the way for Italy's inclusion in the Anti-Comintern Pact (November 6, 1937). He possessed one special talent in particular: that of adjusting his own behavior to the register of those he encountered, of humbling himself, if in his best interest, without relinquishing his authority: an extremely useful quality when it came to convincing others, to obtaining concessions and achieving ends. Like an expert politician or the best of professional diplomats, he knew his interlocutors in an instant, their nature, the precepts they were operating under. In virtue of such a talent, Tucci was able not merely to observe the events and realities of the country around him, all but unknown to the world at the time, but to see immediately through to their dynamics and internal conflicts. From 1925 until he began to organize archeological digs, Tucci placed this talent in the service of Italian politics. In the words of Romano Mastromattei – the son of Tucci's friend, Giuseppe, the prefect of Bolzano – not only was he a prodigious intellectual, he was a true man of power.

This book, therefore, is the first written on this subject, on his relation to Fascism and the policy of Mussolini in India and the Himalayan regions. The brief and sparse writings in his honor that have thus far appeared have been aimed at celebrating his prestigious career and works, with nothing to say of his life, his scientific missions, his surroundings, his loves, his virtues and his vices. Nevertheless, even if commemorative publications do often limit themselves to the usual crop of scientific studies in line with the celebrated theme – apart from the teacher's incomplete bibliography, a brief biographical note, mentions of colleagues and the occasional student – of those that have appeared in Tucci's honor nearly all strive instead to express something more intimate, to remark on certain aspects of his vigorous and multiform personality. In the minds of all those he met, Tucci left an indelible, almost searing, memory.

I have tried, here, to present the man in all his various aspects, both public and private. Those who knew him either hated him viscerally or loved him to the point of veneration, creating almost a cult of personality, an aura of respect and devotion that still hovers about his name. I have attempted to reveal him through facts, documents and information verified by multiple sources, and to refrain from judging by preconceived opinions. If in confronting a historical event – and even more so the history of a man one has known – impartiality is a chimera, I have nonetheless used primary sources without any discriminating ideologies or methodologies. In all cases, I have strived – presenting stories and testimonies, providing information on the habits, customs, and beliefs of the places he visited, drawing on my memories and my impressions – to capture the man. Sources serve only as an underlying support, the warp and weft of a far more complex fabric, bearing a more comprehensive image that may be seen only from a certain, measured distance: the true face of the man. The face I've sought to discover and portray.

Above all, I have been drawn to Tucci's history because he was the teacher of my first teachers, my *paramaguru*, the most glowing figure in my department at the Sapienza University of Rome, and he has influenced the entire course of my adult life; to understand him, I was forced to maintain a certain detachment. It is no simple task, to comprehend the mentality and ethics of a man born at the end of the nineteenth century, who made his career in the era of Fascism: how much simpler it would have been to sing his praises, as do most in Italy, knowing nothing of his history, or to condemn him, as do most scholars across the Atlantic; how much tidier to gloss, to ideologize a life as rich and complex as his.

In weaving together the history of Tucci and his circle, I have hoped to broaden our understanding of the relationship between Fascism and the Orient – Nepal, ruled by a dictatorship; India, under a colonial regime; Japan, governed by an emperor bent on imperialism – to bring forth an entirely new thesis, examining Mussolini's true political vision in regard to Asia, a vision that stretched far beyond his "deep-rooted" interest in India, as De Felice discussed in his brilliant essay, «L'india nella strategia politica di Mussolini» («India in Mussolini's Political Strategy») (echoing, in a certain sense, the historian, Renouvin, and his concept of the "deep-seated forces" that sway the history of international relations).[1]

To arrive at my thesis, I have gathered, chosen, presented, interpreted, and weighed each fact and source carefully, considering all in light of my scientific knowledge and integrity.

With the following statement, Formichi opened his conference, *Nepal*, held at the Augusteo in Rome on February 26, 1934, year XII of the Fasicist Era:

> A trip to Nepal is among the most fascinating experiences, a flood of new and varied impressions, rich with invaluable scientific findings.
>
> Forbidden fruit is always the most attractive, the most desired. Nepal is a forbidden fruit, closed off to foreigners by its government and only the occasional person of high regard is allowed entry, and only if that person can prove that the elevated purpose of study, and nothing else, has driven him to request the gracious permission of His Highness the Mahârâja.[2]

Both Tucci and Formichi had access to this «forbidden fruit», and both corresponded in Sanskrit with Hem Raj. Mediating on their behalf with the current despot, Prime Minister Rana, the pandit facilitated their entrance into Nepal, allowing them to remain there for the «elevated purpose of study». The two were among only a handful of Europeans permitted entry: the English, for example, kept a resident in Katmandhu, though he was not granted access to the more remote regions of the country.

After a stay in India during the academic year 1925–1926 with Formichi, Tucci began his travels, from 1926 onward, through the Himalayan regions, obtaining the priceless manuscripts that now, as a result of his efforts, have left Italy with one of the largest collections in the world of rare Tibetan Buddhist texts. When Tibet was invaded by China, he limited his expeditions exclusively to Nepal, which, owing to its long political and geographical isolation – a «desired» isolation, as Tucci would write, for «no one, certainly, can claim that the Nepalese authorities have been generous with granting permits to foreigners»[3] – remained a precious cultural depository, preserving a way of life almost unchanged after hundreds of years.

The four Sanskrit letters written by Tucci to Hem Raj, the court's high pandit – all original, previously undiscovered letters, translated and published here for the first time – serve as the framework of this book. To them, I have added numerous other letters, all previously unknown – a list of which may be found in the bibliography – of Tucci and other central figures, including a letter in Sanskrit from Formichi, and another in Nepali from Kesar Bahadur K. C. to Hem Raj, as well as Tucci's correspondence with Gentile, which stretches from his first years at university until 1944, and his private correspondence with Andreotti, dating from 1947 to 1984. Among the letters published here, one might add the two Nepali diaries of Hem Raj, which read like letters to himself, and which he kept throughout his adult life: the first, replete with detail, he kept almost daily in small black books, from 1906 to 1953; the second is a neatly unified diary-biography, with just two pages in Nepali and a few brief paragraphs in Sanskrit (to evade certain readers) drafted January 1, 1909 on a small notepad. One might also add the letters held in the Central Archives of the State and the Historic-Diplomatic Archives of the Ministry of Foreign Affairs, as well as in the other institutes and foundations listed in the bibliography, including those in India and Nepal. Of all these documents, the letters held by the State Archives are public; Tucci's correspondence with Gentile, as well as with other members of institutions and foundations, is also public, though viewed with limited access; all the rest is private.

The letters, however, represent only one part of the material collected here. The official and unofficial documents that situate them in time, or in other words, that answer the five, fateful, American Ws – who, what, when, where, why was the document, letter, bulletin, book written, or deed done, or statement published, or article printed (to which I'd add *cui prodest*, that is, who will gain from it, whom will it harm, and to which historical, geographical context does it pertain) – this, too, was part of the work that went into this book. A person can be described, in my view, his actions evaluated, only against the backdrop of the age in which he lives. No human occurrence can be judged in isolation, removed from the external events, whether public or private, that mold and modify all those who partake in it.

In order to understand these letters and the culture of the Orient in Italy, one must take several factors into account: Tucci's work, first of all, carried out in a time when the fate of scientists was in the hands of Fascism, and without whose support he could not have financed his extensive explorations through unforgiving territory, which demanded not only large quantities of money, but also equipment, men, and animals; the diffusion of Eastern culture and Fascist propaganda via IsMEO, promoted and planned by Tucci and founded in 1933 by Giovanni Gentile;

and the archeological missions he spearheaded in the 1950s, during the golden age of Christian Democracy, without considering these elements, one can not hope to understand this expert Tibetologist, among the greatest of all history, and one of the most important intellectuals Italy has produced.

In order to understand Tucci's work, one must not lose sight of the dictatorship and its official and unofficial political stance toward the East Indies, the British colonies in Southern Asia – the political stance not only of the regime, but of Benito Mussolini himself, and of his closest men. As we shall see, Mussolini's position regarding India differed from the official position of his government. Nor can one overlook the political policies of Great Britain in India and throughout the rest of Asia.

To this end, I have consulted several thousand documents at the National Archives, at the Kesar Library and Bir Library (now the Nepal National Library) of Kathmandu, at the Public Record Office, and at the Oriental and India Office Library of London (now The National Archives and British Library). I was able to thoroughly consult the documents contained in the 576 microfiche at Harvard University's Lamont Library, originally held at the India Office, containing formerly classified information of the British secret service on international travelers in India, China, and Tibet, and visa requests for entering into territories controlled by the British Crown. Among the names of travelers: Giuseppe Tucci.

I consulted many thousands of documents regarding Mussolini and his Cabinet, the Ministry of Popular Culture, among other ministries, documents regarding Tucci, Formichi, IsMEO, and the periods leading up to and immediately following the war in the Library of the Central Archive of the State, and numerous documents on Italy up until and after World War II in the Historical-Diplomatic Archives of the Ministry of Foreign Affairs, in Farnesina Square in Rome. Another large source of documents

I had the fortune of consulting, again in the Central Archives of the State, came in the form of several hefty, cardboard boxes. During the occupation of Italy, American Allied troops had transported the documents back to the United States, where they were to be examined and placed on microfilm by the Joint Allied Research Agency, established between July and August, 1945. They were then returned to Italy in the very cardboard boxes I found them in, not yet catalogued, not yet archived, not even opened. I was permitted to view them, though not to make photocopies, in a separate room thanks only to the good sense and kindness of one of the employees there, whose name it's best not to mention, though to whom I still owe my infinite gratitude. In them, I found several large folders of the Ministry of Foreign Affairs containing the envelopes and relative files, all unopened, untouched, caked in dust. As the first to confront the files, not knowing what even to ask the nonetheless efficient librarians and archivists, my research proved difficult. I didn't know where to look and where to begin – and neither did they.

After two days spent blindly rifling through the boxes, I found part of what I was looking for among the documents relative to the Himalayan regions in an enormous folder marked, Political Affairs: Great Britain (until 1931), in several files labeled «Colonies» and «Miscellaneous», and in various others among the folders in the Political Affairs Series (1931–45). The documents were either on tissue paper – yellow, pink, or sky blue, depending on the custom of the time and the type of document – or worse, on beautiful ivory paper, water-marked and bearing official headings, thick and rigid. The thought that many of the documents would be nothing but fragments after the photocopies I'd made, even taking the greatest care, left me feeling somewhat guilty: the remains, too old even to be touched, would soon be reduced to scraps and shreds. Many of the papers were bound with rust-eaten sewing pins – merely removing the pin, the pages flaked away. The cords binding the heavy folders had all snapped, or had been chewed through by mice. Even to use surgical gloves was out of the question, for many of the sheets were already falling apart, and handling them required a certain dexterity, if only to keep from destroying them completely. Even so, I did all I could to preserve the precious sheets and to respect, albeit reluctantly, the future scholars who might come after me.

Tucci, on the other hand, as we shall see, ceded to the temptation of forming his own private collection of some of the more important ancient manuscripts of Buddhist teachers, works of art, and archeological artifacts. An act that, without doubt, casts a shadow on his integrity as a man, though it does little to mar him as a scholar, and could even be said to bolster his reputation as a collector. And yet, in 1953, proving himself a master, as well, of contradiction, Tucci would write that,

> [...] there's nothing less scientific than jealousy hoarding one's discoveries for oneself.[4]

I've attempted to understand his reasoning from a defendant's point of view: in all likelihood, if left to the negligence of man or to the harsh climes of Asia, these very same artifacts would have been damaged; a reasoning which, in any case, stands as valid. Beyond that – as was quite justifiably suggested to me – in donating his collection to IsMEO and to other museums, his contributions have gone on to increase the wealth of the Italian State: though for years jealously guarded and mostly inaccessible to the public, his collection has become a national heritage. Which all goes to show, for as unethical of a topic as it may be, that the high reasoning of a scientist and the high reasoning of morality may not always stand in agreement. As was once said by a professor of mine – by no means a former student of Tucci's – the ethics of research is an ethics *sui generis*, belonging to a category of its own.

I consulted several other archives as well, including those at
the Gramsci Institute in Rome, at the Luce Institute (The Union
for Cinematographic Education), at the Ugo Spirito Foundation,
and several documents from and on Tagore, sent to me with great
care by an Indian friend from Śāntiniketan, in Western Bengal, as
well as others. In the bibliography found in the last volume, I've
included a list of all the letters, of the archives, of public and private collections consulted, of the essential bibliography of books,
articles, manuscripts, catalogues, and films – returning from his
expeditions, Tucci arrived with a mound of photographic material, both photographs and negatives, as well as extensive video
footage. I have included part of this material in each volume as
well. Though by no means does the book contain all the materials consulted, which now fill my (unusable) dining room, aptly
re-baptized the "Tucci room" – an entire bookcase and various
shelves and dresser drawers. I've also included Tucci's bibliography, excepting his occasional and purely journalistic articles,
which I've cited within the text and in the general bibliography,
if of interest to the reader. To his bibliography, however, I have
added a number of works not included in the most complete
bibliographies available before the publication of *L'Esploratore
del Duce. Le avventure di Giuseppe Tucci e la politica italiana in Oriente da Mussolini a Andreotti. Con il carteggio di Giulio Andreotti.*[5] A
brief chronology of Tucci's life has been included in each volume,
as well as geographical maps indicating the routes of his explorations and some of his journeys within India, made using an
original map of Asia, current until the end of the Britannic period
(1947). Most of the photos from Italy, India, United Kingdom, and
Nepal are my own, others have been taken from the journal, *L'illustrazione italiana [Italian Illustration]*, and still others were given
to me by Gilda, the only daughter of Tucci's only son, Ananda
Maria, by Giorgio Serafini Prosperi, the nephew of Tucci's second
wife, by the heirs of Tucci's Nepalese guru, Hem Raj Sharma, by
the Cultural Association "Giosuè Borsi", and by Arte Nomade. I've

also compiled a list of "Tucci's circle", a list of characters including over 1,350 names and persons that appear in the book, with essential and pertinent biographical information, which will be included in volume 9.

To better understand Tucci's correspondence in light of the historical and cultural context in which he lived, I consulted several unpublished documents relating to Hem Raj Sharma and his historical period. No one has yet written of him, with the exception of a few, scattered pages in Nepali and a biography that I myself published in a 2001 scientific article, and in later articles.[6] Those who've written on the tormented historical period in which he lived are few indeed. Even then, a large part of Nepal's historiography was and still is partisan, telling of this or that family, or of a particular ethnic or political group, or of a certain well-known figure. And so, to resolve the hazy image – for even in Italy, up until my article, there were no documents or historical studies available on Nepal – I spent several months traveling there between 1999–2001, in 2003, and in 2006, in order to consult the many documents held in the private libraries of renowned families like that of Hem Raj, or in the Bir Library, the Kesar Library, the National Archives, or, otherwise, in the library of the Nepal-German Manuscript Preservation Project (which in 2002 gave rise to the Nepalese-German Manuscript Cataloguing Project). And Nepal, particularly in past years, was one of the most difficult places to travel in the world – the sense of uncertainty, of anxiety among its people was palpable, and in April 2006 their discontent rose to a boiling point, giving way to the *Jana andolan II*, the second revolution.

Like Tucci, Hem Raj too lived under a dictatorship, which in Nepal was led by the Rana family. Observing the principle that ignorance breeds slavery, no one, by the penalty of death – that is, no one beyond the four or five families most loyal to the regime – was permitted to have books in his possession, especially those in a foreign tongue. Nor could he read them in libraries. Kublaya Raj Pandit, to whom Hem Raj was next-in-line, and Royal Preceptor from 1895 until 1910, was exiled until death in India for having read, in secret, the English books of the Prime Minister – field marshal, Chandra Shamsher Jang Bahadur Rana, who ruled from 1901 to 1929.

And yet, in his enormous house in the center of Kathmandu, known as Bhāratī Bhavan, the «culture house», Hem Raj possessed over 25,411 titles, more than 10,000 of which were manuscripts: most assuredly, the largest private collection of books and manuscripts in southern Asia up until and through the dissolution of the Nepalese dictatorship in 1951. At Hem Raj's death, it was purchased by the government and transferred to the Singh Durbar library. Shortly thereafter, his texts were combined with the comparably vast collection – equal in number of volumes and containing several hundred manuscripts – of Kaiser Shamsher Rana, a friend of Tucci's, and thus was founded the Nepal Rastriya Pustakalaya, or the «National Library of Nepal». Hem Raj had in his service several pandits, and with their aid was able to copy a significant number of manuscripts and to print, or reprint, several rare books using the letterpress he'd set up on the first floor of his home. Essentially, he'd founded a small publishing house.

And so I've asked myself: who was he, this great scholar who may be seen as the other pole of traditional culture in Asia? Who was this man Tucci called his teacher, with whom he sat down to read esoteric texts of immense difficulty, to whom he turned requesting manuscripts, suggestions, opinions, and help? To discover him, given that no history book or Indology book mentioned his name, I consulted official documents, photographs, portraits, the personal papers of Hem Raj's family, stamps bearing his effigy, the letter of his teacher from Benares, his correspondence with other scholars, memories of his voyages in Asia, and, above all, his writings.

Unfortunately, I came to discover, after his death in 1953, when his family sold his collection to the new government in the mid–1970s, they'd also cleared out the enormous room that had served as his library, setting flames to it all in a massive bonfire that many still recall – his correspondence, documents, invitations, announcements, statements, notes, and the many precious papers from Hem Raj's duties as preceptor of the king, of the prime minister, and of all Nepal, as court astrologer at the head of all astrologers in the country, as minister of education, as a judge of the high court, and as councilor of the prime minister. If preserved, these papers would have served as an optimal source by which to reconstruct the events and environment of his time and to increase the accuracy of Nepal's historiography.

Nevertheless, with the written and oral documents I was able to gather, the figure of Hem Raj came into focus – so distinct, so uncompromising, so noble and brilliant, whether donning official, religious or administrative robes, or as a scholar, as a bibliophile, as a man.

While Tucci, a follower of Buddhism, in some ways embraced the "Fascist religion," principally to further his own goals – in a sense, allowing the regime to serve him – Hem Raj was a fervid proponent of Hinduism and faithfully served the Nepalese regime. To his religion, which upheld the caste system and a political and social hierarchy as both an integral part of itself and as the *status quo* in society, Hem Raj felt an intimate bond, from which derived his intense loyalty. Tucci, in the south of Europe, and Hem Raj, in the south of Asia, stood as the foremost representatives and promoters of twentieth century culture. The former wrote prolifically, while of the latter we possess only a few, sparse pages: nonetheless, it would be his grammar to codify the standard Nepali language and to make official its entrance among the literary languages of the world.

Before time swept away the living testimony and, at least in Asia, the documents accompanying it, I thought it of essential importance to collect this data and fix it to the page in a comprehensive study, to see more deeply into the personalities of these two men. Each contributed generously to the culture of his own country, leaving behind priceless treasures and legacies: Hem Raj, from the time he was a boy, gave his money to Motiram Bhatta, the greatest poet in Nepali language, to ensure he'd have food without having to sell his books. I have sought to understand the circumstances that led them to consult with one another and to work, albeit in two different directions – one toward the West, one toward the East – on the same subject and with the same passion: a love for the past, a love for the distant. I have attempted to reconstruct the events, beyond their devotion to culture, that in the same historical period brought them each to accumulate such vast libraries and, eventually, to meet. I have hoped also to understand what drove them to carry on their correspondence: both great men, though in different, often contrasting ways; both powerful, though Hem Raj in the spheres of religion and administration, Tucci in those of politics and culture; both so alike.

Without the many conversations I held with the figures from Tucci's past, who lived alongside him, this book would not be complete.

I interviewed his former students, Paolo Daffinà, Gherardo Gnoli, the one-time president of IsIAO, and another professor with whom he was particularly close and to whom I will refer as the Unnamed, as well as Fosco Maraini, who served as photographer during the 1937 and 1948 expeditions, and Pio Filippani-Ronconi, who learned Tibetan with him, spending nearly 30 hours in interviews. I spoke with Gilda Tucci, his only grandchild, and Usman Erdosy, a student of his students in archeology who had participated in his digs. I also interviewed contacts of Hem Raj, in Nepal and in the United States, and the witnesses, and occasional survivors, of an age of two regimes – Dr. Dilli R. Regmi and Dr. Rishikesh Shaha, who knew Tucci, the old pandit who tended to Hem Raj's library, his personal secretary, Nag Nath Vaidya, the Pant brothers and other intellectuals and scholars including Bishnu Prasad Dhital and Trailokya Nath Upraity, logging in another 160 hours. I participated in the celebrations and commemorations of Hem Raj, contributing as a speaker, and held conferences at the Royal Nepal Academy and at the University of Kathmandu in honor of Tucci and Hem Raj, all experiences from which I garnered new information. I spoke, here and there, with those who recalled Tucci and Hem Raj, or who told of their role in the politics of the time. Wherever I could I cast my line, fishing for information, testimonies, impressions, which I was sure to verify thoroughly, discarding any evidence I found unconvincing.

This proved, in the end, the most difficult part of my research, requiring that I spend extensive amounts of time in Nepal and India, to live a life not of grand hotels but of research in the field (and Nepal, a few years ago, was not exactly an accommodating destination). Linguistically, as well, I was pushed out of my comfort zone, forced to carry on dialogues in English, in Sanskrit, our *lingua franca*, in Nepali, and in Hindi, which I'm able to read, but speak only at an average level, as well as in Tibetan, a language I studied for one exam and immediately shelved. In the case of this last language, I availed myself of a local *bhikkhu*, a Buddhist monk, who kindly served as an interpreter. My interviews in Sanksrit, meanwhile, I made sure to record, which allowed me to listen back to them patiently at home. However, the true problem in speaking with those from a distant country is the profoundly different nature of the mentality, the culture, and the idiomatic expressions that underlie their language, even if we do share the common Indo-European linguistic bond, with Sanskrit as our mutual "older sister." To paraphrase Ingeborg Bachmann, I too would agree that all words cast a shadow, a poetic significance, that accompanies their conventional and symbolic, allusive, meaning. All of it, in the end, is untranslatable. As was said by the great Indian philosopher, Abhinavagupta, an author dear to Tucci, poetic language carries a resonance beyond words, one that stirs the collective chords of artistic and religious sensibility. The movements of a graceful dance seen from an audience, for example, a public concert, a painting, a poetry reading, all give rise to a distinctive feeling, a collective poetic experience that borders on the mystic or religious.

To a word's poetic and allusive meanings, however, I would add also a historical, geographical, and political sense, taking into account that the same words, and their significance, vary according to the country and age in which they're spoken. If a poor man in a developing country speaks of food, is it the same food of which, for example, a politician from the same country speaks, or even, perhaps, a lawyer in America? And if a woman who lives in a skyscraper in Mumbai speaks of freedom, is it the same freedom of which a poor woman speaks from a hut in the furthest removes of Bangladesh or Nepal? A historical base and a social referent are indispensable in understanding a word's meaning and, in turn, making oneself understood. And so, to understand Tucci, the words he himself wrote and the words with which others spoke of him, I have studied the history of the Himalayan countries and have read the accounts of a few of his contemporary explorers and travelers.

And yet, on occasion, in the course of my interviews, I seemed to catch a faint air of this poetic resonance, of an experience which I could not myself partake in or hope to understand in full: the spirit, the shadow of a word that Bachmann spoke of. On occasion, I was cut off from the conversation, just as, in a foreign country, even knowing the language well, we often find ourselves staring on blank-faced as the native speakers erupt into laughter over a joke or a play on words. For we can know the coordinates of another's language, though we'll never have the same internal reference point.

Nonetheless, language and communication proved only a

minimal part of the difficulty I encountered. The true challenge was the locating and gathering of documents. And with the few months I had in Nepal, as many know, even with the full support of Hem Raj's family and their mediation on my behalf with the local authorities, hardly had I found my rhythm and collected all the data available, and unavailable, on Tucci and on his voyages before the days had vanished. Nepal moves at an extremely slow place: you wait, you spend hours in conversation just to gain one piece of information. And at the National Archives, only one manuscript may be viewed at a time. That is, of course, if you're kind to the director and manager: otherwise they're quick to place insurmountable obstacles between you and the documents, whether it's a broken projector – while the new ones, donated by the German government, sit covered in the corner of a large room – or a constantly absent archivist. The political situation, as I've discovered each time I've traveled there, does nothing to put a Westerner's nerves at ease: you must constantly look over your shoulder, must constantly be aware of the famed Maoists – who would go on, eventually, to occupy 75% of the country, and then to become a government party – and the threat that, at any moment, they may storm the capital. The family of Kesari Raj Pandey, the former Royal Preceptor and Hem Raj's eldest son, kept seven soldiers in their service for protection: though in the case of an insurrection, they'd have hardly proven a sturdy line of defense. What kept me even more on guard, however, were the many beggar children, who might surround and assault me, demanding all I had – my money, my clothes, my hat, tissues, precious pens, food: in short, everything on me. Children desperate with anger, aggressive, alone. And extremely poor. Then there were the scheduled hours without electricity in Kathmandu, and the unscheduled outages in some of the isolated territories farther inland, forcing the occasional period of inactivity, or a faceless conversation, or a conversation by candle light, our faces overwrought with expression.

To find the time away in which to interview a Nepali or an Indian is another matter – away from his crowd of wives, his children, the children of others, servants, cousins, and friends, always present, always curious, minding every word, every action, every question, always eager to cordially intervene with a memory of their own, or with a suggestion, or a detail to embellish a story, to interpret and comment upon my every gesture, no matter how insignificant. And always another *chai* to drink, another sweet to chew between every sentence! For all the times these interruptions put me at ease and comforted me, particularly in the cold of the unheated Nepalese houses in January and February, there were others when they drove me to the end of my wits. Many of the interviews, in this way, were fragmentary, held up by domestic issues, by comments on this or that local or national occurrence, by countless questions. And then there were visitors, interruptions of every shape and size, needs of every sort, collective disagreements, bodily expressions, squealing telephones and orders given out to the house attendants. Nearly every interview in India and Nepal came about as the fruit of a collective intervention.

In truth, however, many of the men and women who agreed to speak with me of Tucci, to tell his story and the stories of those around him, to examine or to re-evoke the times, many were so thrilled at the chance to tell of their own life, sometimes heroic, or of their own works, sometimes extraordinary, of the social status they achieved in youth, sometimes staggeringly high, or of their own relationship, real or imagined or simply exaggerated, with the famous Italian professor. All, even those who'd never seen or known Giuseppe Tucci but had only heard him spoken of by their fathers, or their friends, their father's relatives, or friends of friends and acquaintances, all were eager to pass judgment. On the whole, much of it was irrelevant, detached from history, a "false truth" told at a third or fourth remove. Or, in cases where a story did begin to take off, its teller would shy away and withhold important details. Tucci is an extremely well-known figure in Asia, but a controversial one as well, and many were eager to exaggerate the facts in order to present him in a negative light. Many others boasted of a familiarity with him, often imagined, or desired, or, on the contrary, dreaded. Or of a familiarity merely tolerated.

Another important contact, a member of Hem Raj's family, was pained by some of the things I asked or that I sought to verify: as I have already done in person, once again I beg his forgiveness. There were those who suffered in recalling the past, or the ways in which it damaged their lives. In these cases, I've left out any matters of minor importance that might once again bring shame upon them or harm their reputations, as well as any statements that were clearly "historical falsities", intended only to muddy the names of those still living, or even of the dead, whose legacies are alive and well among the Nepalese *intelligencija*. Hem Raj, for many years, in fact, served a brutal government, one that brought great suffering to much of the population and that, in the minds of many, remains a bitter memory. Nonetheless, for several years I kept a regular correspondence with those who knew him and Tucci, and with Tucci's family, the fruit of which proved a precious resource in writing this book.

To search within and rediscover oneself, to fix a memory on the printed page and to verify the historical accuracy of that memory constitute a long and difficult journey, one which remains relatively unknown to the majority of people. Thirty years have passed since Tucci's death, and history takes its time decanting events. What I wanted to write was a biography – though in doing so, as I immediately realized, I'd have also to write, or rewrite, a piece of history. Historians, however, must forgive me if I've fallen short in that respect. It is not a history *per se* that I've set out to write. And they must forgive me if, at times, I've encroached on the objective distance between me and my subject, between me and a man who was not only the celebrated teacher of Italian Indologists and Tibetologists, but the teacher of my teachers. He who wishes to read only of the works and legendary exploits of Giuseppe Tucci must also forgive me: I'm not one for flattery, and after decades of hearing of how extraordinary a man he was, I've set out to discover whether or not this exalted image of him is true, and indeed, how it came about.

Most assuredly, that which I've sought to describe goes beyond the life, the works, the discoveries, relationships and explorations of my subject: it has been my hope to capture his many tastes as well, for manuscripts and art works, for the thousands of books he collected, for travel, for archeological artifacts; his relationship to power and the pleasure he took from it. I have tried to discover his spirit, the spirit of an age and of all those who entered his life. And that which I've sought to discover in Tucci, I've sought as well in the words of those who knew him. Though nearly all writers or scholars themselves, accustomed to thinking on paper, the men and women I interviewed could not have known that I was eager to gather their emotions as well, their tastes and passions, the facts surrounding and informing a piece of their lives. And yet they stood by me, bearing my questions with kindness, and, at times, extreme patience.

I can only hope that what I've written in this book will bring neither shame nor affliction on any of those who shared their memories with me.

But why search predominately in Asia for the traces and living memories of Giuseppe Tucci? Because in Italy the documents related to him are inaccessible; in fact, according to the IsIAO, they do not even possess them. Only in recent months were the records of the former IsMEO's verbal exchanges made available online, though not the letters and documents, nor the personal papers relative to the scientific activities of its presidents. But how could this be? Tucci served as course director at the institute and executive vice-president during Gentile's presidency, before taking the presidential seat himself. Doubtless, the official correspondence was preserved. And yet, in 2002, I was told by Gherardo Gnoli – who followed Tucci as president of IsMEO and maintained the position with IsIAO – that the institute had nothing. I was, to my good fortune, able to look over certain documents held by the Cabinet of Italy; however, no records from the institute were made available for consultation.

As for his students, those still living are by now retired professors at the Sapienza University of Rome, the University of Naples "L'Orientale", and the University of Bologna. Vittore Pisani, who Tucci took under his wing, died in 1990 in Milan. All remain eager to paint a glowing portrait of their teacher and his conduct; or else, are so troubled by the specter of his personality that they refuse to speak of him, for fear of rousing a painful and long-buried memory. I have not set out to write a hagiography of Giuseppe Tucci, and neither am I interested in judging or condemning him. I have sought to tell his story, he who played such a great role in the history and culture of his time.

Among the Italian academic world "that counts," Tucci is regarded only with high praise. Only one, the late archeologist, Maurizio Taddei, held a more complex and realistic opinion of his teacher, and he wasn't ashamed to admit it: no human can be described in terms of black and white. Taddei wrote as much in the *Annali* of the Institute of Oriental Studies (Istituto Universitario Orientale – IUO, now *Annali dell'Università di Napoli "L'Orientale"* – AION):

> At times, Giuseppe Tucci could also be harsh and dismissive of those who seemed, in his opinion, to act outside of the proper code of conduct, which,

though unwritten, was to be respected by all. How
many countless times did we, faced with certain of
his obstinate proclamations, stand perplexed, only
to discover later, perhaps too late, that it was not a
matter of stubbornness, but of a man standing behind
a precise intuition!

Behind his enmities, his aversions and dislikes
– of which he held many, and not casually, and at
times unjustly – was always the fear that someone, in
some way, was attempting to foil his one true goal and
driving force: to furnish Italy with a group of scholars
and the infrastructure necessary for broadening their
knowledge of Asia; or, in other words, for arriving
at the very heart of an understanding of Eurasian
cultural unity.[7]

A student of Tucci's, the brilliant and encyclopedic professor,
Pio Filippani-Ronconi – although heavily involved with Nazism
– speaks of him with a special blend of annoyance and disdain.
With certain good reason, in his own way, as we'll see. And when
judging his character as a man, Fosco Maraini is hardly more
complimentary.

It will take several decades before every repercussion of Tucci's activity comes to light. For such a task, two groups of scholars
would be needed: one familiar with him and willing to speak
openly, and to demonstrate openly any documents recovered;
and a second, not dependent on the first for purposes of academic
hiring, to organize the papers that were held by the now ex-IsIAO.
Substantial traveling funds would be needed as well, to retrace
the great scholar's steps and measure what he witnessed against
what now remains, in light of the latest research. And even still,
in the meantime, all, or nearly all, of the documents and living

witnesses will have disappeared. Remnants vanish, lives end. In Tucci's case, they become phantom documents, spoken of by all, seen by none. To give only one example, a few years ago an American scholar made an official request to consult Tucci's famous diary, still spoken of widely in Asia. Tucci's wife, Francesca – who in 2008, at ninety-one years old, was still lucid, as proud and exuberant as ever – claimed to have destroyed the text with her husband, together with other personal papers and letters, just before he passed. So was I told by the Unnamed. Perhaps it's true, perhaps it isn't. Or perhaps it's a bit of false information, spread by the very person who still possesses the diary. The spiritual heirs of Tucci, real or supposed – as demonstrated by the books written in his honor – never once mention word of it.

Some years ago, a professor and former student of the Sapienza University of Rome – doing research for a book which he would go on to publish with the same University – attempted in vain to consult the folder on Tucci in the archives of the IsMEO. Where the folder should have been, he claims, was only a large, empty gap. I know for a fact, on the account of a former guard of the archives in the Palazzo Brancaccio in Rome, where the institute resided, that the folder was there up until the end of the 1980s. Perhaps, now, it no longer exists. Or perhaps it's been misplaced, who knows. Whatever the case, the president of the IsMEO, and then of the IsIAO, he too a student of Tucci's, and the Unnamed sorely denied possessing any document relative to him, whether public or private.

Faced with all the good and bad that can be said of this renowned and controversial figure, in order to withhold bias I have been forced to adapt my method carefully: I have tried, in particular, to view Tucci from the eyes of an Asian: from the point of view, if such a thing can be claimed, of Asia. Those whom I interviewed resided principally in Asia, and in my travels I collected several of Tucci's photographs still held there. I observed his past both through the lens of written documents

and through the testimonies of men and women who were born
and live in that part of the world. With impartiality, I listened to
the tales and events recounted by men, even when those among
my witnesses expressed an intense bitterness or judged him
negatively. In writing a biography, I know, there can be no true
objectivity: nonetheless I have strived, wherever possible, to
be objective, to speak of him without being swayed one way or
the other intellectually, toward adulation or vilification – polar
extremes that, in the end, can easily ensnare an author. I, too, am
left with the memory of a pivotal encounter with Giuseppe Tucci
– an encounter I'll be certain to discuss in the course of this book.

The evocative power of an image is immediate, and seems
almost contrary to the mediatory and conventional written word.
In my research, I was able to view several hundred of the nearly
14,000 photographs, negatives, and slides taken by Tucci and others with him in Asia, between 1926 and 1954 – whether by his
assistants, his second or third wife, or a hired photographer from
the area – which serve to fill out the tales and studies considered
in this book. The photographs were donated by Tucci to IsMEO
in 1975 and subsequently filed among the Photographic Archives
at the National Museum of Oriental Art. I also consulted Tucci's
photos and film reel, or those relative to him, in the Historical
Archives of the Luce Institute, invaluable sources of information,
recently made available online, even if some of the details reported by the telejournalists of the time have been revealed as
false or imprecise. Rounding out the material collected for the
book are the photographs I took in Nepal, a few portraits of Hem
Raj and of his predecessors, as well as others in his circle, an oil
portrait of Tucci in the Kesar Library, photos of the palace where
Hem Raj resided and kept his library – whose halls Tucci graced
on several occasions – and of his bungalow in the countryside,
photos of figures in Europe with ties to Tucci, of documents, of

manuscripts, and, lastly, photos published in magazines of the epoch, such as *L'illustrazione Italiana*.

Also of great importance are the travel articles published by Tucci in Italian newspapers – the majority of which I have in my possession – and which he reworked and expanded into books. In a category all their own, not least for their ability to transport one magically back in time and into the atmosphere of the Fascist Era, are the documentary films held in the Historic Archives of the Luce Institute and in the archives of IsMEO. These, of which I was kindly gifted copies, contain footage of Tucci's 1933 expedition in western Tibet, of the Formichi expedition of that same year, in which Tucci also took part, of Tucci's 1948 expedition in Tibet, and of his travels through western Nepal in 1954.[8] Unfortunately, I was able to read only some of the lectures Tucci gave around the world, in addition to those in Italy, delivered principally during missions in England, Germany, France, Belgium, India, the Himalayan countries, in Iran, Pakistan, Indonesia, Ceylon (now Sri Lanka), Thailand, and Japan, all either requested or authorized by the Ministry of Foreign Affairs. Accompanying these appointments was, without fail, a healthy back-and-forth of letters and notes between Tucci, the Ministry of Foreign Affairs, the Ministry of Public Education, the President and Dean of Faculty at the University of Rome, as well as several telegrams from the Ministry of Foreign Affairs to Italian ambassadors, to assure that all proceeded smoothly, and the various informative notes, however brief, of the President of the university to the Ministry of Public Education, regarding Tucci's travels. These lectures, as I came to discover, had long been held under the wary-eyed guard of Francesca.

Until March 4, 2014, when she passed away, she was still there, living in the house of San Polo dei Cavalieri. Though I did write to her, share with her some of my work, and speak to her at length on the telephone, I chose in the end not go and visit her. Meeting her face-to-face, I feared, despite her churlish manner, would have roused my instinctive sympathy and, even knowing how favorably she greeted the news of this biography, would have compromised my objectivity, perhaps bringing me to set aside all that I thought might trouble her.

But all of it, the letters, the documents, the manuscripts, books, interviews, photos and film, would be without a soul if not for the vision, there in the background, of the mountains – their towering crests, glinting icily and vibrantly and crowning one side of the Kathmandu Valley, rising beyond the hills, beyond the stratum of clouds, hovering over the Srinagar Valley, and capped with the plateaus that stretch toward China, through former Tibet.

When I saw the peaks in the clear light of early morning and my breath first caught in my lungs, I knew I'd never be able to understand the intense passions of this man, who'd dedicated his life to an ideal, the Orient, and to the mountains, without seeing, at least once, the chain of the Himalayas, and the Karakoram, and the Hindu Kush, extending from the plateaus of the Pamir. Such an intense love for all that is born there, for the piece of yourself you find there, could not be, not without first loving the mountain summit.

As I've followed Giuseppe Tucci through his life and through his voyages, I have attempted to *fictionalize history*, a practice far less common here in Italy than in the United States: that is, to unfold the facts of history in the style and register of a novel. However, no events in this book have been invented, none exaggerated or purposefully disregarded. And even in those moments where the "fiction" writer seems to take the reins, as in the narration of Tucci's voyages, whatever occurrences have not been reported directly by him in published accounts have, nevertheless, taken shape from other written and oral sources, which have permitted me, from time to time, to fill in the gaps. All that is presented here is rooted in fact, interpreted in light of the available documents, my background, and my own discerning judgment. In recounting them, I have sought neither to bore myself nor, I hope, the reader.

Many of my colleagues at the university will turn up their noses at such an approach. But the history of each of us, like life, is full of beauty and heroism, just as it is of misery and banality, of decisions and of escapes, cold calculation and warm generosity, poetry and the crudest realism: all of which can be found among these pages. It has not been my intention to speak only to scholars and, as I've pointed out, this is not a purely historical work: I have filtered the events through my own style and have told their story in my own words, as if telling it to an old friend.

Tucci, after all, was not merely a leader in his field: his style left its mark on an entire age, on a way of teaching and of applying oneself as a student of Eastern studies in Italy. He profoundly influenced my own approach to studying, throughout my years as a student in the Oriental department at the University of Rome and beyond, playing a large role in my decision to leave Italy and teach abroad. Seeking to know him and to understand him further has been, in a way, a mode of coming to know and understand myself. The journey in search of Tucci and the politics of Fascism in Asia was a journey in search of my own roots. And if, at times, the terse language of history gives way to the emotion involved in writing of facts and characters that I myself have confronted, this is why. And it's also the reason this book does not speak solely of Tucci, of his circle, of his age and his travels, but encompasses the tale of my own research as well, and of the events that marked it, my experiences in retracing his footsteps, and personal anecdotes that may help to better understand the reality in which Tucci lived and worked. As a consequence of this personal involvement, the refusal to conceal myself behind a falsely "objective" and impersonal style, the reader will find me peeking out every now and then between the pages, alongside Tucci: I hope only that my presence does not overbear.

If, today, the Orient is far more open to travel, and far more facilitating of study, with many of its texts translated into Western languages and an ever-lengthening bibliography of in-depth studies, I've nonetheless found, and continue to find, that Asian culture is largely unknown to the West, even its basic principles, no matter a person's level of education or erudition. For which reason, in cases where I've seen it fit to elucidate any Eastern concepts or practices – or to comment on Tucci's work as a scholar – I've been careful to provide the reader with a wealth of detailed information.

Of all the documents I consulted, the one element which I could not reproduce here, and which I've labored to describe, has been the emotions of others: the pained voices of the witnesses, their faces lit up or turned away as they delved into personal memories, the deep melancholy in their eyes. An epoch had passed and, with it, their affections and a piece of their lives. At such sentiment, I've been able only to hint and to suggest; the rest, I leave to that indefinable space that readers must confront in every book, even a scientific text – a space in which to wonder, in which to project their own dreams, their own imaginations and desires.

With the aid of my sources, the correspondence, the libraries, the documents, works, voyages, testimonies, photographs, and films, I have sought foremost to recount the history of the many discoveries, the archeological missions, the writings, and the life and thoughts of one of the greatest scientists, explorers, bibliophiles, collectors, archeologists, practitioners of Track II diplomacy, and cultural advocates of the last century, together with the lives of the people, the events, and the ideas surrounding him. Above all else, I have strived to view my subject in the cultural context of the age, to understand not only Tucci himself, but all that made him who he was: not only his personal decisions, which, as Origene says, are always within reach, but of the decisions, the opportunities, and the difficulties associated with holding an important role in a totalitarian regime, as well as the decisions, opportunities, and difficulties of the regime in dealing with a personality of such proportions: for as we'll see, the regime did support him, though not without a certain level of suspicion.

In its journey through Tucci's life, through time, and through the territories of Asia, this book is an affirmation of the tremendous power and promise of discovery, of choice and of action, capabilities that lie not in Tucci alone, but in all of us; in a quite opposite sense, this book stands also as a demonstration of the way in which our actions, and even our passions, are tied, inevitably and interdependently, together.

ACKNOWLEDGEMENTS

The seed of this book was carried from Africa and Asia, long before I was born, by my father, Elpidio, a volunteer among the first seventy soldiers in the Folgore Parachute Brigade and a hero of the African campaign, and by Giuseppe Tucci, the protagonist of this story and the teacher of my teachers. The tree of knowledge that these two extraordinary men gave rise to, each in his own way, was nourished by the memories and tales of the Fascist period bequeathed to me by my father and by the works and teachings passed down by Giuseppe Tucci. Their words and deeds have vanished with time; but the manner of these two men, the spirit of an epoch, and the school of thought that found life's principal validation only in works of great merit and in acts of fearlessness and valor have persisted and have left us with the essence, the feeling, the idea of the age and characters described in this book. Both men, my father and Tucci, instilled in me a love for the "Italian colonies," real or imagined, of Fascism: Africa and Asia. From both, I inherited a manner, an approach, *un modo di vivere.* The historical research, the documents, and the testimonies would all come later.

During the years in which I wrote this book, I traveled widely through Asia, Europe, and the United States, reading every source I could find that would permit me to understand an epoch and a mentality very distant and very different from my own: the Fascist mentality. I was gripped by an almost obsessive need to understand, not only the documents and events, but the ideas, the ideals, the hopes, illusions, and disappointments of the men who lived in that age. During this long pursuit, I encountered so many men and women to whom I still owe my sincerest gratitude – who, for brief or extended stretches, journeyed alongside me, who shared with me their experiences and entrusted me with their memories, who helped me, or who simply stood by my side.

A thank-you of particular note is due to Giulio Andreotti, for the generous contribution of his original correspondence, of over thirty-seven years, with Giuseppe Tucci, for having, on countless occasions, responded to my countless questions, and for the truly moving gift of the commemorative placard with which India, in 1985, sought to honor the guru. The openness and promptness with which he responded to my requests and resolved my several doubts were exemplary.

A note of overwhelming gratitude goes to the former Royal Preceptor of Nepal, Kesari Raj Pandey, the eldest son of Hem Raj Sharma, to his wife, Kiran Pandey, and to his children, Jyoti Pathak, and, above all, Prakash A. Raj, for providing me with Hem Raj's correspondence in Sanskrit—including the letters with Tucci reproduced in this biography—with documents, with publications on his family, and for the precious information regarding their native country, all of which would have otherwise been inaccessible. A note of equal gratitude goes to Albrecht Wezler, the former director of the Nepal-German Manuscript Preservation Project, for having supplied me with several of the pages missing from among Tucci's letters on microfilm.

I'd like to thank Giuseppe Tucci's only grandchild, Gilda, who so kindly opened the doors of her home to me, who allowed me to use the photographs of her grandfather, and who shared with me her memories. I thank also Francesca Bonardi, Tucci's last wife, for the joy and generosity with which she received the news of this biography.

I thank Giorgio Serafini Prosperi, grandnephew of Giulia Tucci Nuvoloni, for the three documents sent from the Central Archives of the State and several photographs, and for the valuable information regarding his family. And by way of him I thank his aunt,

Enrica Sleiter Nicolini, for having shared the story of Giulia's wedding. Thanks are due also to Carlo Adorni and the "Giosuè Borsi" cultural association for two original photographs.

I thank Nicoletta Pescarolo Gentile, who waited patiently for me to write this book and partly supported it, and Francesco Perfetti, for the care and consideration with which he regarded this project, even at its earliest stages.

I remain indebted to Marco Goldoni for the beautiful maps, including that of India, reproduced here with the aid of the originals. And to Guglielmo Duccoli – and by way of him, to MyWayMedia – for his sage editorial advice and several articles from *L'Illustrazione Italiana*.

My most sincere thanks to Roberto Donatoni, Giancarlo Maggiulli, and Carlo Molinaro for their careful readings of the manuscript and for their advice and suggestions, and to Donatoni in particular, who reviewed those passages having specifically to do with Oriental scholarship. Though he has left his earthly body, I'm certain that Donatoni would have taken great joy in the publication of this work.

I thank Hervé A. Cavallera, for having combed through a final draft of the manuscript with a scholar's critical eye.

I thank the friends and readers of the Asiatica Association, and in particular the scholars who serve on the scientific committees of the *International Journal of Tantric Studies* and the *Journal of South Asia Women Studies* – as well as the many libraries who support these publications – for their collaboration these past twenty years and for their patience of late, as I've been particularly occupied with the drafting of this work.[1]

I thank Riccardo Redaelli for his support in scientific matters; I am indebted to him for some information on the Iranian oil companies; and Fiorenza Ferrini, who provided me with materials regarding one of Mussolini's private libraries. I am grateful also to Carlo Brioschi and Claudia Gualdana, who, from the very beginning, greeted this work with enthusiasm and encouragement.

I thank Jed Wyrick for his help, and his friendship.

My heartfelt gratitude to Henryk Hoffmann – time reveals all that is hidden. And a thank-you also to Vincenzo Castigli, whose esteem and affection are still a boon to me.

I thank Princess India d'Afghanistan, a true champion of human rights, for the information regarding her country and for her dear advice, which guided me through this project, and for twenty-nine steady years of friendship.

And lastly, I thank Lupo, for the precious jewel of life and death.

I thank the universities, the institutes, and the institutions that made my research possible and that supported me with unfaltering dedication, as well as their many employees for their kindness, their professionalism, and their courtesy – *in primis*, the Ministry of Cultural and Environmental Assets (now renamed the Ministry of Heritage and Cultural Activities), and particularly, Paola Carucci; the Ministry of Foreign Affairs and the Historical-Diplomatic Archives, in particular, Giovanni Cassis, who permitted me to view and photocopy documents unavailable to the public regarding cultural and political exchanges with Nepal, India, and Europe; the Widener Library at Harvard University, for having welcomed me for over twenty-three years and for having helped in every possible way to locate rare and ancient texts; the National Archives, the British Library, and the Royal Geographical Society of London, all remarkably organized and efficient; the Bir Library (now the Nepal National Library), the Kesar Library, and the National Archives of Kathmandu, all of which made manuscripts readily available and responded to my doubts and requests even in the difficult years of civil war and technological shutdowns; the Bhandarkar Oriental Research Institute in Pune, the Rabindra Bhavan Archives and Library at the University of Shantinkiketan, and the Library of Tibetan Works & Archives in Dharamsala, India; the Internationale Balzan Stiftung in Zurich; the studio Arte Nomade, in Macerata, for sharing some pictures; the Giovanni Gentile Foundation – and so, Nicoletta Pescarolo Gentile – which provided me with copies of parts of Tucci and Gentile's correspondence; the Luce Institute, the Ugo Spirito Foundation, the Gramsci Institute Foundation, the National Institute of Roman Studies, and the Library of the National Academy of Lincei – Corsiniana Section, Rome; the National Library "Vittorio Emanuele III" in Naples, and particularly Antonia Cinnamo, for her diligence in sending materials to which I'd have otherwise had no access; the Central Public Library of Milan, in Palazzo Sormani, and notably Aldo Pirola and Gianni Pizzi; the open-shelf library, Crociera e Sottocrociera, at the University of Milan, which greatly facilitated the consultation of important national and international periodicals; and the Ambrosiana Library of Milan, a temple of silence, which provided me with several original documents.

I am sincerely grateful to scholars and friends in Canada, in Finland, in Germany, India, Israel, Italy, in Nepal, Romania, in the United States, and in Switzerland for their interviews, for biographical or bibliographical information, or for sending publications, short films, and documents: Rammani Acharya, Marilia Albanese, Paul Arpaia, Enrico Astuni, Gustavo Benavides, Bindu Bhatt, Vittorio Caratozzolo, Claudio Cardelli, Eugen Ciurtin, Stefano Cordero di Montezemolo, M. G. Dhadphale, Bishnu Prasad Dhital, Kamal Mani Dixit, Jérôme Ducor, George Erdosy (Muhammad Usman Erdosy), Giuseppe Flora, Marcello Foa, Alessandra Gatti, Janet Glausch, Gherardo Gnoli, Hans Thomas Hakl, Klaus Karttunen, Toke Knundsen, Sergio Lambiase, Pasquale Lebano, Matteo Luteriani, Davide Magni S.J., Luca Mancini, Romano Mastromattei, Klaus-Dieter Mathes, Yoram Mayorek, Federico Migliorati, Roberto Moschini, Andrea Munno, Claudio Mutti, Luca Maria Olivieri, Dinesh Raj Pant, Mahes Raj Pant, Raniero Paulucci Di Calboli, Roberto Pignani, David Pingree, Mario Prayer, Anna Maria

Rossato, Farian Sabahi, Vito Salierno, Maurizio Serafini, Somnath Sogdyal, Elliot Sperling, Elliot M. Stern, Shiva Ram Shrestha, Patrizio Tanzi, Allen W. Thrasher, Kapila Vatsyayan, Piero Verni, Alexander von Raspatt, Michael Witzel.

Among my acknowledgments, I could not fail to mention Luca Conti, who suggested I open the first informational website on Giuseppe Tucci, and Alberto Fanelli, photographer.[2] I also thank Francesco Abruzzo, Lorenzo Cairoli, don Guerino Dozzi, Agostino Regnicoli, Edmondo Rho for their intriguing, interdisciplinary discussions.

Here, I reserve a thought for those who have stood beside me for the greater part of these last fifteen years, first among which the pandit, Nityanand Sharma, who helped me out of countless binds and who led me by hand, with affection and blind trust, to discover an India that is no longer; the civil rights champion, William P. Homans, who taught me the basic principles of law, by word and by example; the scholar, Giorgio Orvieto, who urged me to follow my path as if there were no other. To three of Tucci's students I owe my utmost gratitude, for their unbounded support and for the trust they've placed in me over the past decades: Pio Filippani-Ronconi, of whom I'll speak in the course of this book, who aided me to publish my first translations from Sanskrit and served as an important source of information; Luciano Petech, the incomparable teacher and scholar, and a former professor of mine, for his wealth of precious advice; and another former professor, Paolo Daffinà, who taught me to use my doubt as a tool, to never lend my complete faith to the words written or spoken by others, and to verify my sources thoroughly. It was he who convinced me to write this history, providing me with the first bibliographical and biographical references. The seriousness with which these men approached their studies – though their choices in life may have differed greatly from mine – has been an example to me.

Doubtless, I must mention my closest friend Virginia Prosdocimi, the psychoanalyst and university professor, who for over twenty-seven years has made an indescribable contribution to my life. Above all, however, I have been inspired by the attention and respect she paid to those whom life has forgotten – like the scraps of a manuscript long since lost, that only an act of love can piece together. With her, I have shared doubts, laughs, hopes, and passages of this book, adopting her motto as my own: «Tomorrow is another day».

I reserve a thought here, as well, for the many scholars who so kindly and patiently allowed me to interview them and have since passed on, among whom Fosco Maraini, Dilli R. Regmi, who also provided me with one of Tucci's letters, Rishikesh Shaha, and others, across three continents, whom I've mentioned in the introduction. I thank also Nag Nath Vaidya, who, despite his many years, responded to my questions with great care.

To two books in particular, which served as a source of inspiration and serenity, I owe a great deal. The first is *The Story of My Experiments with Truth*, the autobiography of Gandhi. As a young girl, I purchased a cheap reprint of the original Italian edition; one lazy summer afternoon, thoughtless, I pulled a copy from the shelf and the words struck me immediately. In a fury, I read it from beginning to end. Then I re-read it, more patiently, in English. That was the beginning, the spark that lit the fire of my life to come. The second is *Albert Speer: His Battle with Truth*, by Gitta Sereny. I would read it twenty years later, and of all the books I encountered in my life, it affected me most deeply. At the center of both works is the theme of truth: Gandhi's experiments with it, and Speer's struggle with it as the architect of Nazism. The first convinced me to follow my path, at any cost, with simplicity and without fear; the second, to seek out the truth even in unlikely places – and to write it down. That I've pursued this work at all, I owe to them.

As a final note of gratitude, I thank my family, who have stood by me and supported me in innumerable ways, and in particular, Andrea Rachele Fiore, the most exquisite *fiore* in the garden of my life. Also Emi Bianchi del Torre, Salvatore Celani, Angela Celani D'Aversa, Antonio Cosimelli, Wanda Cosimelli Garzilli, Fabrizio Maria Ruggero Fiore, Alessandra Fiore Garzilli, Friccico Fiore Garzilli, Nina Fiore Garzilli, Titta Fiore Garzilli, Blanche Garzilli, Brigitte Garzilli, Charlie Manas Garzilli, Crescenzo Garzilli, Elpidio Garzilli, Giuseppina Garzilli Celani, Enrica Garzilli Santoro, Ormindo Lucchetti, Zaira Lucchetti Zerbini Regini, Beatrice Magnocavallo, Lalè Magnocavallo, Lili Garzilli Magnocavallo, Ludovico Magnocavallo, Silvestro Magnocavallo, Maria Antonietta Magnocavallo Barassi.

This book is dedicated to my father, Elpidio Garzilli (March 25, 1921 – February 12, 1984), among the first seventy volunteers in the parachute brigade, Folgore (7th battalion, 21st regiment) and subsequently in the Nembo brigade, decorated for campaigns in Africa, including El Alamein. From his battles, he came back with disfigurations, with wounds and sicknesses that in time proved fatal, though never once did he back down, not even in the battle of his too-brief life on earth. It is he, a painter, who instilled in me a love for beauty and a hunger for truth, and in his generosity, his forthrightness, and his reserved tenderness he remains close to me to this day. Like an ancient, flourishing tree he still casts his protective shadow and scatters his fecund seeds of clarity, honesty, and hard-to-achieve simplicity. There are those who wrote on behalf of their native land; my father gave his life for it.

In life there is no choice: you're either friend or enemy. Such is the path in life for the strong-willed; not that false courtesy that hangs over all Europe like a shroud, a conformism, lacking forthrightness, lacking reciprocal trust, in which relationships soften and at last liquefy in a cauldron of lies. (Giuseppe Tucci)

NOTE ON THE TEXT

All documents and citations in this book have been reproduced here to the letter, in a diplomatic transcription, including their unique orthographic signs.

All translations from eastern and western languages, unless otherwise specified, are the author's own. The letters in Sanskrit and Nepali have been emended.

When not used within citations, the characters in Sanskrit, Tibetan and Chinese follow the most widely-accepted usages, that is the IAST system for Sanskrit, Pāli and Nepali, Wylie for Tibetan, and Pinyin for Chinese, in which case the reader might find, for example, Lao tze in a citation and Laozi within the text. The use of diacritics has been limited, in most cases, to the names of gods and mythological figures.

In cases of certain, commonly used terms, the simplified form has been used, such as in the case of «gompa». In regard to toponyms, the spellings used by Tucci have most often been preserved; in other cases, place spellings in Southern Asia vary according to the speaker, with no standard of reference (even if, for clear historical motives, English usage from geographic maps of the *Survey of India* has been favored).

All characters of Asian descent have been referred to using their first names, their last names or their appropriate titles, according to current practice. Certain names may be referred to in slightly different forms: Kaiser Shamsher Rana, for example, may be referred to variably as Kesar, Keshar, Kaisher, Kaisar, or Kaiser. On occasion, names in Tibetan, Sanskrit, Hindi, Pāli, and Nepali have been simplified, according to the most widely known pronunciations.

The historical dates in reference to Nepal have been calculated using the local calendar, the Vikram Saṁvat (V.S.), a lunar
calendar whose beginning date varies, causing the months to
shift out of sync with the Gregorian solar calendar; 2010, for example, corresponds to 2066–67 V.S., depending on the month
in question. The dates of historical Indian calendars have been
recast in terms of the Gregorian calendar. Many of these cases,
however, save a few exceptions, are already widely known.

The value of the lira throughout the historical periods covered
in this book has been calculated according to data reported by
the Sistema Statistico Nazionale / Istituto Nazionale di Statistica
[National Statistic System / The National Institute of Statistics],
Il valore della moneta in Italia dal 1861 al 2004, Informazioni [*The Value
of Money in Italy from 1861 to 2004, Data*], n. 24, 2005. Likewise, the
value of the pound has been calculated using *Global Financial Data*,
edited by Global Financial Data, Inc., Los Angeles, CA, ca. 1990.[1]

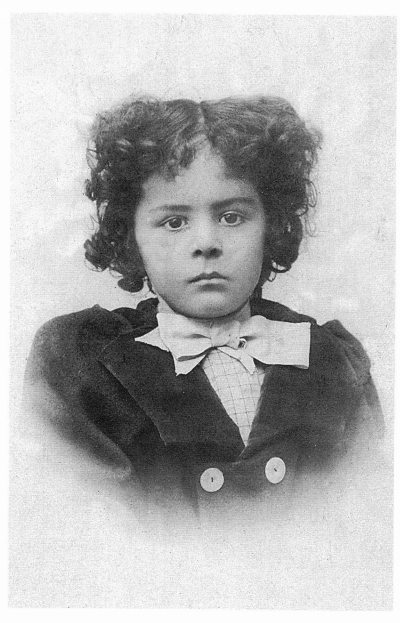

Figure 2: Giuseppe Tucci in Macerata, 1902.
Courtesy of Arte Nomade

Figure 3: Giuseppe Tucci in Macerata, 1907.
Property of Francesca Bonardi, courtesy of Arte Nomade

Figure 4: Giuseppe Tucci during World War I, 1915–1918.
Property of Francesca Bonardi, courtesy of Arte Nomade

Figure 5: Giuseppe Tucci reading, Rome, 1919.
Property of Francesca Bonardi, courtesy of Arte Nomade

Figure 6: A young Tucci in Italy.
Property of Francesca Bonardi, courtesy of Arte Nomade

Figure 7: Giuseppe Tucci near a *chorten*, India, 1926–30.
Courtesy of Arte Nomade

CLASSICI

D'ORIENTE

RĀJAÇEKHARA
LA KARPŪRAMAÑJARĪ
Dramma pracrito volto in italiano
A CURA DI
GIUSEPPE TUCCI

"IL SOLCO„ CASA EDITRICE
CITTÀ DI CASTELLO

Figure 8: Giuseppe Tucci (ed.), *La Karpūramañjarī.*
Dramma pracrito volto in italiano, front cover, 1922.

Figure 9: Giuseppe Tucci (ed.),
Saggezza Cinese. Scelta di massime – parabole – leggende, front cover, 1926.

BIBLIOTECA DI CRITICA
RELIGIOSA
–

GIVSEPPE TVCCI

IL BVDDHISMO

F·CAMPITELLI·EDITORE
FOLIGNO

F C
F

B·DISERTORI

Figure 10: Giuseppe Tucci,
Il Buddhismo, front cover, 1926.

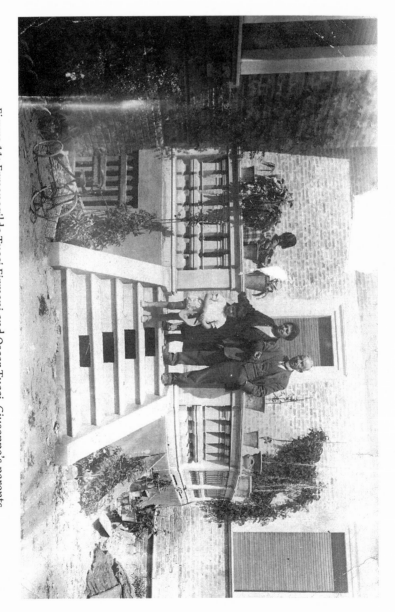

Figure 11: Ermenegilda Tucci Firmani and Oscar Tucci, Giuseppe's parents, with Ananda Maria in Macerata, ca. 1926–28.

Figure 12: Ermenegilda Tucci Firmani and Oscar Tucci, Giuseppe's parents, with Ananda Maria in Macerata, ca. 1927–29.

Figure 13: Ermenegilda Tucci Firmani and Oscar Tucci, Giuseppe's parents, with their grandson Ananda Maria in Macerata, ca. 1927–29.

Figure 14: Ananda Maria Tucci at age 15-17.

Figure 15: Ananda Maria Tucci at age 18-20.

Figure 16: Ananda Maria Tucci and his wife Bice Tucci Pascali in the Fifties.

Figure 17: Giuseppe Tucci in Bengal with a local, 1926–27.
Courtesy of Arte Nomade.

Figure 18: Tucci's second wife Giulia Nuvoloni and the caravan
in Tibet or Ladakh, ca. 1928–1939.

CHAPTER I

FROM YOUTH TO THE FIRST VOYAGE: ENLIGHTENED BY THE BUDDHA

> I found Buddhism to be much simpler. It is an ethical doctrine, and nothing else. All is based on sincerity, and you are completely free.
>
> —*Giuseppe Tucci, 1984*

On February 16, 1983, in the opulent Palazzo Brancaccio on Via Merulana in Rome, the foundation of the Italian Institute for the Middle and Far East (IsMEO) celebrated its fiftieth anniversary. Among pink marble and heavy red velvet tapestries, gilded salons and ornamental plaster friezes, in a room facing out on the Baroque garden, a group of Italian scholars presented a new project: a book collecting a variety of studies in homage to the man who served as «both the founder and the brilliant, energetic, and enthusiastic leader» of IsMEO – that is, GiuseppeTucci – overlooking the true founder, Giovanni Gentile.[1] Tucci, rather, had been its initial promoter. The miscellany would be a collection of studies by students, collaborators, and «eminent specialists from around the world», and the intention was to present the multi-volume book to their teacher on his birthday, June 5, 1984, «as a gift from his many students and admirers and a sign of their devotion and affection». Tucci, unfortunately, would never see its publication: on April 5, 1984, exactly two months to the date of its promised arrival, he died. He would have been ninety years old.

The three volumes *ad honorem* compiled by IsMEO – not the only volumes to have been dedicated to him by his students – came out in 1985–88, covering the numerous studies initiated and conducted by Tucci on an extraordinary range of subjects, both geographical and cultural: from the historical and pre-historical archeology of Iran, India, and Pakistan, to explorations and discoveries in Nepal and Tibet; from Tibetology, his preferred field of study – thanks to his fluent knowledge of literary and colloquial Tibetan– to Indology and Sanskrit; from Buddhism, a religion he studied with particular interest and which he himself practiced, to Indian and Chinese philosophy; from the Roman world to Japanese culture; from the discoveries of *stūpas* – Buddhist mausoleums – of monasteries, monuments, inscriptions, frescoes and paintings, to the restoration of works of art. Neither architect nor restorer, Tucci would spearhead Italian archeology and archeological restorations in Asia. Standing as proof of his fervent activity is the National Museum of Oriental Art, now dedicated to him, on a floor of Palazzo Brancaccio, which as a result of his efforts holds the largest European collection of Gandhāra art. Tucci was all of this – one of the most prolific and profound scholars in the field of Asian studies, and on the most widely diverse subjects – though, as we'll see, he was also much more.

Giuseppe Vincenzo Tucci was born in Macerata, June 5, 1884. His father, Oscar, first secretary of the Revenue Office, and his mother, Ermenegilda Firmani, had emigrated to Marche from Apulia. Giuseppe was an only child. In 1902 the family relocated to Novara, only to return again to Macerata one year later. It wasn't until 1917 that they would move permanently to Ancona, when Giuseppe was already living in Rome.

Perhaps it was the nearness of his birthplace to the water, which separates distant nations and peoples just as surely as it draws them together, or perhaps it was his ties to a region that had given rise to so many discoverers and explorers with their gaze set on the East – whatever the case, Tucci proved himself early on as an *enfant prodige,* with a special interest in the Orient: according to his own accounts, by the age of twelve he'd learned

Sanskrit, Hebrew, and Iranian. Macerata had been made famous bythe Ricci family: Father Matteo Ricci, the celebrated Jesuit missionary of the sixteenth and seventeenth centuries, established contact between the most ancient European and Chinese civilizations and wrote important treatises on astronomy and geography,and would eventually die in China. His tomb in Beijing has been destroyed and reconstructed on three occasions in the past four centuries – the last of which came only in recent years, after the Cultural Revolution – and his name appears among the few foreigners given mention in the national Chinese encyclopedia. In 1982, celebrating the fourth centenary of his arrival in China, Pope John Paul II gave a lecture at the Pontifical Gregorian University tracing his life, and comparing him, no less, to the Church Fathers. One of Tucci's great patrons, Giulio Andreotti, would publish a book on him as well, *A Jesuit in China (1522-1610): Matteo Ricci, from Italy to Pechino*.[2]

Another native of Marche, from the city of Pennabilli, was Father Francesco Orazio della Penna, a Capuchin missionary who reached Lhasa on October 1, 1716, together with Father Domenico da Fano,prefect of the evangelical mission in Tibet. On January 2, in the Rimini edition of the newspaper, *Il Resto del Carlino*, it was reported that his Italian-Tibetan dictionary had been uncovered in a dusty crate in Calcutta.[3] Before them, still other Capuchin Fathers from the Marche region had left for Lhasa, on the initiative of the Frenchman, Father Francesco Maria da Tours. Having recently returned from missions in India, Father Francesco proposed to his order's superiors and, through them, to the Sacra Congregatio de Propaganda Fide, that a mission be carried out in Tibet, where he'd heard rumors of an ancient Christian communitystill in existence. Shortly thereafter, a group of Capuchins from Marche left for India, choosing to travel by land. The band of friars, however, was literally decimated by the harsh travel conditions: some were forced to stay behind, others died en route. Nevertheless, on June 12, 1707, Father Giuseppe da Ascoli and

Father Francesco Maria da Tours crossed into Lhasa, where they would remain until late 1711, when, in fear that they would not survive the brutal winters, the vice-prefect called them back to Chandernagor – a city on the shore of the Ganges in western Bengal. The two friars obeyed, despite the fact that their work in Lhasa had at last begun to take off, thanks in large part to a Tibetan translation of the Catechism, prepared by Father Domenico with the help of an interpreter.

As a region, Marche never could boast of descendants famed for their conquests at sea and on land or for the plundering of great treasures, but instead proved fertile grounds for Church Fathers – Cassiano Beligatti da Macerata, Carlo Horatii da Castorano, Vito da Recanati, Costantino Cruciani da Loro, and many others – who would leave for countries still largely unknown to the world, for lands whose very borders remained a mystery, jotted in with a touch of imagination even on the maps of the great Dutch merchants of the seventeenth century, who'd traveled the globe far and wide.

Voyaging to the East, the evangelists and travelers from Marche brought with them the Catholic religion and, to a lesser extent, the practice of Western medicine. On their return from Asia, however, they arrived with far more than religions, gold, and spices: they brought new languages, composed of bizarre characters, with strong aspirants, gutturals, and dentals; they told of an extravagant wedding in Lhasa, between a Chinese princess and a Tibetan king; they spoke of inaccessible monasteries with large, golden-faced buddhas, blackened by incense smoke; of gigantic statues, nearly two hundred feet high, and stone bodhisattvas stretched out in sleep, bearing the blessed, elusive smiles of the Enlightened. The maps of the heavens were redrawn, with a new and more sophisticated base of mathematical and astrological knowledge; they spoke of «certain Saracens from the westerly regions, who knew much about Europe, India, and Persia» and who had visited the court of Beijing, like Father

Ricci. Ricci himself told of the many Mohammedans he'd met in China, who «in nearly every province gather in their sumptuous mosques, where they recite prayers, perform circumcisions, and hold their many ceremonies».[4]

In 1907, Tucci enrolled at the superb Liceo Classico, "Giacomo Leopardi" in Macerata – a secondary school for the humanities, founded in 1861 and which, in 1876, was given high marks by the then governmental inspector, Nobel laureate Giosuè Carducci. He obtained his diploma in 1912. Starting from 1909 Tucci published several cultural articles in the local newspapers. "Peppino," as he was called at home, was peevish as a boy, ornery, introverted, a writer of poetry. His parents worried for him – not only had he come from a bourgeois family, but his clothing, they noticed, was shabby, his hair long and messy, his social relationships negligent. He had only one friend, Lucia, a neighbor girl his own age. In compensation, however, he was extremely close with his grandmother, Teresa, who lived with the family at 6 Via Felice Cavallotti, in Macerata. As a high school student, he went on several archeological expeditions outside of the city. Despite the early interest in Asia of many of his distinguished countrymen, however – and despite his own precocious knowledge of difficult and abstruse languages –Tucci turned his attention first toward his native land and the study of ancient Rome. In 1909, at only fifteen years old, he completed the study,«Illustri città romane del Piceno poco conosciute: Elvia Ricina» («The Illustrious and Lesser-Known Roman Cities of Picenum: Helvia Recina»), which, though unpublished, he dedicated to his parents and grandparents,

> the fruit of long study – for the honest efforts of their son and grandson are best rewarded by their high regard.

Helvia Recina is an ancient Roman city, nearly 2.5 miles to the northwest of Macerata. Even as a child, as is manifest in this work and its dedication, Tucci demonstrates a strong inclination for study and a fascination with the unknown, for that which must still be discovered. He expresses likewise a strong desire to be well regarded by figures of authority, a desire which will become evident in his relations with Mussolini: to Gentile, he would lament often that his studies and expeditions were not sufficiently well-recognized by Italy's "Capo".

In 1911 came his first publication, a brief article regarding the Latin inscriptions then recently discovered in the Macerata countryside, printed among the pages of the German Archeological Institute's prestigious journal, *Mitteilungen*: he was seventeen years old.[5] And yet, it seems, he'd already begun his study of Buddhism. After receiving his high school diploma in 1912, Tucci had no choice but to flee his native city in pursuit of a university education – though the first documented mention of a Law School in Macerata dates back to 1290, the Faculty of Literature and Philosophy would not be established until 1964. In 1912, as well, he would publish his «Ricerche sul nome personale romano nel Piceno» («Studies on the Use of Roman Personal Names in Picenum»).[6] He was just eighteen years old. Even at that age, so commonly an age of transition in a young man's life, of self-discovery, of dreams, a passage from the twilight of childhood into the first fledgling months of manhood, Tucci's personality and character seem already well-established: he was a scholar, a discoverer.

In his writings one recognizes a profound interest, and even a love, for Marche, though he'd persistently claim to be, and in fact was, detached from his native land and from his own origins: throughout his life he sought to overcome his roots, to transcend them. When he presented himself in full regalia or insisted upon being referred to by all as "His Excellency" (as Conze notes, «And then the great man, *Professor Tucci* himself, the *Senator, His Excellency,* arrived with a company of some twenty or thirty others trailing behind him»),[7] and, when in Asia he continually reminded his traveling companions of the weight he carried in Rome, was he not, in some way, seeking to conceal his bourgeois, provincial background, to be recognized as a man without country, far removed from parochial frivolities – a man who, in truth, could claim as his home only the vast expanse of the globe itself? In his later years, however, after having spent the majority of his life from 1925 onward in the East, Tucci would declare his love for Marche in a lecture delivered at the Merchants Lodge in Ancona, on March 14, 1959, praising its skies – pure, almost translucent – its hills – the gentlest, perhaps, in all of Italy – and claiming that he himself returned there often and with pleasure:

> Which is why – if you'll allow me to end on a prayer– I would like that it be a native of Marche, my home, to continue this proud tradition [of Oriental scholarship], a native of this land to which I return so often, to breathe again its vital air, to discover still more beauty in its bounteous landscape, to run my gaze along its gentle slopes and to dream beneath its skies.[8]

And again, on June 29, 1961, in another lecture held in Ancona:

> I am not one given to flights of sentiment, though the inevitable spell of nostalgia does draw me back, when I'm most distant, to consider these hills, these skies; though there is a deeper motive and, for a man of science, a more valid and justifiable motive: if there is one place where a new wing of IsMEO truly belongs, it is in Marche. We natives of Marche are by our very nature filled with a curious and vagrant spirit; and it

is to the Orient, above all, that we are drawn, called
forth by the sea.[9]

Who's to say if these belated declarations of love were genuine
or simply an elegant plea to win the hearts of the people and
the approval of the local authorities?Tucci had come to deliver
these lectures, after all, with the intention of opening a new wing
of IsMEO in Marche – a project which, for various reasons, was
never realized. And Tucci was no stranger to the dramatic arts.
Wielding this talent to great advantage during his expeditions,
he often played the part of an ardent Buddhist in order to gain
entrance into sacred temples. In this case, perhaps Tucciwas just
buttering up his audience, doing as performers do when they
take the stage in smaller cities – cities where they may never
have even stepped foot – and swoon over the incomparably warm
welcome they'd received.

In 1922, he would publish a short, 48 page work on another
city in Marche, together with C. Mariotti – perhaps the historian,
and art-historian, Cesare, who wrote several fine works on the
marvelous city of Ascoli Piceno – entitled, *Iscrizioni medievali ascolane [Medieval Inscriptions in Ascoli]*, which incorporated a large
number of illustrations.[10] From that point on, Tucci would rou-
tinely include drawings and photographs in his published works.

Initial Contact with Gentile
and First Publications

The first letter addressed to Giovanni Gentile, whom he knew
from his early years at university, dates back to the beginning of
the period between 1916–18, when Tucci was a soldier and his
family had moved temporarily to Ascoli Piceno. Even at such a
young age, it seems, Tucci had his sights set on a brilliant career.
In the letter, he humbly requests Gentile's opinion on the prospect
of republishing a philosophical work of Tommaso Campanella: a

project, in truth, somewhat distant from Tucci's own interests, though very dear to Gentile. Whatever his intentions, in the end the project fizzled.

In 1937, on occasion of the inauguration ceremony of the Lombard branch of IsMEO, Gentile introduced Tucci as a former student:

> [IsMEO] was proposed by me and a close group of friends, experts in all that is of the Orient, at the head of which was a former student of mine, who, with his sharp intuition, his scholarship, and his unceasing and brilliant activity as a pioneer in the discovery and study of the most mysterious regions on earth and Oriental souls, stands as an honor not only to the Roman school, but to all of Italy: Giuseppe Tucci. And Il Duce, always quick to perceive the value of all ideas inspired by our nation's true interests, has approved of and encouraged his efforts; [...].[11]

It is unclear whether Tucci attended the philosopher's lectures and, therefore, met him in the classroom, or whether they were introduced by Carlo Formichi, who for many years had been carrying out official duties for the government. As the first world war approached, Tucci's star was rising as a young intellectual. He'd stepped on the scene of Oriental studies in Italy as an anthropologist, a scholar of Iran, and a sinologist. In 1913, Tucci's «Totemismo ed esogamia» («Totemism and Exogamy») would appear; the following year, he published four studies on the prehistory of Asia and on the rites and customs of ancient Persians.[12] In these years, as well, was born a love that Tucci would cherish for the rest of his life: the work of Laozi and Chinese philosophy. In 1914, he would also publish a brief essay on *Coenobium*, entitled, «Il Tao e il Wu-wei di Lao-tzu» («The Tao and Wu Wei of Lao-tzu»), and, in 1915, «Dispute filosofiche nella Cina antica»

(«Philosophical Disputes in Ancient China»),[13] a brief article on Han Yu, «Un filosofo apologista cinese del sec. IX» («A Ninth Century Chinese Apologist Philosopher»),[14] and a critical review of Tacchi Venturi's *Opere storiche di P. Matteo Ricci [The Historical Works of Father Matteo Ricci].*[15]

Up until 1922, Tucci threw himself wholly into his passion for Taoism and its traditional founder, Laozi, and for Chinese literature. In 1916, he published «I mistici dell'Oriente» («The Mystics of the Orient»), an article on Liezi, the great Taoist sage, and his first work in the field of Indology, a critical review of Ferdinando Belloni-Filippi's book, *I maggiori sistemi filosofici indiani [The Major Philosophical Systems of India].*[16] His profound knowledge of Chinese language and culture would serve him, as well, in his famous comparative studies of Buddhist texts in Chinese and Tibetan, at which he'd labor until the 1950s. These texts had been carried by itinerant teachers into China and Tibet and translated there into the local languages, in order to spread the True Law, the word of the Buddha. In this way, when the original Sanskrit text was lost, comparisons were made between the various translations to determine the proper interpretation of the text, to weed out false or poorly rendered passages, and to fill in the *lacunae.*

In 1917, when his family relocated to Ancona, Tucci published the first part of «Note cinesi» («Chinese Notes»), a critical review of the volume of Buddhist hymns, *Gaṇḍīstotragāthā*, edited by Baron Freiherr Alexander von Staël-Holstein, and the article, «Aspirazioni di pace e necessità di guerra nell'Estremo Oriente» («The Aspiration for Peace and the Necessity of War in the Far East»).[17] Two years later, he completed his degree in Letters and Philosophy. On April 19, 1920 he was married in Spoleto, at the bidding of his father, without ever having met his bride: Rosa De Benedetto, the daughter of a family of prosperous butchers in Macerata. That same year, it appears, he began his studies of the Tibetan language, of which he would soon become one of the world's leading experts. From 1920 on, his publications began to appear in a steady rhythm, with eleven works in 1923 alone. Only in 1974, at the age of eighty, would Tucci's production begin to decline.

A FRENZY OF PUBLICATIONS

Attributed to Tucci's name are over 365 works, some of which are new editions of already-published works, or translations of works originally published in Italian. Some of the works number only two or three pages, others are monumental – as in the case of the seven-volume series, *Indo-Tibetica*,[18] 1,353 pages in all, including hundreds of colored charts and diagrams, and the volumes of *Tibetan Painted Scrolls*.[19] This last work, translated from Italian into English by the scholar, Virginia Vacca, with its fifteen-page introduction, its two volumes totaling 798 pages (or nearly 17 inches of glossy paper), and a portfolio of 256 original, color plates stands not only as a mine of information and descriptions of *thangkas* – available neither in Tibet nor elsewhere – but constitutes a veritable *opus magnum* on the country's religion, history, and iconography up until the years preceding the work's publication in 1949. Unfurled along the walls of a temple or rolled into a scroll when transported or preserved, a *thangka* is a painted or woven depiction of buddhas and bodhisattvas or their disciples, of divinities, of famous lamas and yogis and episodes from their lives, of *maṇḍalas*, or, in some cases, a symbolic representation of the teachings and doctrines of Buddhism. The canvas is most often a light cotton, treated with a plaster paste and rabbit-skin glue. The value of a *thangka* is determined by the number of divinities represented and by the gold used in its decoration. Once the figure is complete, a fine gold is applied to the image, obtained by melting a small nugget with a solvent.*Thangkas* consist principally of five dominant colors – white, yellow, red, black, and green – each with its own symbolic meaning. In Tibetan *thangkas*, the subject is typically the Buddha, in one of his many forms, and the image is executed according to a precise order, beginning first with the jewel that sits beneath the bun, or protuberance, atop his head, and ending with his eyes, which are painted last. In order to paint the *thangkas*, one must wait for a favorable lunar phase, and perform the ritual "opening of the eyes".

To this day, though nearly seven decades have passed since its publication, it would be impossible to dedicate oneself to Tibetology without having carefully studied *Tibetan Painted Scrolls*.

Not only does Tucci approach a wide spectrum of topics and objects of study, but the tone and register of his writings vary greatly as well, ranging from explanatory accounts of his expeditions to didactic descriptions of religions, from translations of texts from Sanskrit, Pāli, Chinese, and Tibetan, to articles on Tibetan medicine, Indian filmography, and the means of meditation. Tucci was also a brilliant and pioneering scholar: his 1949 best seller, *Teoria e pratica del Mandala, con particolare riguardo alla moderna psicologia del profondo [The Theory and Practice of Mandala: With Special Reference to the Modern Psychology of the Subconscious]*, was the first instructive text on the *maṇḍala* as a method of meditation and the first study linking the Oriental sciences to Jungian psychoanalysis, a science still widely unknown in Tucci's time.[20] In 1949, Tucci published his translation of *Il libro tibetano dei morti [The Tibetan Book of the Dead]*.[21] In 1944, Jung suffered an accident, a fracture, succeeded by a heart attack. While in a coma, he experienced a near-death vision, which he would describe in his 1962 semi-autobiographical text, *Erinnerungen, Träume, Gedanken [Memories, Dreams, Reflections]*.[22] But it was Tucci who first linked the near-death experience, as interpreted by Jung, with the experience of the spirit's journey before reincarnation, according to the belief of Tibetan Buddhism. Jung's interest in Tibetan teachings, meanwhile, would continue to grow, and in 1954 he wrote a commentary, through the lens of psychology, on Walter

Yeeling Evans-Wentz's *The Tibetan Book of the Great Liberation*, on the possibility of ultimate liberation according to the tradition of Padmasaṃbhava.[23]

As a scholar, Tucci covered all 360 degrees, with publications in every field: from volumes of Tibetan art to archeological studies of the ancient Near East; from *Storia della filosofia cinese antica* [*The History of Ancient Chinese Philosophy*] in 1922 to his classic 1957 text, *Storia della filosofia Indiana* [*The History of Indian Philosophy*], which followed the traditional division of Indian philosophy into six principal systems; from brief, explanatory texts on magic in the Orient to articles in daily newspapers and on the *Bollettino della Reale Società Geografica Italiana* [*Bulletin of the Italian Royal Geographical Society*].

The cultural importance of Tucci's works is highly variable. In 1930 and 1932, for example, he published studies on Buddhist logic comprehensible only to few experts around the world, while in 1956, the Roman Camping Club would release his eighteen page booklet, *Vita nomade* [*Nomadic Life*], said to have been read by thousands. He published dozens of excellent journalistic articles on various Oriental disciplines, thirteen of them alone on Japan. In 1924, as part of the well-regarded series of Angelo Fortunato Formiggini – or the "private, dilettante editor," as the internationalist Jewish publisher was wont to label himself – Tucci published his delightful *Apologia del Taoismo* [*Apology of Taoism*], on the ancient philosophical-religious systems of the Japanese. In this endeavor, Tucci had followed in the footsteps of his teacher, Formichi, who knew the Modenese editor well and with whom, in 1923, he'd published his *Apologia del Buddhismo* [*Apology of Buddhism*].[24]

Tucci wrote night and day, at a grueling pace. Among his many works, one must also count the encyclopedia entries, book reviews, chapters in books complied by other authors, reports from archeological digs, presentations, and lectures. With increasing frequency, from 1974 until 1983, he wrote the introductions to

books of other scholars, mostly those of his students or others
involved with IsMEO. His last scientific articles are «On Swāt.
The Dards and Connected Problems», and, what many believe
to be his self-declared cultural legacy,«New Areas of Research
for Archeologists and Buddhologists».[25] Both were published
in 1977, at the ripe age of eighty-three. In 1980 he would edit,
with the aid of Joseph Mitsuo Kitagawa and other scholars, the
forty-seven page entry on «The Buddha and Buddhism» in *The
New Encyclopaedia Britannica*, with two of the sections bearing
his signature alone.[26] He was then eighty-six. In his final years,
between 1977 and 1983, he would maintain the strength and lu-
cidity to publish seventeen brief works, including his eight-page
acknowledgment speech on occasion of receiving the Jawaharlal
Nehru Award for International Understanding. Due to limited
mobility – as an eighty-six-year-old in ill health he was no longer
so agile – he wouldn't deliver the speech until October 3, 1978,
in Rome, though he'd been awarded the prize in India two years
prior.

Tucci's bibliography has been included in this biography in
its entirety – with the addition of several works not included in
the most current bibliography compiled by his students – for the
express purpose that, merely scanning the titles, one can trace
the cultural, spiritual, and social journey traversed in the life of
this exceptional man, whose wealth of cultural knowledge was
as deep as it was broad.[27] In fact, in the field of Oriental studies
– and I avoid the term Orientalism, which in recent years, with
Edward Said, has come to take on a strong political connotation
– the sheer breadth and depth of Tucci's cultural knowledge remains unparalleled in Italy to this day.[28] And as Tucci himself
said, what counts are the words we put down, that which is documented: despite his noted eccentricities, he himself wished
to be remembered only for what he'd left to us, whether written, photographed, filmed, realized, or projected. The rest, as

he said, is ineffable and ephemeral, looked on with same light, quasi-impermanent smile of the Buddha. The rest is nothing but a mind game, an illusion maker which is itself nothing more than an illusion.

This is the mentality, the creed Tucci would gradually come to adopt. And one cannot say with certainty whether this mentality was derived from his studies or if, instead, it was the mentality itself that brought him to produce his exceptional body of work and drew him toward a Buddhist vision of the world. Indeed, just as Formichi had before him, Tucci would embrace Buddhism; and even here, one cannot say whether it was his belief in the world's impermanence that brought him to Buddhism, or his Buddhism that would bring him to believe in the world's impermanence.

BUDDHA SMILES UPON HIM

As for determining when, in Tucci's life, he chose to follow in the path of the Buddha, no clear date can be specified. Like the majority of children in Italy at the turn of the century, he was baptized in the Christian faith, as a Catholic – even if, as he himself would insist, he spent his entire adult life as a Buddhist. A. N. Dar, a journalist for *Indian Express* – one of the most widely read Indian newspapers, circulated in Delhi, Bombay, and Madras – interviewed Tucci when he was just over eighty-four years old, and would ask how his interest in India and in Buddhism had developed. At the time, in fact, when Tucci was still in his youth, Buddhism was a religion and a culture all but unknown in Europe, other than to a few intellectuals of the likes of the Schlegel brothers, Schopenhauer, Nietzsche, Jung, and, of course, scholars of the Oriental sciences and theology. As early as the pre-war era, and even in Italy, groups of enthusiasts had begun to form around Theravāda Buddhism, its original branch – understood, however, as a rationalistic, individualistic, and elitist doctrine, a "non-religious religion," according to the nineteenth century interpretation. Tucci's response to Dar was that his attraction had probably developed in a previous life. His interpretation of Buddhism, however, was *sui generis*. In truth, there are five, obligatory precepts every monk and layman must strive to follow – Tucci, as we'll learn, will obey some more faithfully than others:

> *Abstain from killing*
> *Abstain from taking what is not given*
> *Abstain from sexual misconduct*
> *Abstain from false speech*
> *Abstain from fermented drink that causes heedlessness*

There are other, optional, precepts – among which, the call to abstain from public honors and ranks – recommended to all practicing Buddhists. As a scholar, Tucci rose to the highest ranks in his field and was showered with medals and honors. But then, as Buddha says: «What would you think if the man, having crossed over the river, then said to himself, Oh, this raft has served me so well, I should strap it on to my back and carry it over land now?» So it is with the vehicle of doctrine: as soon as the shore of Enlightenment is reached, the raft must be tossed aside and abandoned. In just such a way must the believer act, having achieved the highest state, in regard to the Buddhist precepts which form its doctrine: he must liberate himself of them and behave only according to his own principles. Even still, he can't possibly disobey the precepts he's abandoned, for all motive to do so, including desire itself, has been conquered. Tucci considered himself an Enlightened One, one for whom the raft of doctrine and rules was no longer necessary: in determining his actions, he needed obey only his own conscience.

More so than a religion, Buddhism is a moral doctrine and an ethical discipline, founded on the theory of the transmigration of souls. Some five hundred years before the appearance of Christ, the prince of the Śākya clan realized that life inevitably brings pain – the pain of distance and detachment from the people and objects we love, the pain of being joined to that which we hate, the pain of sickness and death. The essence of life is pain. And so he set off in search of a way to avoid suffering and, ultimately, to avoid rebirth, and thus a new life burdened with the very same sufferings. One day, while meditating in the shade of a tree, he came to the understanding that our normal perception of the world is illusory and that only in relinquishing each and every attachment to the world – every desire and aversion, whatever its object, friend or enemy, material goods, convictions, feelings – could a man avoid suffering, and therefore, rebirth: he'd reached Enlightenment. From then on, he became known as Buddha, which in Sanskrit means «awakened»: he'd woken from the long sleep of ignorance, to reality as it truly is.

Gautama Buddha – the Tathāgata, as he would call himself, according to scripture – by his radiant example and his many sermons, transcribed by his disciples, revealed the path to the absence of all pain, the simple road to reawakening, rousing the mind from its state of illusion. All had been clearly laid out, like a trail marked on a precise map, indicating each house along the way, each tree, bridge, fountain, even the vagrant flocks, leaving traces of their gray fleece as they passed: dreams, desires, fantasies, memories, regrets: in a word, the sediment of our hearts and minds. The Buddha merely showed the way, the simplest road from ignorance to Enlightenment. We are free to choose our own path, to continue in our suffering or not, though as long as we cling to the illusion of life we fall deeper into the pit of unconsciousness and ever closer to rebirth. In his first lecture, referred to as the Sermon at Benares, the Buddha expressed the core of his teaching:

Now, this, O bhikkhus, is the noble truth concerning suffering: birth is attended with pain, decay is painful, disease is painful, death is painful. Union with the unpleasant is painful, painful is separation from the pleasant, and any craving that is unsatisfied, that too is painful. In brief, bodily conditions which spring from attachment are painful.

Now this, O bhikkhus, is the noble truth concerning the origin of suffering: verily, it is that craving which causes the renewal of existence, accompanied by sensual delight, seeking satisfaction now here, now there, the craving for the gratification of the passions, the craving for a future life, and the craving for happiness in this life.

Now this, O bhikkhus, is the noble truth concerning the destruction of suffering: verily, it is the destruction, in which no passion remains, of this very thirst; it is the laying aside of, the being free from, the dwelling no longer upon this thirst.[29]

Temptation – a desire present even in devoted followers, no matter their level of awareness –the want to take pleasure in life, or, more precisely, to live life as if it were real and bind oneself to the transitory, was embodied by Māra, «he who kills», a demon who, in later texts, came to be defined as «the ruler of desire's kingdom». He was destruction personified, depicted as a devil who, at the sight of the Buddha meditating and on the verge Enlightenment, unleashed his armies of poisonous snakes, of arrows and fire-spewing mountains. But before the young prince, Māra's weapons turned to so many pleasant breezes, palaces decked with flowers, halos of light. So powerful is the illusion that the very same image that might arouse in us a great fear can awaken us to great beauty. Then came the daughters of Māra – craving, boredom, and passion – to assault Siddhārta, «he who's achieved his goal», driving him toward temptation. They too were defeated: lust, the thirst for power, the desire to possess, all that saps the adept of his energy, neither do these have any basis in reality. Our needs and sensations imprison us, forming part of *māyā*, the entrapping net of the perceivable world. Though to free oneself is simple, once these trappings are recognized for their true nature. We are like children, haunted in the dark by monsters and ghosts or, quite the opposite, overtaken by a splendid vision: nothing, in the end, but the fruit of our imagination, our fears and desires. One need only flick the lights and the images cease to exist. Buddhism, in this way, is the refusal of a return to infancy. It is a habit of living and an internal discipline that combat our tendency to turn back.

In Tibet, the demon Māra and his daughters are commonly depicted in frescoes, paintings, *thangkas*, carvings, and, ifless often, handmade goods – wooden or silver teapots, tea cup saucers, the silver or gold necklaces in which mantras are kept, sacred lamps and sheathes – where represented instead are the eight auspicious symbols, the *makaras* (or, sea monsters), winding rivers, dragons, or stylized Chinese characters.

Non-attachment, or detachment from all things, the refusal to take anything but that which is given or to disturb the natural harmony of the universe with one's actions, is a simple path to set out on, though difficult to keep. With each rebirth, each life, one purer than the last, the believer comes closer, searching deeper within, practicing the tenets with greater devotion, striving. Only after several incarnations of a life lived in strict adherence to non-attachment – whether to thoughts, words, deeds, or emotions – and an unwavering benevolence toward all living creatures can one hope to eradicate all desire, even the desire involved with achieving the ultimate goal itself. In this way, we nurture the hope that we may one day slip from the bonds that tie our bodies and hearts to the external world and be born again enlightened, freed from passion, weightless yet filled with love for our neighbors, like the bodhisattvas, the buddhas, who do not merge with a final *nirvāṇa* or *paranirvāṇa*, but remain on earth, to guide men in the ways of conquering ignorance and draw them toward the nature of the Enlightened One.

To merge with the pure light of *nirvāṇa* – the very absence of *karman's* lingering effects, which cloud our mind and weight us down – a devotee, regardless of sex or cast, must follow in the path of the Buddha. In so doing, man cleans his flesh of all that is of this worldand liberates himself from the five aggregates (form and body, feelings and sensations, perceptions and memory, mental states, and consciousness). He must do so, however, without subjecting himself to exaggerated displays of asceticism, or, of course, indulging in passions of any kind.

Buddhism, as it was originally developed, is not a religion, in the sense that it does not demand that its devotees worship one or more gods, but that they live by a series of practical, ethical and moral norms, as a shield against worldly troubles and concerns – to overcome suffering. Buddha himself was not a god, but a man, an exceptional being of exceptional virtue: man perfected. According to the precepts of Mahāyāna, the largest branch of Buddhism, the Buddha did not distance himself or cut himself off from men in reaching the supreme light, but instead continued to demonstrate a profound love for the world around him, to share his teachings with men, with plants and animals, with the entire universe, showing the path toward absolute internal peace, as symbolized by his weightless smile. In the Mahāyāna tradition, the historic figure of the Buddha is viewed as an eternal and omnipresent principle, which manifests itself in numerous ways, while humans follow along the path of the Bodhisattva, seeking to master six, or ten, Perfections – or, in Sanskrit, *pāramitās* – including generosity (*dāna*), patience (*kṣānti*), perfection of meditation (*dhyāna*), and knowledge (*jñāna*). In so doing, an adept dedicates himself to the attainment of Enlightenment, not only for himself, but for all beings.

Kṣānti stands for «patience», «acceptance», «tolerance». To master it, one must face pain and affliction with a determined patience, free of anger toward the suffering which others inflict upon us, and approach the more difficult teachings, such as emptiness (*śūnyatā*) without fear of their implications. One must confront life with a spirit of immense goodwill and, as the Dalai Lama says, of kindness toward ourselves and toward others. I've claimed that Buddhism is not, in the strict sense, a religion, and yet it stands as one of the great religions of the world, offering a comprehensive view of life in all its aspects, of the cosmos, of the natural world, and of the realms of culture and emotion. It lays out precise guidelines on how to treat animals, on what to eat, how to travel, on philosophy, on how to view ourselves, what to wear, which colors most delight the spirit, on the origin of the universe, on how to behave and to interpret every single act and phenomenon in life, on myths and rites, which are symbolic and, at times, historic expressions of religious truths. Within only a few centuries after the birth of Buddha in a region of southern Nepal, the religion had spread throughout India and China, Tibet, Mongolia, Japan, and Southeast Asia.

In the case of Giuseppe Tucci, one of few such cases in Italy, it was Buddhism in its original form to which he would devote himself, Buddhism at its humble beginnings – without the countless sects and temples, the endless rites, rosaries, mantras, and prayer wheels, the holy name of Buddha repeated a thousand times, the powerful incense andthe overflow of colors, sounds, and visions so characteristic of the religion in its later forms, as it would be observed by the masses throughout half of Asia. A Mahāyāna of a thousand gods, a thousand bells, a thousand invocations recited in a hypnotic trance. Among the scholars of Oriental studies prior to the 1950s, it appears that only Formichi, Fosco Maraini, and the scientist, Giuseppe De Lorenzo, professed the same belief, at least publicly.

When, in his interview «A Love Affair with India», A. N. Dar asked Tucci what he thought were the most pressing issues in modern India, Tucci responded that the principal issue, the country's greatest problem, was overpopulation.[30]

– I firmly support birth control methods. In our case, unfortunately, we have the Pope. You, however, do not. Japan has already taken advantage of this fact, and already we see the benefits of such action –Tucci replied.

Tucci's open and fearless opinion on birth control, as well as on abortion, did not quite earn him the affection of the Vatican. And yet, as it seemed, he remained untroubled by the church's disapproval.

– I am a Buddhist. In Buddhism, there is no church. One answers only to one's own conscience.

Such a Malthusian view of population control had been expressed already in 1925, and with great conviction, by Rabindranath Tagore, during his first visit to Italy, which will be addressed in the following chapter. When questioned of India's most dire problems – in an interview recalled by Formichi in *India e indiani [India and Indians]* – the Poet would cite excessive population as the sole cause of economic inequality in Europe and, to a greater extent, in India. A recourse to science, he believed, was necessary, to seek out methods to destroy life in its germinal state. As long as its population continued to multiply without restraint, India would find no salvation.[31]

His attraction to Buddhism, a lack of access to Tibet – then in the hands of the Chinese – and, above all, a desire to venture down unexplored paths in search of documents and remnants of the past, would together lead Tucci to Nepal. There, he developed a profound interest in so-called, "erotic sculpture" – Tantric sculptures and bas-reliefs. Up until the last half-century, the Tantric arts have been unpopular with scholars, disturbed as they were by their seeming amorality. Unlike his contemporaries, however, Tucci held no qualms and began carrying out studies in the field, which would take root and flourish with the efforts of his students. Neither would he view Nepali sculpture as obscene, nor the famed Hindu art in the Khajuraho temple, in Madhya Pradesh, charged as it is with eroticism. In adopting such a point of view, singular in its time, Tucci stood in opposition not only to the opinion of amateurs, but to that of dedicated scholars as well. Orthodox Hinduism states that *kāma* – that is, love, the sixty-four arts, and life's other pleasures, such as music, dance, painting, reciting poetry, cooking, preparing perfumes, chess-playing, book-binding, and other crafts and skills – is, in fact, one of the four aims of all men who adhere to *dharma*, the personal and universal law that regulates *karman*, or, all actions and their consequences. Only by passing through these two filters can one achieve *mokṣa*, ultimate freedom. *Kāma*, in that sense, is a moral and religious precept as well, one of the four great «aims of man», the *puruṣārthas*. Proponents of the Tantric schools would go even further, claiming that everything, even eroticism, may serve in the pursuit of our final liberation: that which binds us may also lead to our freedom.

As Tucci said, in response to Dar:

– We must transform our passions into a means of liberation.

With the sincerity permitted to all great men and women late in life, he confessed that his turn to Buddhism had come as a result of disenchantment with the Catholic church and its priests, adding:

– I found Buddhism to be much simpler. It is an ethical doctrine, and nothing else. All is based on sincerity, and you are completely free.

Tucci was a Buddhist insofar as he believed in a certain dimension of life, an alternate reality, safe from suffering and complications; a reality which our words and thoughts can neither describe nor disturb. He was, in that sense, an atheist, without belief in a god, though respectful of religion in all its forms. Upon entering a temple, he felt himself neither Hindu nor Buddhist, as he would repeatedly attest. He did not worship the statues of their gods and goddesses, but bowed when others bowed, prayed when others prayed. In every place of worship, he perceived a special aura. On a more pragmatic level, Tucci also believed that in order to connect meaningfully with those of another culture one must first adapt to that culture's habits and customs.

From Buddhism came his tendency to regard any attachment to personal emotions with a certain distaste; even if, in the end, he often found himself strongly inclined toward one person or another, or felt himself partial to this or that project, or bound heart and soul to ancient manuscripts, rare books, works of art, *thangkas*, archeological remains and objects of exceptional craft; even if, in other cases, and with no apparent motive, he would develop an instinctual antipathy toward a student, a colleague, another scholar – even those from distant countries – or a particular work. If anything at all, Tucci was not a man to take the middle road, to reveal himself as passive or mild-mannered, at least not as long as such behavior did not strike him as advantageous.

Speaking of his own character, Tucci often declared himself to be as dry and unfeeling as desert grass. Which was, perhaps, a mere affectation – his way of saying that, as a Buddhist, he'd surpassed the realm of emotions and passions common to all mortals, through which we inevitably perceive the world and which we attribute, often erroneously, to those around us. Rather than recognize them as our own mental construct, we bind ourselves to them inextricably and observe them in others as if they were facts of reality. If, however, by sentiment one intends that spontaneous empathy that opens us now and then to the suffering of our neighbors and constitutes one of the highest forms of *karuṇā* – Buddhist compassion, Christian *pietas* – Tucci's absence of emotion was undeniable. Indiscriminately, and with the exception of only his closest students, all those who came to know Tucci and spend time with him declared him a frigid and calculating man – amiable and charming one moment, callous and scornful the next, whichever he found most opportune. All of his magnificent works as a scholar, his expeditions and activities under the Fascist regime and throughout the golden age of Christian Democracy, demonstrate a clear detachment, as well as a capacity to foresee, to equip, to plan, and, in part, to manipulate others, bending them to his own inflexible and most uncommon will. He also possessed a particular knack for ingratiating himself with men of power, as well as an impressive ability to maintain his focus and to overcome any obstacle – man, object, or mountain – that dare come between him and his aim: he was a tireless walker and an expert climber.

Toward those most in need, Tucci held none of the compassion that would take root in his travel companions – Giulia Nuvoloni and Francesca Bonardi, both of whom he would marry, Eugenio Ghersi, Fosco Maraini, Felice Boffa Ballaran, Pietro Mele, Concetto Guttuso, Regolo Moise, Vito Amorosino. Only on rare occasions would he go out of his way to help those in need, and even then, only once his fame had spread. An explorer of unlikely character, he exuded a coldness, a detachment, an inaccessibility similar to that of the pure and insurmountable peaks of the Himalayas, among which he'd spend decades of his life. Only in the final pages of *Tra giungle e pagode [Among Jungles and Pagodas]*, the account of his penultimate expedition in Nepal, would a flicker of compassion reveal itself, as a shadow of remorse for the men who, bearing his belongings up the mountain, had been swallowed by its gorges, and of whose very names he remained ignorant:

> And I knew that the memory, at times, would be cast in the grim shadow of the three bearers who lost their lives, whose names I do not know, nor ever knew, who, driven by meager wages, followed me up the mountain and were stolen from their families by the pitfalls of the journey.[32]

As a young man, however, Tucci held out hope that his men would, in some way, look on him with affection, as he would express of his caravaneers on the 1933 expedition in western Tibet:

> At Scipki, on the border separating Tibet from the state of Bashahar, we wave one last goodbye to the distant peaks we'd scaled, and my caravaneers, though used to such dangers and hardships, pray to God that they never again be made to traverse such a harsh landscape. And yet, I'm certain, were I to call on them for another expedition, they would agree immediately: they had grown fond of us. And now, writing at such a great distance from their land, I think with nostalgia not only of the hushed immensity of Tibet and of my unforgettable experiences there, but of my humble companions as well, who struggled with me and served me, for compensation, yes, but perhaps also out of a growing understanding and, as it may be, affection.[33]

Among the various lists of the world's most renowned Buddhists, Tucci is the only Italian whose biography appears, along with the Venerable U. Lokanatha Thera.[34] His philosophy of life, his non-attachment in regard to passions and emotions so permeated his works – or rather, his works and studies so permeated his life – that Tucci would name his first and only child, with his first wife, Rosa, after the Buddha's most beloved disciple. The child was born on May 5, 1923, in Ancona, and baptized Ananda, which in Sanskrit means «bliss», with the middle name Maria. He was raised by his paternal grandparents, after the marriage of Giuseppe and Rosa was annulled, on April 4, 1927, by the tribunal of the Roman Rota, and Rosa stripped of custody. Ananda would go on to become a reputable doctor, though no one in his city knew him for the son of a world-renowned Orientalist. I spoke with two men from Ancona, both well informed and culturally engaged, asking of Ananda's reputation before he died. They replied that he treated his patients «in something of a Buddhist manner». Giving no further explanation, their response seemed to speak of a certain oddness in his medical practice, or perhaps something unusual about his behavior. Gilda Tucci, Ananda's daughter, would later tell me that in Libya, where he'd relocated for his profession, he would treat lepers with immense dedication. Outside of work, however, when they called after him or tried to touch him in demonstration of their gratitude, Andanda would call on the askari appointed by the king to lash them and drive them away.

As if the Buddha himself were mocking Tucci's choice of such a loaded name for his son – reminding that all is impermanent, all an illusion – poor Ananda was referred to by all who knew him in Rome with the diminutive "A' Nando . . .", a typical Roman expression used to mean "whatchamacallit" or "what's-his-face."

Tucci requested, and his request honored, that in his obituary he be described as having reached the supreme light. In his life and work, as noted before, Tucci evidently believed to have liberated himself from the karmic chain of rebirths, from body to body, from mortal shell to mortal shell, and to have reached Enlightenment, thus, *paranirvāṇa*, attaining the perfection of the Buddha, the state of Buddha himself.

THE GURU

Raniero Gnoli, who may indeed have been Tucci's most beloved student, wrote in his account, *Ricordo di Giuseppe Tucci [A Memory of Giuseppe Tucci]* that «knowledge, by its very nature, is a unifying force, and in so being it stood for him as a true means of ethical purification and the principal duty of man».[35] Tucci, speaking at the University of Naples "L'Orientale" in 1974, where he was presented with the volume *Gururājamañjarikā: Studi in onore di Giuseppe Tucci [Gururājamañjarikā: Studies in Honor of Giuseppe Tucci]*, would have the following to say of the central role of knowledge in his life and on science as a way of life:[36]

> You have called me a guru [...] and a guru, as you know, shares with his disciples all that he thinks, imagines, learns, intuits, by way of a living relationship, which the Indians call *govatsanyāya:* much like the vital nourishment a mother cow passes to its calf, infusing it, so to speak, with its own vitality; *śuṣkatarka*, on the other hand, dry reasoning, has nothing of the warm, and life-giving vibrations of the spirit. Science is not merely the reporting of facts, formulas, comparisons, and data: it is a way of living, of feeling, of reacting...

In the name of this formative science, which is life itself, and fueled by his impassioned interest in Western origins and cultural traditions, Tucci would take time nearly every day, up until the very end of his life, to study classical Greek and medieval Latin. Perhaps as an act of rebellion toward the rhetorical and philological tradition that dominated the schools of his time, Tucci displayed no particular interest in Cicero, Quintilian, and Virgil, the three Latin classics *par excellence*, whose well-known passages were the bane of entire generations, including my own, as we were forced to translate them into modern Italian. Instead, he fell for a Doctor of the Catholic Church, St. Thomas Aquinas, whose *Summa Theologiae* he'd read multiple times even before completing grammar school. Just before his death, he would comment on this lifelong passion: «He, St. Thomas [...] who never left my side and to whom I owe, if indeed any remain in me, the clarity and logical soundness of my thought».[37]

In regard to the Italian canon, he preferred the writers of the 1300s, and Petrarch over Dante. He loved and admired the poet Giacomo Leopardi and Daniello Bartoli, the seventeenth century Jesuit who wrote a history of China, as well as several other works, including the essay, *Dell'huomo di lettere difeso et emendato [The Learned Man Defended and Reformed]*, in which he announces the two greatest enemies of educated man: vice and ignorance.

Tucci conceived of culture as an abstract good, with its own, transcendent ethical system, unbound to humanity or humanism. At the center of his studies is not man, but the search itself; and he did not see himself as "only" a man, but as a scientist and an explorer. Put in such terms, it would seem to reveal him as an unfeeling scholar, greedy and indifferent: and yet, one need only read his students' accounts to perceive his spirit, his ability to incite their passions and inspire their unconditional reverence, the reverence of his friends and of his wives – or, at the very least, of his last wife. He was a cold, impassioned scientist, so filled with contradictions that it seems a far stretch to imagine them coexisting in one man. In the course of his long life, however, he would not dedicate himself to science alone, but also, through IsMEO, to the development of a clear cultural policy.

Tucci studied in the Liberal Arts Faculty at the Royal University of Rome, today called La Sapienza University of Rome. As a student, he migrated gradually from the Western classics to the East and Asia, in whose books and in whose «clairvoyant insights» he began to «espy new answers to the doubts» that had been tormenting him. In 1963, he would describe his passions for the lands of the East and Oriental studies in the following terms: it was, for him, an escape from the «dull and dry philology worship» that the university's archeology department had come to practice, imprisoning rather than giving form to the imagination:

> And so I crept, further and further, into the labyrinth
> of Oriental studies, which was to me a fascinating
> and radiant guiding light, and gradually, as I gained
> a greater familiarity with the texts and the clairvoy-
> ant insights of Asia, I began to espy new answers to
> the doubts that had been tormenting me. I was at-
> tracted to the philosophical subtleties of India and
> China, the logical structures of certain systems, their
> mythologies interspersed with flashes of insight and
> terror, at once corporal and metaphysical, like the
> apparitions of a world which at first seemed so dis-
> tant from ours, but which revealed itself, as I began
> to decode its languages and symbols, as intimately
> linked on both a spiritual and human level. There,
> I found more life than in the dull and dry philology
> worship that, in my time as a university student, had
> ensnared the study of archaeology, which seemed
> utterly lost in particulars, and at times, mere trifles,
> while I'd thought it was the duty of archaeology to
> equip the imagination, to enliven, if only for a brief
> moment, the lives and objects of past civilizations.
> So I abandoned archeology and turned, with great
> hope – with hope that would not be spent in vain –
> to the Orient.[38]

Tucci's first voyage, it could be said, one which would mark him for the rest of his life, was a voyage through time, to under-stand the culture of men and the life of objects from ages past. In 1942, he said *in memoriam* of the Tibetologist, Sándor Csoma de Kőrös (Alexander Csoma De Körös):

> Mankind is not enriched only by an insatiable plow-
> ing forward, a relentless conquering of new ideas and
> inventing of new devices; we must also pause now
> and then to reflect, to understand our distant and
> nearly forgotten thoughts: for nowhere is it said that
> the new is better than the ancient, and even in the
> imaginations of those separated from us by time and
> space, we may catch a flicker of that eternal light,
> that light which, beneath every sky, man has ignited
> or discovered, to serve as warmth and comfort in a
> life of pain and suffering.[39]

Throughout his life, Tucci dedicated himself to the study of Sanskrit and Chinese. Not for a love of the language in and of itself, nor for the sake of mere philology – that field which exhausts itself, as a Harvard professor once said to me, «in the study of a single world» – but to better understand the religious conceptions, beliefs, and modes of thought of the Indian and Chinese peoples, to give form to the spirit of these cultures, whose origins lie in the remotest stretches of time and space.

Early on, Tucci would turn his attention to a twelfth century historical text, Kalhaṇa's *Rājataraṅgiṇī*, consulting the edition of the great Hungarian archeologist, philologist, and explorer, Aurel Stein. Of the texts and epigraphs discovered to this day, Kalhaṇa's work remains the only medieval history of Kashmir, and of Southern Asia, ever written. In the case of Indian culture, however, one cannot speak of history in its modern conception. Up until British rule and, in fact, on into the 1970s, scholars of Greater India and Southern Asia, India's former territory – comprising modern day Pakistan, Kashmir, Nepal, Afghanistan, Tibet, the states of Sikkim and Bhutan, Bangladesh and Sri Lanka – had no understanding of time in its Western, historical sense. Years were not measured continuously from a specified starting point, like the birth of Christ or, in the case of the ancient

Greeks, the "I" of Herodotus. With the rise of each new king began a new era, and a new measure of time, as happened on October 29, 1922, the day after the March on Rome, when Mussolini gave rise to the Fascist Era. With each new dynasty the sense of time, and, with it, the sense of history, was thus reborn, and all that came before that moment, when another dynasty held sway, was erased. A new epoch was born – the world renewed, new principles established, new rules and new values. In the Era of Fascism, the style of calligraphy reverted to that of Roman inscriptions, to indicate Italy's return to grandeur and the new empire's colonial expansion, a journey back in time of sorts, a rehashing of the most famed and glorious period of Western civilization, which had its seat in Rome. Not only was a new political structure established with the new era, but a new order of thought, a new conception of art, of architecture, and with it, a new dimension of space, which stretched to cover new territories and to uncover a former glory: an utterly modern antiquity.

But turning back to Southern Asia – here, one speaks not in terms of history, but of royal lineages, or, in fact, chronicles; with each new king and emperor not only is there no absolute time established, but neither is there a relative time between one kingdom and another, and the dates are not sequential. The only exception is the relative dating system put in place by the great Buddhist king, Aśoka, ruler of Magadha, of the Maurya Indian dynasty, who died in 232 BCE. In his forty-first year of reign, ruling an immense kingdom that covered a large part of India and the modern day states of Nepal, Pakistan, and Afghanistan, Aśoka began to spread the Good Law – the *dharma* of Buddhism – issuing edicts. Inscribed on rocks or stone columns in the local language, or else in Sanskrit, or bilingual, in Greek and Aramaic, the edicts told of his reforms and incited the people of his kingdom to follow in the path of the Buddha and to respect other religions. He urged them to follow an individual morality, based on respect for one's parents, elders, teachers, friends, servants, and Brahmins, encouraging generosity toward the poor, ascetics, friends, and relatives, non-violence toward life in every form, moderation in spending and saving, and kindness toward one's neighbor as a value of greater importance even than ritual ceremonies, which stood as the focal point of religious practice in India. This Buddhist apostle, who claimed himself to be «dear to the gods», allowed us to determine the duration of his rule by having mentioned a few of his neighboring kings, of whose dates we have a sure record.

Tucci studied the *Rājataraṅgiṇī* so thoroughly that his students, after his death, often recalled its worn and tattered pages. So deeply did he cherish this book that he would bring it with him down into the trenches, when he was sent to fight in the Great War, serving twenty-eight months. And as he did throughout his life with the books he loved, he filled the margins with notes, comments, and cross references, which often ran over to the back pages of the volume. It's not hard to imagine a young Tucci, his back to the wall of a trench, struggling to read his book in the cold and dark, grenades harassing the air around him, indifferent to his status as an officer.

GAZING EAST

An interest in China swept through all Europe in the seventeenth century. And in the two centuries to follow, the trend spread to Italian literary culture as well: Ugo Foscolo, Giacomo Leopardi, Carlo Cattaneo, and Giuseppe Ferrari would all pen essays on China. But their works were not true Sinology. The scientific study of China's language and culture would arrive later, with Antelmo Severini, who graduated from the Faculty of Law in Macerata, and whose publications marked the birth of Sinology and Japanology.

Indology, or the science concerned with the language and culture of the Indian subcontinent, had its birth in Italy in the second half of the 1800s, with the studies of Angelo de Gubernatis in Florence and Rome, followed by the work of Michele Kerbaker in Naples, and his student, Formichi, in Rome, as well as that of Valentino Papesso, Ferdinando Belloni-Filippi, and other scholars throughout Italy. Tucci, a student of Formichi's, came as a fourth generation scholar – though he would act, as we'll see, as a pioneer in numerous branches of study.

Tucci studied Chinese and Indian philosophy every day; he also read – «out of penance», as he would jokingly remark – classical Sanskrit literature and poetry, the so-called *kāvya*, which he held to be indispensable in understanding the history and culture of India. *Kāvya* refers to the lyric poetry and prose of India, its theater work, novels, biographies, and its two great epics, the *Mahābhārata* and the *Rāmāyaṇa* – above all, however, it denotes the highly stylized courtly poetry of India. There is the question, then, of why Tucci would consider the study of *kāvya* an act of penance. As his former student, Paolo Daffinà, would astutely describe it in a lecture, *kāvya* is a literary style which «managed to express even the simplest ideas in complicated terms». Each poetic technique is employed to excess, even in a single verse: objects, persons, and emotions are described in the most ornate manner possible, with word-play, the infinite repetition of a specific term or syllable, or *double entendre*; anacoluthon, allusion, analogy, and allegory abound; in other words, every possible weapon of poetics and rhetoric is employed, resulting in contorted, convoluted, baroque lines of poetry. There are poems constructed of a single, two-syllable word which, read in various ways, produces different meanings; others are formed from the repetition of the same word, which in Sanskrit may take on a variety of meanings, sometimes contrary. And so two syllables give rise to an endless line of poetry. All of which is complicated further by *sandhi*, or the euphonic combination of letters, which effects changes not only within the word itself, but also when that word is united with others to form a single word, sometimes across several lines, which must be interpreted from end to beginning. Of course, in poetry and prose, *sandhi* is used both internally and externally.

Classical Indian poetry is much like a cocktail with too many ingredients – a profusion of flavors, colors, and scents.

As a young man,Tucci was essentially, or so he considered himself, an autodidact. He attended university, though he would hold little esteem for the institution throughout his life, even when he himself became a professor. The Italian university, which in his time followed the rhetorical model of German universities, he saw as crushed beneath the «squalid weight of pointless notions». Tucci would hardly reserve memory of his Sanskrit professor, Formichi, though Formichi would reserve the highest respect for his student, aiding him throughout his career. Commenting on the institution of the university and its teaching methods, and therefore, indirectly, on his teacher, Tucci would write:

Right off, I must say [...] that upon first entering the university, I found it a disheartening and dwindling reservoir of outdated and exhausted teaching methods... More an autodidact than a student, I left high school fresh and filled with the hope of finding in the University a guiding light and inspiration, what I found instead was a University bogged down in the methods and model of German institutions from the 1870s; too far had men and the sciences come to ignore the consequences of their progress. Dead was that mutual bond that links student and teacher in a true and inventive consanguinity, that living relationship, that prodigious exchange of ideas and emotions which teachers in India refer to as *govatsanyāya*. And in fact, if you'll allow me to linger in my memories, when I began attending courses at the university I found myself nearly overwhelmed by academic assertions and defenses, *in minoribus*, crushed beneath the squalid weight of pointless notions. Gone was the passion, the vibrant exchange that enflamed young students; our professors, in approaching the literature, whether by classical or Eastern authors, rather than shed light on the work through active participation, whether fruitful or unfruitful, fleeting or lasting, lost themselves in menial chatter, in a complaisant and meticulous listing of the opinions of others, all seemingly removed from the discussion and all of which any student could, at any time, find in a book and consider on his own; thus all critical examination, all intimacy with the text gave way to such rigid preoccupations.[40]

And yet Formichi, in promotion of a governmental reform that would open the University to the world and encourage an encounter between East and West, had published a booklet entitled *Il tarlo delle università italiane [The Ails of the Italian Universities].* In it, he would assert that the university system as it currently stood discouraged, and even hindered, Eastern studies.[41]

As we've seen already, Tucci began his studies of Sanskrit and Hebrew while still quite young, progressing to Iranian studies and Sinology. He would begin, as well, his studies of India, not only of its history, but delving into an as-of-yet unexplored branch of knowledge in Italy: Hindu materialist philosophy. This stood in line with his vision that India, as he would continually insist, was not merely a land of mystics and meditation. There are, of course, the philosophical schools that place all in the figure of the supreme *brahman* - the transcendent principle, identical to *ātman*, which resides in the fortress of the heart – and those in which all leads to the supreme God of the *Bhagavadgītā*, but in addition, there are still other philosophical schools that do not, to such a degree, negate external reality or depend upon a god figure. All, however, with the exception of the school of the materialists – called the *nāstikas*, *cārvākas*, or *lokāyatikas* – submit to the law of *karman*, by which a lowly life may be redeemed through noble action. With each virtuous act a seed is planted, which then flowers into a rebirth as a being of a higher order. This process continues until the soul is exalted and purified, liberated from the karmic bonds, and therefore no longer subject to rebirth. According to the inexorable law of *karman*, a woman may merit rebirth as a man; or, on the contrary, if a man's deeds violate *dharma*, the cosmic order, the laws of his caste, or those of his country, he will be reborn as a being of a progressively lower order, from man to woman, from woman to casteless – the famous untouchables, who lie outside of the caste system and are therefore of a special impurity – from casteless to dog, and so on. For the Hindu, then, the lowest status possible is to be reborn as a female dog, or as a woman in the caste of untouchables: a status which, in truth, was held as lower than rebirth as an animal.

For Buddhists, inferiority is determined as a measure of one's consciousness: animals, therefore, though living beings deserving of respect and help, just as all beings in the universe according to the Buddha, are inferior to men – without the ability to amend their behavior and slip from the karmic bonds that tie them to the earth they have no hope of achieving *nirvāṇa*. An animal must suffer rebirth until the tendencies that bind it in such a state have exhausted themselves. If indeed the cycle of rebirth is sustained by the maltreatment of other creatures – whether one of your kind, a cockroach, or a blade of grass – by desire, the seed of all action, and by action itself, carried out for the purpose of satisfying a desire, it is clear how difficult it would be for an animal to evolve and escape this vicious cycle. Lacking the consciousness and the freedom necessary to act of its own will, it cannot lift itself to reincarnation as a being of a higher order.

The *Jātakamālā*, the «garland of birth-stories [of the Buddha]», serves as an excellent illustration of the Enlightened One's compassionate love toward all forms of life, including animals. One famous tale recounts how the Buddha, by way of aquiet self-sacrifice, saved a being from its own voracity: in order to appease a starving tigress, on the point of completing the horrendous sin of consuming its own cubs, he killed himself to offer his body as food.

Though if honorable actions lead to honor, dishonorable actions, too, come with their negative consequences. In carrying out a base action, we do harm not only to ourselves – in that the action's negative effects harm us directly – but we disturb the balance and harmony of all creation. We mar ourselves within and debase the world around us. That single action, for as small and insignificant as it may be, generates a chain of negative events. As when a stone is tossed into a pond: the circular wave that forms around it disturbs the water's peaceful surface, the disturbance expanding outward with each subsequent, albeit weakened, ripple. And even below the water's surface, how are we to know what damage the stone has done there? Each action carries with it unforeseeable repercussions, for which reason we must always act honorably, or not at all. We must be mindful of all we do, say, think, and desire for ourselves and for others. Though it be beyond our knowledge or imagination, all, in its own way, is of extreme importance, and all has its weight in the universe.

Once, the Bodhisattva was born to a respectable family of scholars and mastered the lessons of several sacred scriptures. Soon, however, he grew disillusioned, and renounced his worldly life in pursuit of spiritual elevation. In the course of time, he proved his excellence and became the guru of several ascetics.

One day, while wandering through the forest with his disciple, Ajita, he saw from the top of a hill a tigress, pacing hungrily around its cubs. Moved by compassion, he thought to sacrifice his own body, as a means of feeding the tigress and saving the cubs. He sent his disciple off in search of food for the tigress, lest he grow fearful of his teacher's sacrifice. No sooner than Ajita left the site, had the Bodhisattva leaped down from the mountains that stood across from the tigress, offering his body. The clatter of the fall caught the hungry tigress's attention; without delay, she pounced on him and tore his body to pieces, feasting upon him with her cubs.

When Ajita returned, he saw his guru was missing. He glanced around and was surprised to find that the tigress no longer appeared hungry. Her cubs, too, seemed content. But before long, to his astonishment, he noticed the blood-stained rags of his guru's dress scattered about the scene. He knew, then, that his guru had offered his body as food to the hungry tigress, protecting her young ones in an act of immense charity. And he knew, as well, why his guru had sent him away. Out of reverence for his guru, who'd demonstrated the supreme sacrifice, he bowed his head.

Lo! The way of the world:
To appease her hunger, this beast transgresses all
limits of affection
and seeks to devour her own cubs.[42]

In the Buddhist and Hindu texts of the time, hardly any mention – beyond brief references and fragments – is made of the materialist school, which was often neglected for its refusal to believe in reincarnation. Before the war, Tucci began patiently collecting these sparse sources, seeking to piece together their mode of thought. Only several years later would he complete his efforts, publishing his results in two parts, in 1923 and in 1929, under the title «Linee di una storia del materialismo indiano» («Tracing the History of Indian Materialism»).[43] To this day, nearly eighty years on, these studies remain of fundamental importance and are considered essential to the understanding of the materialist school.

As evidence of his realistic and stringently unsentimental view of India, the first text in Sanskrit that Tucci placed in the hands of his students was the *Nyāyasūtras*, the verses of logic attributed to Gautama in the second century CE, which he considered essential reading for anyone who wished to understand Indian thought. Tucci would then turn his interests to the Buddhist logicians, such as Vasubandhu, Diṅnāga, Dharmakīrti, requesting their manuscripts from the powerful Guruju, Hem Raj Sharma – of whom we'll speak extensively later on in this book. Parts of these texts were thought to have been lost in their original Sanskrit, surviving only in later Tibetan and Chinese translations. For which reason, Tucci – whose interest in Buddhism, around the year 1920, had pushed him to study Pāli as well, the language in which the Buddhist canon was most widely available – translated some of these Chinese and Tibetan logical treatises back into Sanskrit, including the *Tarkaśāstra*, or «Treatise on Sound Reasoning». In 1929, the Baroda Oriental Institute published the book, *Pre-Diṅnāga Buddhist Texts on Logic from Chinese Sources*, which included the re-translations in Sanskrit of the *Tarkaśāstra* and the *Upāyahṛdaya*, the English translation of the Chinese and Tibetan version of Nāgārjuna's *Vigrahavyāvartanī*, and an English translation of the Chinese version of āryadeva's *śataśāstra*.[44] That same year, Tucci would publish «Buddhist Logic before *Diṅnāga* (Asaṅga, Vasubandhu, *Tarkaśāstras*)», an article in two parts.[45]

In India, as must be noted, *tarka* is a valid technique, and not merely a technique of reasoning. It is the process of debate, guided by rules and well-defined aims – an argument between two parties that leads to conclusive results, for which reason it stands as a valid method of obtaining knowledge. Since the Medieval period, two types of debate have been recognized among scholars: that which is held before the public, often under the protection and with the economic support of a king, coordinated, directed, and judged by one or more examiners; and that which is held between two scholars and is referred to as *tarka*, which translates as «logic». In certain philosophical schools, *tarka* refers to a complex and rather elaborate process, carried out in several, predetermined phases, and guided by rigid terms and precise objectives, so as to reach a succinct explanation on the nature of the substance, on its qualities and other ontological categories.[46] Of course, these methods gave rise to several valid treatises, referred to, precisely, as *tarkaśāstras*.

At the thought of translating a text back into Sanskrit, available only in medieval Tibetan or Chinese, I can't help but recall the laborious Greek translations we were forced to produce as teenagers, in our shaky Latin, of passages from Cicero; I can still see the German book of Latin Classics translated into Greek, with its greasy and worn black cover, from which our high school teacher made her selections. Though the Tibetan versions of the manuscripts are all but perfect renderings of the original Sanskrit – with uncertainty only in cases of commonly used words (given the many synonyms in Sanskrit) and in questions of syntax, particularly in works of prose – whether one can re-translate a translation remains a subject of cultural and philological debate. To translate in the language of an ancient or medieval philosopher, one must enter into the mind-set and cultural and social environment of the age, and into the very mind of the author. And even still, though the words and syntax of the text be rendered with near perfection, one can never reconstruct the text in its entirety, down to the last detail, including its style. Nevertheless, Tucci's translations into Sanskrit demonstrate an exceptional mastery of Chinese, Tibetan, and Sanskrit.

In 1920, after completing his degree in 1919, and after a two year break in scientific production due to the Great War, Tucci published the second part of «Note cinesi» («Chinese Notes»), the article «Dei rapporti fra la filosofia greca e l'orientale» («On the Relationship Between Greek and Oriental Philosophy») in the first issue of the *Giornale critico della filosofia italiana [Critical Journal of Italian Philosophy]* founded by Gentile, and his first work on Indian art in Tibetan texts, a review of Berthold Laufer's book, *Das Citralakshaṇa nach dem tibetischen Tanjur [The Citralakshaṇa according to the Tibetan Tanjur].*[47] Shortly after, with the cultural prescience that would characterize his entire career, he began to publish on a topic very much in vogue with scholars today, interreligious dialogue, with the article «A proposito dei rapporti tra cristianesimo e buddhismo» («On the Relationship between Christianity and Buddhism»).[48] It would also be his first article on Buddhism. At twenty-six years old, his areas of interest were already well laid out: Indian and Chinese philosophy, the history of Indian art and, later – the art it so influenced – Tibetan art.

THE SCIENTIST, THE EXPLORER

We have said thus far that Tucci's first voyage was a voyage into the past, a quest to understand the civilizations that had come before him and which, in Asia, at the turn of the twentieth century, remained nearly unaltered after hundreds of years. It was this mental journey that would lead him first to India, then to the most impenetrable and unexplored regions of the Land of

Snows and Nepal, and, at last, to the promotion and coordination of archeological digs in Pakistan, Iran, and Afghanistan. But why did he come to be one of the great explorers of the modern world? How did he manage to convince those in power of the scientific importance of his missions, to obtain the funds and necessary support, to procure himself the men and the means? Three factors, essentially, served as his source of strength and energy. As he himself would explain, his journey into the past was a mode of fleeing the facile and superficial encounters favored by the commodity culture and modern communications. It was a journey, as well, in opposition to the flattening out of culture, against the globalization and homogenization of societies that, nearly a half century ago, he predicted in all its disheartening effect. The third element was his aversion to monotony, of just the sort implied by cultural uniformity. But his most powerful impetus, the internal force that would spur him to cross thousands of kilometers through hardly known regions of the world and fill his life with adventures that stretch beyond fiction, was that which he himself referred to as an unceasing restlessness, which drove him to wander even from his childhood. Restlessness is the soul of scientific inquiry: we are all of us in search of one thing, which ultimately may be described as happiness:

> [...] that disquietude that drives me, almost against my will, to return to the impenetrable paths of the roof of the world.[49]

Action, however – as he would reflect in 1940 – is realized only in relation to others. One must find the courage to live one's ideas utterly in the world, transforming them into actions:

> To contemplate is to participate in the eternal: to act is to return to earth. [...] Action presupposes a relationship, it cannot be effected by a man on his

> own; it lifts me outside of myself and gives me a place among others.
>
> [...] And so we come to realize that to truly live on this earth, and not merely contemplate eternal truths, one needs, above all, character, and no amount of philosophizing or reflecting can sculpt that character, for a man will still lack the strength to live out his own ideas; our words, too often, are not followed by faithful, willing and courageous action. [...] It is not enough to have ideas, one must live them.[50]

Fueled by these reasons, by his intellectual curiosity, by his search for a more authentic connection with the world around him, his firm sense of individuality, his lust for adventure – all animated by his characteristic restlessness –Tucci would set off in search of the past, chasing down its remains and carrying out scientific explorations of extravagant means. All he did reflected the grandeur of his own "I," his own self. For Tucci, these distant voyages – whether metaphoric, through time, or real, in Asia – were his great adventure, his realm of freedom. There, more so than in his encounters with politicians and in the halls of universities, he felt truly himself. To press forward in a caravan over thousands of miles, in search of the vestiges of unknown and inaccessible civilizations, still untouched by the masses, was, for Tucci, a means of expressing the full force of his personality – a personality which, as we'll see, gave form and direction to everything and everyone around it, leaving the mark of his extraordinary individuality.

Though Tucci's love for the Orient expressed a need, as well, to liberate himself from the individual "I", no less important a motivation was his thoroughly Western mentality and the exultation of the personal "I" and its conquests, which acted as a driving force behind his arduous intellectual achievements. Such a mentality stood firmly in line with the Fascist culture of the time, which favored a strong-willed, masculine personality and emphasized originality in intellectuals – in whom all was to obey the intensely egocentric will of the "I," the reflection of a leader, who forged all according to his own image and likeness. By the journalists of his time, Tucci was referred to as *"l'ardito italiano"* ("the ardent Italian"). He considered himself the final explorer. After him, Tucci wrote, nothing on Earth would remain to be explored, as if beyond Tibet and Nepal there was no land left to discover, as if knowledge was limited to something pure, something static, the capturing of a moment or of a period whose form, trapped within its own rigid contours, would never alter in time and space. Scientific and technological advancement, therefore, could not occur. Quite the opposite, in fact – from an initial virginity and authenticity, the inevitable progress of science and high-speed communications were driving the world toward decadence. From a past, golden age, men were sinking into an age of iron – as he would express in his last travelogue, *La via dello Svat [The Road to Swat]*, published in 1963:

> After all, I am who I always was: I have not become an archeologist. More so than ever, I remain faithful to the study of philosophy and the religions of the Orient, eager still to retrace the paths along which Europe and Asia, in a dizzying series of events, at times drawn to one another, at times repelled, in moments of great decline and renewed greatness, shared with one another the very best of their thought; drawn together even more so by the political events of the time, which, in their futility, though they cause war and disagreement, though they build and foster commercial relations, nevertheless encourage spiritual encounters; and these encounters redeem all the horror, the blood, the pillaging, and

survive beyond the collapse of empires, just as no storm can forever obscure the sun.

It is only that my journey, now, is no longer a journey through space. In suspicion and doubt, we seal our borders and the gradual uniformity of customs and habits, this monotony that chains us, this leveling out that drowns everything, this inhuman overflow of societal living, this erosion of the resistance with which thinking men defend themselves from the masses, it is hollowing out our days, reducing them everywhere to ashes by the same presumptions. And no more is there solitude; everywhere you go, someone is watching, prying into your life, and even into the core of your thought and heart. To travel in a world stripped of its variety is to shuffle about in a hospital of the dying; to watch as the last flickerings of ancient habits go out in a swirl of fading embers. No choice remains but to journey back in time, to wake the dead.

There is nowhere on this earth left to explore; with Tibet and Nepal I completed my explorations; and even there, all is changing. Now that the Orient is absorbing our poison, there's nowhere left to turn but into the past; and there, dealing only with shadows and images, the soul is at peace. All else is unimportant.[51]

And yet, as we'll see, despite his negative view of scientific achievement and his proclaimed hostility toward all that is mechanical, from the automobile to the camera, when it came to his explorations, his archeological missions, and the restoration projects he promoted, Tucci would furnish himself and his crew with the most advanced scientific and technological equipment of the age.

Of Tucci's life before his voyages in Asia we know very little, beyond that which he himself recounted in popular accounts and lectures. His early years are cast in the almost legendary aura of the young, brilliant scholar, enshrouded in a tale that reads almost as a hagiography. Upholding the legend are his scientific writings, begun at the age of fifteen. And though his brilliance was widely acknowledged from an early age, Tucci would go about bolstering his fame through his own efforts as well: as happened frequently in Nepal – and there are those who still recall him doing so –Tucci began proclaiming himself a «famous professor» even before he became one.

Between Tibet and Nepal he would complete thirteen or fourteen expeditions, alternating between his scientific and professorial duties.[52] And though teaching was by no means the central focus of his mission, a few select students would look to him for guidance, respecting him as a guru. Not one, however, would be capable of absorbing the sum of his cultural insights nor attain the completeness of his erudition. The various disciplines in which his students specialized had all of them been previously investigated by their teacher.

HUNTING FOR TEXTS: ORIGINALITY OR TRADITION?

Setting out to write this biography, I worried that in having descended from my teacher's same line of thought I might be putting myself at a disadvantage – particularly as I'd be reconstructing the history of a man of such singular personality, a man who influenced not only his own epoch, but whose unparalleled methods of study imprinted entire generations of scholars, and whose work heralded the years to come, both culturally and politically, altering the very mode of understanding and representing the Orient in the collective imagination. How could I hope to approach my subject with impartiality? With time, however, I realized that this very factor could instead prove itself an advantage: I was a student of his students, I met him personally, and who better than an insider to uncover the behind-the-scenes events of an official biography, which is otherwise nothing but a work of praise *in memoriam*? Who better to capture the chorus of contrasting voices behind each fact and to calibrate the truth? Could we possibly negate, for instance, the historical and documentary value of accounts on racism by blacks or on anti-Semitism by Jews? I, in large part – whether directly or indirectly, through his students and through the institutions he founded – experienced first-hand the actions of Tucci, his style of organization, the consequences of his choices, his particular tastes and even his personality, and I stand in a better position than most to recount his life and to separate the wheat from the chaff. When I first began collecting documents on Tucci, I was met at times with silence; other times, I was ostracized. In reconstructing history, as in life, the silences are much like the spaces in architecture and calligraphy, or the pauses in a dance: not an absence, but a reminder of fullness, a complement to movement. And they stand, also, as an outline of the central event, giving it voice and defining its shape. Silence accentuates words just as rests accentuate music, just as space gives weight to calligraphy and dance. Silence is analogous to the concept of «emptiness», of vacuity or the Buddhist concept of *śūnya*: not nothingness, as is often claimed, but a space charged with possibility.

I would have liked, as well, to recount the history and travels of the manuscripts and xylographs Tucci uncovered in Tibet and Nepal. But my intentions were dashed along the way, for lack of funds, for lack of time, and for the unfortunate misunderstanding that, as I worked on the project, I would have at my disposal the catalogue of manuscripts conserved in the Tucci Center of IsIAO, the large part of which instead came to be published long after I'd begun work on the book, in 1999.[53] A few of the texts, in Tucci's day, were already available in printed form, though Tucci nonetheless returned with both the printed copy – or copies – and manuscripts. But then why bother searching for a copy of the original if a version of the text has already been edited, emended, and printed? It seems a pointless labor, particularly when we possess only a few copies of a particular manuscript – and in some cases, only one. How much different a case than that of the Latin and Greek classics, whose manuscripts and recensions have come to us by the dozens!

Yet, as in all that Tucci did, there was a logical reason behind it. The texts in Sanskrit, Vedic (or ancient Sanskrit), Newari (a native language of Nepal), Tibetan, or in one of the many languages heard throughout the continent of Southern Asia, all came to us, whether recited or sung, by word of mouth. At the advent of the written word, the first lines to be written onbirch bark, on palm leaves, on stones, on whatever surface available, were those recording administrative and commercial acts. Traveling from land to land, hunting for new roads by which to carry their goods, merchants were the ones in true need of travel documents and written agreements, precisely because written agreements are more difficult to dispute. Throughout history it has been the merchants, forever in search of ways to render their commerce more efficient, that have discovered a new way forward: Mongolian merchants, for example, were apparently responsible for the invention of paper money, seeking to lighten the load of metal currency. After the merchants, the next to put word to paper were the priests: the sacred word, and sacred rites in particular, demanded preservation. But priests often hired scribes, who were, at times, unaware of what they were writing, transcribing the words mechanically. And therefore they were prone to making errors, just as any man would be, who spends his days reading only the newspaper, if asked to copy out the *Divine Comedy* or an abstruse text on astrophysics in fine calligraphy. The scribe's attention, especially in cases when forced to copy and recopy a single text, faded quickly. And the errors inevitably made

were not always the same. If, for example, he were to commit
as banal an error in devanāgarī, the most used script to write
Sanskrit, as to exchange the letter "p" for the letter "ṣ", which
are written with an identical character, other than the addition
of a diagonal bar, there's no guaranteeing that such a mistake
will be repeated. It may very well happen, out of ignorance or
inattention, or he may instead mix up the characters for "m"
and "bh", which differ only in one, discontinuous horizontal line,
and so on and so forth. Many of the letters, at dusk or in faint
candlelight, appear identical. But even within the same texts
the errors tend to differ. Another frequent mistake results from
differences in local pronunciation, which can occasionally lead
to an errant phonetic transcription: to write a "b" or "bh" in
place of a "v", for example, a sound which for the Nepalese is
unpronounced.

As a matter of fact, therefore, even employing the same *devanāgarī* alphabet in the same historic period, no uniform manner
of writing existed among scribes. Add to that the endless hours
of writing while seated on the ground, with a low bench for a
writing desk, with the heat gusting in from the room's one tiny
window, or the relentless mosquitoes, or the rain, which in monsoon periods soaked a man through to his thoughts, as well as the
fifty-two simple letters of the *devanāgarī*, sometimes written in
different manners depending on the position of the word, and the
nearly 1,000 combined letters – the symbols, as one can imagine,
start shifting on their own. Soon the scribe forgets or adds a line
to a certain letter, mistakes a long vowel for a short, and *vice versa*:
and so, a new word is born.

Nevertheless, I'm amazed to find even excellent scholars now
and then launching into imaginative interpretations of the orthographic and grammatical oddities of a text. We humans, as
they fail to consider, are the ones who make the errors, and so
too did the scribes of the past. And as happens in life, the errors often varied without reason, particularly in those cases in

which a scribe was copying a manuscript that he himself could not comprehend.

On occasion, rather than rely on a scribe, learned pandits and lamas copied out the books on their own. In virtue of their knowledge, they felt themselves authorized to change the text – except when dealing with divine revelations and books of rituals – here and there adding a word or a sentence they felt to be important, or cutting a line that seemed superfluous, or annotating a particularly difficult passage with notes from a textual commentary. Which is to say, they altered the text with their best intentions, interpolating and "bettering" it where they saw fit. Now, hundreds of years later, only an expert eye can distinguish their additions. And who knows how many *chai* breaks interrupted the work of these learned men, leaving time for idle chatter and the wanderings of the imagination? A rich Nepalese maharaja could afford to keep several pandits in his service at once, working out of his personal library. Now and then, of course, these men spoke to one another – and their crude humor and grammatical jests remain, to this day, greatly appreciated – exchanging ideas, launching into erudite disquisitions or astute grammatical exegeses or impassioned discussions on the nature of the eternal *brahman*, or on the state of emptiness which the soul must reach before dissolving into the Eternal. In such a way, and without intending to, they changed the text. On certain occasions, they added colophons. Placed in the margins of the manuscript or, every so often, at the bottom, these stand as precious sources of information, indicating the dynasty currently in power, the location, the gods worshipped by the author or commissioner of the work, and various other bits of information. Not only do they aid us in reconstructing the history of the text, but the political, social, and cultural history as well. They are a true mine of information, and in fact a large part of the historiography of Asia could be written in light of the colophons included in manuscripts in Sanskrit, Newari, Tibetan, Pāli, Sinhalese, or in any of the hundreds of other local languages.

Until recent years, any changes to the original text were interpreted solely as extrapolations, additions, or distortions, with no just cause for their existence. Using several criteria – an analysis of as many of these instances as have been collected and collated, the variants, errors, omissions, etc. – scholars constructed a *stemma codicum*, that is, a genealogical tree of textual evidence. Any evidence that proved redundant was discarded, and from the remaining information the principal text was reconstructed in its true, original form, from which other recensions of the text had arisen. Combing through a text to discern between original elements, elements added or omitted, and instances of human error, as well as to determine which are the various recensions of the text, has always been held as important. Now, however, with our increased understanding of ancient religions and writings, scholars have recognized the importance of the changes in a text as well: often, these alterations will shed light on an otherwise ambiguous text, informing previously held conceptions with new knowledge, clarifying any unresolved ideas, or offering a point of view subsequent to the compilation of the text. All of which, particularly in the case of writings of a religious-philosophical nature, is of extreme importance. Even in cases where a sacred text reaches us in its exact, original condition, the interpretation of that text, often so difficult, is facilitated by the cultural and critical intrusions of the scribes and learned men who copied them out, either expanding upon the text, shrinking, or "correcting" it. Of prime importance is to distinguish creative contributions form mere errors: this task, however, just as in the case of modern books, does not present too great a difficulty.

In different locations, furthermore, the same book may come to us in different recensions, arising from the different schools to which the learned men and scribes who copied the texts belonged, or from different regions and languages. And so today, as it rightly should, a text is edited according to that which we presume to be the original, which is then used to form a so-called *editio princeps*, a first printed edition of the original. Variants of the text, however, are also printed, as was done, for example, in the extensive notes of the critical edition of the *Mahābhārata,* produced in Pune. Not all that differs from the original text is to be considered an error: in different geographical regions, there are various and specific modes of reciting, passing on, and finally, writing a text. In certain cases, cantors expanded upon more popular texts – as in the case of the *Purāṇas*, «the ancient histories», which narrate the origins of the world, the gods, and the cosmology and first kings of India – including stories, legends, myths, or local history, to provide listeners with a more intimate point of reference. These local elements are of extreme importance in reconstructing a text's history, in determining the location from which it derived and the dynasty which commissioned the recitation. In the case of more narrative texts, then, several different recensions may arise, though one cannot speak of a single, "original" text, reconstructed by examining and sifting through the various manuscripts of the many regions of India. In the course of their production over the centuries, these popular works took on an encyclopedic character. Which is to say, if one were interested in translating a book from a language of Southern Asia, one must take into account that yes, there was an original text, which may possibly be reconstructed, but that in certain literary genres, such as the epic, the variants of the work arenearly as important as the original.

Many families of pandits and lamas possess sacred texts "of their own," particular to a given school, or their own recension of a certain text – their private manuscripts. In many religions, especially in Tantrism, Sikhism, and Islam, the sacred word is of comparable importance and power to the sacrament in Catholicism. The Word is the goddess, Vāc, which means, precisely, «word», who was worshiped from the time of the first Vedic text,

the Ṛgveda. To preserve a sacred book is what, to a Catholic, would
be to preserve the reliquary of a saint. If a pandit's family mi-
grates to another region – an event that occurs quite frequently
in Southern and Central Asia – they bring with them their own
sacred texts, their own prayer books, their own images of the
tutelary divinities, their own statues, just as they bring their own
language and culinary habits.

The different recensions of a single text, whether printed or
not, aid us therefore not only to understand the social history of
India, but also the particular paths traced by certain families, or
groups of families, or even castes – such as the Brahmin of the
Gangetic Plain in Nepal – over the course of years or centuries,
as well as the settlements, the histories of particular locations,
the topography, toponymy, and much more: in short, the cultural
history of a specific geographic region or social group.

Furthermore, Sanskrit may be written using other alphabets
than *devanāgarī*. A single manuscript may very well be drafted in
Sanskrit, but in *śāradā* script, in use in Kashmir, or in one of the
many other scripts used in India. The text might also be written
in Gupta characters, or others that precede the classic characters
of *devanāgarī*, and undergo several phases of transformation and
evolution.

These reasons, taken together, are what would push Tucci to travel into ever more impenetrable regions, in search
of manuscripts or their various recensions. Each monastery,
each home of an abbot or village leader, might possess new
manuscripts, or manuscripts written in different ways. They
might hold books long thought to have been lost, cited in other
texts but never before discovered.

This digression, as it may be, from the central theme of Tucci's
life, has been made in order to stress the scientific importance
of his work, to describe his passion and the various pursuits of
his expeditions – the very tasks at which he excelled. His search

was one of philological reconstruction, the search for the original word of an original culture, which, for Tucci, came to be a search for happiness, a search, in some sense, for the garden of Eden. His philology however, never stood as an end in itself, but was employed to interpret cultures of origin. His unrest, his imagination, his love for the sun and mountains transformed what might have been a cold scientist's work of pedantic philological reconstruction into a great adventure:

> two things, he claimed, to have loved above all others: the sun, like Julian the Apostate, and the mountains, like the shepherds [...].[54]

This digression has served also to illustrate the principal aim of his scientific missions: the pursuit of manuscripts, inscriptions, works of art, the vestiges of fallen dynasties, pre-historic and archeological remains. What Tucci initially set out to accomplish was to reconstruct a way of thinking, via the study of original texts, according to the philological method taught to him by Formichi, perfected at Tagore's school, and broadened with the aid of Hem Raj.

In discussing original and re-worked texts, however, we must consider for a moment the concept of originality, its particular significance in Asia and the weight it holds in artistic, philosophic, and religious creation. It is well known that originality, in the East, is not seen as a positive and absolute value, one to seek out manically and at all costs, as in the West. The cult of individual personality does not, or at least did not, exist. In valuing a work of art, it is not so much who executed it, but how well the teachings of the school to which it belongs are represented – for art is, essentially, religious art. In Tibet, as Tucci noted, paintings are always «symbolic reproductions and sacred iconography», the art of which should be developed in great monasteries.[55] Even in

Zen painting, for example, perfection is a measure of one's ability to most closely imitate the work of a teacher, to reproduce not only the images, but the hues, the colors, the subtle energy that emanates from every work of art. Few paintings, whether they be Japanese landscapes or representations of symbols or characters of the alphabet, bear the name of their author: to achieve perfection is to copy, as faithfully as possible, the school's founder, to improve upon the work without making any substantial changes, to express as truly as possible the ideas and spirit of the school without the addition of any new elements. For a painting is a religious illustration, of the same importance as a religious text, though more direct: that which cannot be understood by the less literate in readingis comprehended by looking. An image is pressing and immediate, allowing the observer to interpret its message almost instantaneously. The value of a sacred image, even a work of art, rests in its religious impact. Whereas in the West we might stand before the *Annunciation* of Piero della Francesca and reflect solely on its beauty, without a thought for its religious significance, in the East such a reaction would be unthinkable.

Doubtless, however, each artisan and artist, no matter the subject represented, leaves his own personal touch and stamp on the work: a quality which, to the eye of a calligraphy student, leaps immediately off the page. Depending on who drafts it, an identical passage with identical characters – Gothic, Roman, Carolingian, or otherwise – will appear completely different.

In Hindu and Buddhist Tantric schools especially – such as those in Tibet, which Tucci came to know so well, and of whose scholarship he stood as an unrivaled authority – perfection is a measure of one's faithfulness in representing a religious ideal, as laid out in religious texts or as embodied by a guru, a figure of particular importance in Tantric schools: as faithfully as he can, the artist must portray the canon of his school. With new words, he must tap into the same devotional impulse as the school's founder, reenter within the established parameters, and thus recast himself within the same spiritual line of descent, the same *paraṃparā*; on the other hand, perfection consists also in coming to be recognized by the teacher as an integral part of the school. As diligently as possible, the student must express the values and precepts of the line of thought laid out by the *paramaguru*, the initial teacher, without altering them: in all aspects – religious teachings, whether expressed in art or in literature, in dance, etc. – the student must conform. To revolt in any way is to abandon one's right to belong to that particular school. Rebellion, the ability to seek out aesthetic solutions and new iconographies – these are the freedoms of the individual; the disciple, however, must fall in line with the canon. Tradition is held as a value in and of itself and an author's authority counts more than the truthfulness or beauty of the lines thathe sets down, the images he paints, or the philosophical arguments he proposes. It is the student's duty to pass on a school's beliefs and values, and the measure of his authority depends upon the quantity and quality of the lessons he absorbs from his predecessors and from his own religious experiences – not from innovation. As in all oral traditions, he who knows the most is held in highest regard. Hence the importance of age – with a broader knowledge base, the eldersof a group represent its historical and cultural memory, and are therefore viewed with greater respect. We must not forget that, for millennia, Indian literature was transmitted only in oral form, memorized with the aid of numerous mnemonic devices – the many methods of reciting a text in rigorous prosody, for example. Hymns, philosophical papers, *thangkas*, paintings, sculptures, music, dance, all served as methods by which a student could establish his identity, prove his faithfulness to a school's precepts, and so come to be recognized as one of its representatives.

Authority and antiquity, therefore, are the essential traditional values of Asian cultures, not originality and individuality.

The teacher was Logos incarnate, while the student was regarded by the teacher as a vessel for the Word itself; when the
student becomes the teacher, therefore, he or she becomes Logos.
In this way, the Word is passed on unaltered, by way of a living
relationship, a constant, nurturing link between a teacher and his
students: precisely what Tucci, as a student, sought in vain at the
university, and what he himself would enact as a professor with
his own, prized students, transforming them, in a way, into disciples. In the past, a guru's disciples would take up residence in his
home and regard him with the respect and devotion due to a god:
in several passages of the *Mahābhārata*, in fact, the guru is said
to be ten times superior to a god. To his own favored students,
Tucci opened the doors of his enormous private library.

To conclude, it can be safely said that today we no longer
search only for the "original" text: of critical importance as well
are the various recensions of a text, which all together form the
image and creed of a school and its history. Tucci did not seek
out only original manuscripts, but also their recensions, hunting
for the most ancient among them: those nearest to the Word of
origin.

The more ancient a manuscript, moreover, meant also a
greater commercial value. Some of the manuscripts donated
by Tucci to IsMEO on June 4, 1959, for example, date back to
the ninth and tenth century, others are extremely rare, and
still others are in fact the last remaining copies. In 1954, the
collection of manuscripts alone was valued at 26 million lire,
the equivalent of 660,249,200 lire in 2004, by the director of the
Executive Office of the Single Directory of the Italian Libraries,
Professor Camillo Scaccia Scarafoni. His highly detailed report,
measuring the worth of Tucci's library as a national cultural
heritage, was completed for the General Directorate of Antiqui-
ties and the Fine Arts.[56] It goes without saying, however, that
for a scholar or a collector, the vast inheritance of Tibetan and
Sanskrit manuscripts is an invaluable treasure.

Among intellectuals in the West, Tucci was not known for his extensive expeditions in Asia – though they would earn him the renown of the general public – but for his prodigious cultural knowledge and the rich abundance of manuscripts and art works he brought back with him. In Asia, too, it was this treasure hunt *sui generis* that earned him his legendary status. In 1999, in a small town of Newar culture in the valley of Kathmandu, I spoke with a wizened old pandit, Dhruba, who worked in the library of the Nepalese general, Kaiser Shamsher, a friend of Tucci's. Discussing Tucci and the documents I was collecting, Dhruba showed me a half shrunken little book published in 1958, entitled *The Mountain is Young*. It was the fictionalized tale of Rosalie Elizabeth Kuanghu Chow's travels through Nepal, who wrote under the pseudonym, Suyin Han. While Dhruba forced me to promise that I'd never reveal his exact identity or where he lived, for fear that the new government leaders would punish him, he allowed me to make a few photocopies, from which I here transcribe:

> The Field Marshal then abandoned his hookah and showed her old Nepalese manuscripts written in gold upon handmade paper. "I leant one of these to a white man who told me he was a famous professor in a European university, and vowed he would return it. Yet he never turned up again, and nor did my manuscript. But we must not generalize; this man may be shame to his own country and his seat of learning; but my heart has not hankered after the manuscript, for he must have wanted it very much to keep it to his dishonor. It was the will of the gods, or God, and who knows? He may still turn up some day..."[57]

As Dhruba told me, it hardly took a leap of imagination to recognize Tucci as the white man, covetous of manuscripts. He told me also that, as early as the 1920s, Tucci had begun declaring himself a famous professor and that they knew immediately what his intentions were in Nepal. Nevertheless, he added, to remove ancient manuscripts from the country was illegal, and Tucci could not have done so without the authorization of the government.

In October 2003 a famous Indian scholar, who for many years worked in governmental positions, told me that when Tucci stepped foot in the halls of the National Archives of India, in Delhi, where the manuscripts are held, they would take a careful count after his visit. She too requested I withhold her name, so as «not to upset the politicians in Italy».

Tucci's journey, nonetheless, whether among manuscripts or in nature, is truly unique: as we'll come to learn, by the end of his explorations he'd fallen deeply in love with the humble men and women who'd hosted him in Tibet and Nepal, and with the slow, plodding marches, with the landscape, the silence.

Of course, to go searching for manuscripts is all very well, but why search for the Buddhist and Hindu Tantric texts in Nepal, as did Tucci? Why not remain in India or travel solely to Tibet, where visas were easily obtained through British and Tibetan authorities? Tibet, after all, was a theocratic government pre-dominated by Tantric Buddhism – though other religions were present as well, such as Bon – and stood as a true manna in the hunt for manuscripts. Yet Nepal, too, held an abundance of texts. Muslims, in fact – first the Arabs, then Turks and Persians – from around the year 700 had settled in Sindh, the northern most region of India, which following Independence became Pakistan. There they plundered and destroyed, tortured, raped and raided all that was of value. So feared were they that the women would kill themselves before their villages were conquered, just as in the fourteenth century when the Afghani Muslim, 'Alā'-ud-Dīn Khaljī, conquered the palace of the splendid queen, Padminī, in

Rajasthan. Together with hundreds of slaves, attendants, and friends, the queen took her own life: fearing the victory of their savage enemies, they commited *jauhar* – a mass suicide by self-immolation committed in advance (that is, before the murder of their husbands) in order to avoid dishonor at the hands of the invaders. And again, a century earlier, in the 1295 sack of Jaisalmer, when 24,000 women burned themselves at the pyre.[58] When life turns unbearable and the most precious gifts in the world, dignity and honor, are jeopardized, what better refuge than death?

Kashmir, situated in the shadow of the western Himalayas and blessed with a temperate climate – spared, that is, from the sweltering heat of the desert plains of southernmost India and the devastating monsoons, which reach Kashmir as only a brisk rain shower – was a particularly fertile ground in terms of culture as well, and stood as a central hub for the exchange of ideas between dozens of different schools, whether Buddhist or Hindu. Protected by the mountains, the territory was unharmed by the initial invasion. Some centuries on, when the Muslims closed in on Srinagar – its beautiful capital, encircled by bodies of water – some of the families of Brahmin put up a brave resistance, others were forced into a mass exile. A great number of pandits were able to traverse the hills and mountains and take refuge in the valley of Kathmandu, sheltered by the jungle, the mountains, and the surrounding hills. At the time, no road had yet been constructed from India to Nepal, which was then better linked to Tibet. For millennia, in fact, the land remained logistically isolated, due both to natural causes and political calculation. When, in England, the Prime Minister Chandra Shamsher Rana, who governed with absolute power from 1901 to 1929, was questioned on the state of communications in his country, he responded: «We do not construct roads, for roads would allow foreign powers to invade our country».

During the Rana dynasty, which ruled Nepal as a despotic power from 1846 until the revolution of 1951, the country was

held in a state of external isolation, both logistically and culturally, even with the internal improvements enacted by Chandra,
which saw for the construction of major pathways through the
hills and bridges to cross the rivers. This condition of isolation
only heightened at the beginning of the 1900s, when fear spread
that tsarist Russia was planning to extend its influence into Tibet. Lord Curzon, the Viceroy of the British Empire, dispatched
an expedition there in 1904, to convince the Tibetans to form
commercial and political ties with British India, rather than with
Russia. Chandra supported the policy fully, and the Nepalese representative in Lhasa became an extremely important figure for
the English, both as a vital source of information and a mediator
with Chinese authorities. As a result of the operation, a new trade
route opened between Tibet and India, by way of Sikkim, which in
only a few short years replaced the old road through Kathmandu.
And so, while India constructed its important railroad lines and
the rest of the world laid down the infrastructure for the great
roads of communication, Nepal sank further into isolation, cut
off from the principal road to India. In compensation, they maintained the privilege of independence and, as no other country in
Asia, freedom even from British influence.

Most assuredly, such isolation protected them from being ab-
sorbed as colonies, but it also allowed for the Rana dynasty to
maintain its absolute power – not solely because no other power
existed to supplant them, but because the population over which
they ruled held no knowledge of the outside world, were illiterate,
cut off from all modes of communication, and living under an ob-
scurantist despotism. To invade Nepal, or even to merely cross its
border, was never a simple matter. The Brahmin fleeing Kashmir
and the Gangetic Plains hoped to find refuge in a secure location:
the valley of Kathmandu, to the northeast of Kashmir, isolated
from the political system, unthreatened by Islam, with fertile
soil and a mild climate ideal for the preservation of manuscripts.
When, in the fourteenth century, the Muslims were at last able to

enter Nepal, the bold spirit of the first conquerors had already faded: the country was pillaged, though not annexed. Up until the revolution of 1951, Nepal remained isolated, inaccessible, closed off to all foreigners unless they were granted a special permit by the Prime Minister.[59]

This, in the end, is what drew Tucci to embark on his famous expeditions, to recover the texts carried by pandits in their migration to Nepal, texts which were preserved thanks precisely to the country's isolation and climate. These manuscripts were regarded by the families who possessed them as their true tutelary divinities. Hinduism is a religion of many faces, with numerous gods to worship, and each school, consecrated to a particular god or goddess, has its own prayers, its own texts, its own philosophical program, its own line of thought; and each school, without discounting the methods of others, sees in its own methods the true path to liberation, as revealed by their particular group of texts. Hinduism was quick to welcome the experiences and divinities of other religions, incorporating them and rendering them unique to itself. As Tucci would write:

> Never has India done otherwise; never did it turn away an experience, but welcomed all ideas, and opened the doors of tolerance to faiths of every sort. Though neither did it bow in worship to them; all was filtered through its own mode of perception, reconsidered, altered, and adapted, like an ancient tree that buries its vital roots in the earth, that grazes the sky with its branches, and transforms the earth's sap and the air's light into life and vigor.[60]

To this day in Nepal, and especially in its least accessible regions, it is no rare occasion to come across a monastery isolated in the mountains or a Hindu or Buddhist family – and to be of both religions is not unfeasible – who in their libraries still jealously guard their most sacred books, the images of their tutelary divinities, or the recension of a well-known text prepared by a particular school. To acquire the most precious manuscripts, Tucci often paid. But some were priceless, to be had only by gaining the trust of their owners, forming a personal relationship, speaking their language, calling upon the help of a local pandit or lama, observing their customs, and approaching the matter properly, with due respect; and then came the contracts, the negotiations, the waiting. In all of these aspects, Tucci was a true master – as proof, the 1,515 Tibetan and Sanskrit manuscripts, or photographs of Sanskrit manuscripts, he brought back with him to Italy. The decision of when, and whether, the transaction between money and manuscript, xylography, or artwork would occur, was in the hands of the pandit or the abbot of the monastery. All was done in secrecy and bogged down by long periods of waiting. Generally, if the process was dragging on too long, it was best to feign disinterest and deliver an ultimatum: as often happened, the owner of the precious item would begin to worry that the entire deal might fizzle or that the uncomprehending Westerner was losing interest – and so contractual agreements would begin.

Of extreme importance for the buyer was to avoid, at all costs, giving any indication to the other party that what was at stake was the simple sale of a precious item: each owner displayed the utmost devotion to his sacred objects. One must give the seller an excuse to sell: a dream often worked well; the premonition of a well-respected – and well-bribed – figure worked even better. In all cases, to make an offer was obligatory. One must also consider that, following World War II, the sale of ancient objects in Southern Asia was deemed illegal: the high price, therefore, reflected the seller's risk. Though more than all else, itwas the fear of social reprobation that caused the seller to hesitate. Tucci, as always, kept a lama or local guide in his company, whom he would send, at night or in secret, to negotiate the price with representatives of the monastery. In Asia, to negotiate a contract is not an act of business, but an art. No less a help in winning the trust of his sellers was Tucci's extraordinary ability to speak their language and to respond to any philosophical query with his astonishing wealth of knowledge, which often proved far broader than their own. In the end, whatever barrier of hostility or mistrust still remained would fall to the substantial price he was able to offer: yet another reason for which his expeditions proved costly. That, however, is subject for later chapters.

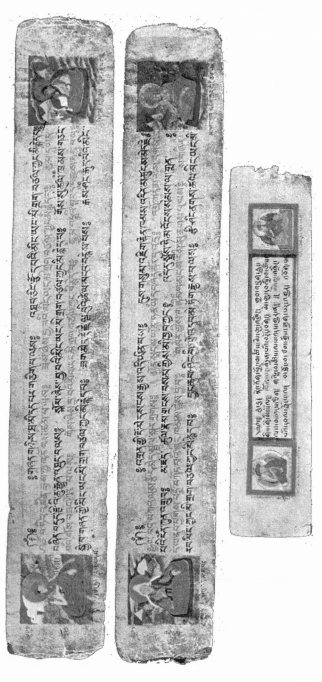

Figure 19: Illuminated Tibetan manuscripts photographed during the 1931 Expedition: the top two represent Padmasambhava's life; the manuscript at the bottom is part of a Bon treatise.

Figure 20: Giuseppe Tucci and his wife Giulia Tucci Nuvoloni (1889–1992)
during the 1931 Expedition.

Figure 21: Giuseppe Tucci and his caravan at the Zoji pass, 1931 Expedition.

Figure 22: Image of a *thangka* representing Milarepa (mi la ras pa, 1051–1135) photographed during the 1931 Expedition.

Figure 23: Carlo Formichi (1871–1943) standing. Originally published in 1944.

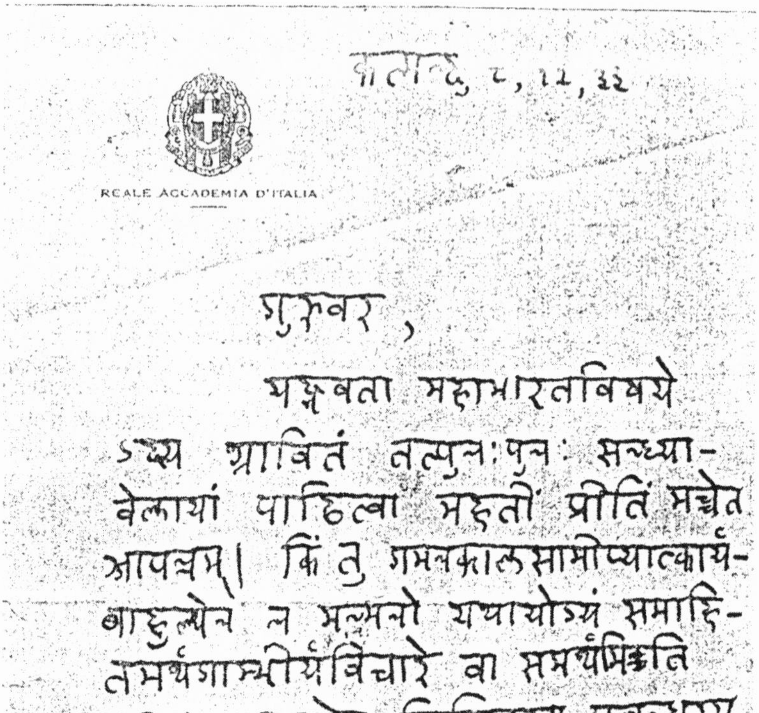

REALE ACCADEMIA D'ITALIA

नालन्दे ८, १२, ३२

गुरुवर,

भवता महाभारतविषये
ऽस्य आजितं तत्पुन:पुन: सन्ध्या-
वेलायां पठित्वा महतीं प्रीतिं मचेत
आपन्नम्। किं तु गमनकालसामीप्यात्कार्य-
बाहुल्येन न भवतो यथायोग्यं समाहि-
तभर्थगाम्भीर्यविचारे वा समर्थभिक्षति
ज्ञात्वा गुरुवरेण लिखितस्य प्रबन्धस्य
यदि भवानितःपरं यथाप्रतिज्ञातं
प्रेषयिष्यति, महानुपकार: स्यात्। इति
निवेदनम्।
भवत्समेलनप्रीतिमनुस्मरन्साधरं सनहुमानः
भवदीय: काल्लो फोर्मीकि

Figure 24: Sanskrit letter by Carlo Formichi to the Royal Preceptor of Nepal,
Hem Raj Sharma, December 8, 1933.

Figure 25: Gandhi at the Sala delle Armi (Weapons Room) in Palazzo Venezia after his meeting with Benito Mussolini, Rome, 1931.

Figure 26: Gandhi reviews the Marinaretti (Young Sailors of the Fascist Youth Organization) of the Caio Duilio legion during his visit to Italy, 1931.

Figure 27: Giuseppe Tucci and his Tibetan mastiff, Chankù, in Rome, 1934.

Figure 28: Traditional palanquin.

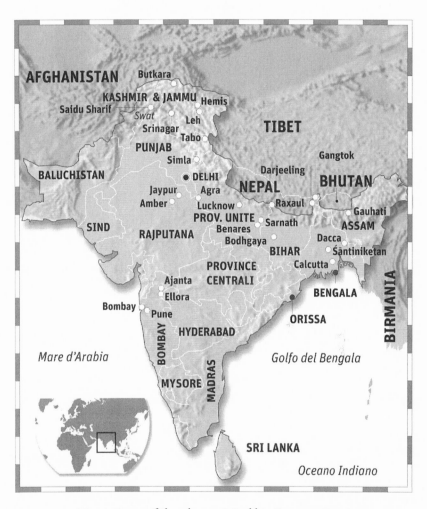

Map 1: Some of the places visited by Giuseppe Tucci
in India in 1925–1955.

CHAPTER II

THE SEED OF HIS GREAT EXPEDITIONS

> The day Tucci and I, approaching a single bookseller in
> Benares, found each and every ancient Sanskrit text we'd
> come for, all at a very reasonable price, and all in pristine and
> I'd even say, artistic editions, was the day we started believing
> in Cockaigne.
>
> —*Carlo Formichi, 1929*

In 1944, in a preface to the collection of Carlo Formichi's
essays entitled *India: pensiero e azione [India: Thought and Action]* –
a publication coordinated by an *ad hoc* committee under IsMEO
to pay tribute to Formichi at the end of his career as a professor –
Giuseppe Tucci and Ambrogio Ballini honored their late friend
and teacher with the following words:

> By word and by example, from his Chair as profes-
> sor and in His life, this remarkable scientist edu-
> cated countless young students who today stand as
> an honor to Italian scholarship and to the Teacher in
> whose footsteps they now follow; through His trav-
> els abroad, most notably in India, Nepal, and in the
> Far East, He taught us to better understand and ap-
> preciate our own country and our own culture; and
> finally, through His numerous and important publica-
> tions, which demonstrate the exceptional character
> of His scientific and educational aims, He sought to
> promote a reciprocal understanding between the Oc-
> cident and the Orient.[1]

Outside of such official, celebratory remarks, Tucci would insistently declare himself an autodidact, thus discounting the importance of Formichi's role in his education. In truth, however, not only did he receive concrete help from his professor – who invited him to submit manuscripts to several journals to which he himself was a regular contributor (such as *Bilychnis*, a spiritualistic journal which later printed the writings of Julius Evola), who helped him to obtain the funds necessary for his expeditions, who proposed to the government that he be sent to teach at Tagore's University of Viśvabhāratī, and who, as its Elder Vice President, assured him membership in the powerful and munificent Royal Academy of Italy – but Tucci also inherited Formichi's direction of study, pursuing and expanding upon the areas of research first explored by him.

Formichi was an Indologist of indisputable renown. Throughout his life, he nurtured a true passion for India, for its «most noble and ancient» language, Sanskrit, and for its culture. A love he would pass on to Tucci, at a time when the study of ancient languages was a purely philological exercise, unconcerned with examining the cultures behind those languages *in loco*, nor with understanding the traditions, the history, myths, and rituals of the peoples who spoke them. In fact, though he defined himself an autodidact, Tucci would come to praise his teacher, as well as many other Italian scholars – Paolo Emilio Pavolini foremost among them– for having guarded the field of Oriental studies in Italy from the

> obsessive dependence on philology still dominating the fields of historiography and classical studies, that for decades has sapped the spirits of our intellectuals, stripping them of all productive thought, forcing them to slave after a subject matter that, with no constructive method to give it life, was never more than fragmentary and extrinsic. Our Orientalists perhaps

avoided these pitfalls, which, being the fashion of
the age, stifled a great much of our scientific activity, precisely because of the arguments they chose to
address in their studies; studies which, by necessity,
center around the philosophical profundities that
embody and enliven all that is best in Oriental literature. As a result came several successful attempts at
synthesis, comprehensive summaries of entire periods of Asian literature. With no base of raw facts to
assure us, our scholars have begun to dig ever deeper
with their studies, probing beyond the merely particular or transitory aspects that appear in one work
or another, to uncover the real forms of the Asian
spirit. In short, a tendency has arisen among our
scholars, clearer and more cognizant every day, to
go beyond pure philology, to reach an organic and
coherent vision of Oriental thought and of its forma-
tion, to understand its terms intimately, to compare
them with ours, to find what is truly alive and akin
to us in their culture, and to incorporate it into our
own.[2]

And in a single paragraph, Tucci set the work of Pavolini side
by side with that of Formichi,

whose work was, instead, predominated, by a philosophical interest: drawn to the profound and specula-
tive thought of Buddhism, and with the same enthusiasm he brought to all his works, he traced its slow
development in the soul of India and shed light on its
essential doctrines. His translation of *Asvagosha* remains a marvelous testament of his scholarship and
his artistic capabilities, on display as well in his translation of Raghuidi's poem.[3] With the exit of Pavolini

and Formichi, so ended the old generation of Italian Orientalism. A generation which, though few in number, nonetheless left its mark, and never once, to put it briefly, lost sight of the brilliant humanistic traditions.[4]

Carlo Formichi, the Teacher's Teacher

Carlo Formichi was born in Naples on February 14, 1871, the son of a wealthy business broker and a Greek mother, who'd completed her schooling in France. He studied at the school of Michele Kerbaker, a professor of Sanskrit at the Royal University of Naples, as well in Kiel, Germany, with one of the great European Indologists of his time, Paul Deussen. In Vienna he came to know the famous Georg Bühler, and at Oxford, Max Müller, the great scholar to whom we owe the *editio princeps* of the Ṛgveda, and in whose name was dedicated the fervent cultural center of the German Embassy in Delhi. For the academic year 1901–02, Dr. Formichi was named Associate Professor of Sanskrit at the Royal University of Pisa, with a salary of 3,000 lire, effective as of the first of November, 1901. Among his students were Vittorio Rocca, Belloni-Filippi, and Pizzagalli – later, a friend of Tucci – who would all go onto become distinguished scholars in their own right. And when Gandhi arrived at Milano Centrale, it was Formichi who was there to welcome him, climbing aboard the train to greet him in Sanskrit.

The following year, December 18, 1902, in his pretty, orderly, and miniscule calligraphy, Carlo Formichi, son of Giuseppe, wrote to the Ministry of Public Education with «a vital request, Your Excellency, that he be granted an increase in salary, from 3,000 to 3,500 lire». This, «to permit him to maintain the decorum required of his social position» for he was pressed with «grave family matters, having to provide for his mother, his sister, and his distant and aging father, no longer able to work». A second letter followed, only a few days later, written by the university president, underlining the «truly grave economic conditions in which the Professor finds himself».[5] The salary increase went into effect in February 1903, but economic troubles would remain one of the central problems in the lives of both Formichi and Tucci: the former, on account of his large family, the latter, as a result of his expeditions and his boundless love of art, books, manuscripts, and travel – a passion that comes, as it always has, with a high price tag.[6]

On June 27, 1904, Formichi applied with the Ministry of Public Education for a promotion to full professorship, enclosing in his letter five scientific articles and three years of didactic materials, from 1901–1904. The Faculty of Letters and Philosophy of the Royal University of Pisa received his request in a meeting of June 30, 1904 «in consideration of his diligence and zeal [...] and the effectiveness [...] of his teaching», and in November 1905 he was promoted. Eight years later, in November 1913, Formichi accepted a transfer to the Royal University of Rome – as it turns out, neither Kerbaker in Naples, nor Paolo Emilio Pavolini in Florence, nor Ambrogio Ballini in Padova could, or had any desire to, leave their current positions.[7] To help with his moving costs, he received 41.95 lire from the Ministry of Education. Among those Formichi taught in Rome was Vittore Pisani, who would be promoted to full professor of Sanskrit at the State University of Milan. Though his most prized student would be Giuseppe Tucci.

From November, 1917 on – prior, that is, to the arrival of Fascism – Formichi was called on by the Undersecretary of State for Press and Propaganda Abroad to aid the News Bureau. He was then sent, by the Ministry of Foreign Affairs, to Paris, as the Italian delegate during talks at the Paris Peace Conference of 1919-20 – a measure «taken with extreme urgency, in view of the binding necessities of our propaganda in France at the current moment».[8] Formichi's involvement with the offices of propaganda abroad would continue under the Fascist regime.

In December, 1920 Formichi once again asked the President of the Royal University of Rome for an increase in salary, with the concession that it be granted one year in advance of normal procedures. The desired increase, however, given that he'd taught Sanskrit in Pisa for only two years, could not be granted – at least three years of service were required. Meanwhile, Formichi was assigned the extra task of serving on the hiring committee of the national competition for a new professor of English Language and Literature.

In Śāntiniketan

On October 3, 1925 Formichi submitted a memorandum to the Minister of Public Education, Pietro Fedele, proposing a mission in India and requesting all the necessary means to guarantee Italy's reputation abroad. The mission arose initially from agreements made with Rabindranath Tagore – educator, poet, playwright, literary critic, novelist, painter, musician, and founder of the international University of Viśvabhāratī – agreements which had already been unofficially accepted and which included a teaching position for Formichi. If Tagore could afford to cover the costs of an Italian professor of Sanskrit, Formichi writes, would not the Italian government wish to reciprocate by offering an Italian course in India?

> Before I accept your attractive offer it is my duty to discuss the matter with my country's Government, not only to request the required leave of absence, but to ensure that my mission is carried out on official terms and with all the means necessary to guarantee the honor and prestige of Italy.
>
> Expenses and living arrangements in Santineketan will be seen to by the University of Vishvabharati.

It is only just, then, that Italy reciprocate such generosity. Of course, I won't presume to say in exactly
what manner my country will do so, but I will take it
upon myself to provide a few suggestions, based on
my experience with India's people and affairs. The
University of Vishvabharati is assembling a library,
and many volumes have been offered as gifts from
the governments of Germany, France, Great Britain,
and the United States of America. Almost entirely
absent from the shelves of this growing and important library are Italian texts. What better occasion
for our government to send, in my care, a collection
of Italian classics and, more importantly, a series of
publications on Italian art?

In addition to these materials, the Government
might provide a teacher of Italian language, literature, and art, a person of great merit, equally competent in Italian and Indian literature. This course in
Italian would be held in Santiniketan alongside my
course in Sanskrit. Such an arrangement would allow for a fluid exchange between the two civilizations
and would foster a set of mutual interests, beneficial
for the commerce not only of ideas, but of things.

Before all else, Formichi's motive was diplomatic:

Ambassadors and consuls are not the only ones to
cultivate international relations. Since in our age
men of culture, above all, form the true links between
one State and another, and are the true founders and
promoters of the very sympathies that grow into a
firm and lasting alliance of interests.[9]

In response to his letter, Mussolini had five-hundred volumes
shipped to the Poet in śāntiniketan, and Fedele granted Formichi

a one year leave of absence from his professorship, for purposes of study, from November 1, 1925 to October 31, 1926, and provided him with a passport «for royal service in the above-mentioned State», that is, India. Formichi also managed to secure the Italian teaching position for his former student, Giuseppe Tucci.

During his year of service abroad, despite the interest in his mission held by the Dean of Letters and Philosophy, Giuseppe Cardinali, Formichi would not be granted the yearly stipend of 9,500 lire for active service that he'd rushed to request by the 2nd or 3rd of April, 1926. It so happens, in fact, that Formichi returned from India earlier than scheduled, on March 30, 1926, in order to prepare for Tagore's second visit to Italy. However, the Ministry of Foreign Affairs did issue a report to the minister informing him of the positive outcome of Formichi's time studying and teaching in India and of the «great affection and sympathy Formichi managed to garner for himself and for his Country», requesting that he receive «the highest honors as a sign of recognition for the service performed on behalf of the Country»; and on June 13, 1926, Formichi was awarded the degree of Knight Commander of the Order of the Crown of Italy.

Formichi left us with a detailed account of his sojourn in Śāntiniketan. In *India e indiani [India and Indians]*, writing of his «friend, Tucci», he depicts his former student and the life he led at Tagore's center:

> Leaving the Poet's house I always took a walk, short or long, in someone else's company. That someone else would soon cede his place to Tucci, who was quick to join me in my peaceful refuge, to teach Italian language and literature and add to the prestige of Italy and the Italian Government.

Giuseppe Tucci, whom I'm honored to count amongst my former students, is without doubt an exceptional man. Having only recently turned thirty, already his wealth of knowledge is astonishing. In addition to Sanskrit and the literary dialects of India, he knows Chinese, Tibetan, and has delved into the study of Iranian and the languages of Central Asia, which have only been discovered in recent years. In evidence here is that natural gift which allows only a few privileged men to learn even the most difficult languages with breathtaking facility and speed. Giuseppe Tucci, in other words, is in full possession of that quality which we call a knack for languages. Such a gift, nevertheless, often produces a mere polyglot, which is to say, that human parrot who can speak, read, and write in a myriad of idioms, and who may make for a fine interpreter or librarian, but is absolutely clueless in the realm of scientific research. Ninety-nine percent of polyglots are men of limited wit, and in a certain sense, ignorant. In Tucci, the miraculous ease of absorbing languages is combined with a scientific temperament of the highest order, characterized, that is, by a thirst, a passion for knowledge, which takes hold of a man as if he were possessed, obsessed solely by the idea of learning, searching, clarifying, which forces him to pass hours, night and day, among books, scrolls, papers, and relics. A willful act of martyrdom, so to speak, at the core of which man finds a certain, undeniable pleasure, and which becomes the very reason for his existence.

In Santiniketan, with his exemplary life as a scholar, the immensity of his linguistic knowledge, and his magnificently sharp wit, Tucci elicited the

general wonder and unbounded admiration of the
Poet, who immediately recognized in him the future
prince of Oriental scholarship.

That I love Tucci as a son, that I'm ever with him
during the few free hours left to us, that I seek out
his company on my daily walks and excursions, is a
fact readily understood by all.[10]

Tucci set sail from Bombay in November 1925, on his way to
Śāntiniketan, the «abode of peace», in West Bengal, where he
arrived on the 28th of that same month. As is understood from
the above account and from documents held by the Ministry of
Public Education, in Śāntiniketan Tucci taught, at least officially,
only Italian – language, literature, and art – and not Chinese, as
was recorded.[11] He would, however, study Chinese and Tibetan
texts with local pandits.

In addition to accounts of their daily life in Śāntiniketan,
Formichi provides us with vivid descriptions of Indian habits and
customs. On the evening of December 19, 1925, in the company of
Tagore and a few other guests, he went to the theatre in Calcutta
(now Kolkata), where he saw a melodramatic production, in Bengali, of Tagore's *L'entrata nella casa nuova [Entering a New Home]*.[12]
After having described the theatre and the division between men
down in the orchestra and woman up in the boxes – each box
equipped with curtains to keep the women hidden from «indis-
creet and wandering eyes» – he proceeds to a description of how,
during the intermissions between one act and another, one heard

a shouting from above: women, acting as ushers,
to allow the female spectators in the upper balcony to
communicate with their men below in the orchestra.

In the boxes with no curtains, *in the European fashion*, one might say, I was able to admire the beautiful,
chubby brunettes, that remind of our Sicilian women.

> In their gazes was no hint of impudence, only modesty and timidity, too much timidity, rather.[13]

His final twelve days he spent in Śāntiniketan Formichi would dedicate to his students,

> doubling and tripling the number of lectures and conferences, leaving the door of my hermitage perpetually open to all who might come, seeking advice, certificates, clarification, or helpful scientific and literary opinions.[14]

He concluded his courses on the political science of ancient Indians, on the great Buddhist poet Aśvaghoṣa, and «wound up the demonstration of the dynamic currents in the religious evolution from the hymns of the Rigveda to the Buddha's sermons». Hardly had he a moment to himself, so constantly was he surrounded by students and pandits.

When Formichi left Śāntiniketan, Tagore was held up in Calcutta with cardiac troubles – and what may likely have been one of his nervous breakdowns – and was therefore unable to attend the festive and affectionate farewell ceremony. In his stead, he sent the director of Viśvabhāratī, Vidhushekhara Bhattacharya, who in honor of Formichi read a speech in Sanskrit, transcribed on parchment in his own hand, and most likely composed by Bhattacharya himself: he was an excellent pandit.

On February 5, 1926, Formichi took his official leave from the representatives of Viśvabhāratī. Together with Tucci and Tagore he was headed to Dhaka. The Poet and the Italian professors had been invited to deliver lectures at the university there. They first stopped off in Calcutta, where in December, 1925 Formichi had already given a speech, as part of the first Indian Philosophical Congress, founded that year by Tagore, who served as its President General, and the philosopher Sarvepalli Radhakrishnan, the future president of India, and inaugurated by Lord Lytton, the governor of Bengal. At the conference, Tucci spoke of Indian materialism – Indian materialist philosophy being one of his prime interests, as we've seen – because, as he wrote in the article «La religiosità dell'India» («The Religiosity of India»),

> The widely held perception in the West of India as a country lost in the clouds, an idealist, deeply mystical and religious country, does not correspond to reality.[15]

He would later publish the paper delivered at the conference, under the title, «A Sketch of Indian Materialism».[16] Tucci and Formichi remained in Dhaka in February 7–15, and were once again, as always in India, swept up in a whirlwind of visits, lectures, and presentations. Formichi held five lectures, two of which took place in the university's *aula magna*, Curzon Hall, a «magnificent hall, with enough room to fit two-thousand people comfortably». As Formichi recalls,

> between the lectures, the visits to be made and visitors to receive, the ceremonies, banquets, and *garden-parties* to attend, there were days when our natural stamina was stretched to its very limit.[17]

Tagore, Formichi, and Tucci left for Assam, where Tucci quickly learned that mere permission from the British authorities to visit the monasteries and other institutions would not suffice. In addition, one must appeal to the local authorities. As was officially specified, the possessor of a travel permit, "may not visit monasteries or other institutions without the express approval of the proper authorities".[18] Some years later, Tucci reflected on his time in Assam:

In the city of Gauhati, in Assam, for example, when I sought to visit the renowned Kamakia Temple, famed for its tantric rituals, the appeal of a few Indian friends was of no worth at all. And even when they attempted to accompany me there in person, the doors of the temple would not open. I returned alone: with the Pandas, or temple guards, I struck up a discussion in Sanskrit of religious and philosophical arguments; and after three hours of rigorous examination not only was I granted entrance into the *Sancta sanctorum*, but was given full permission to view the many manuscripts held there under the careful guard of priests and citizens alike. In Nepal, I was forced to repeat this same process, and indeed, the great wealth of scientific material I was able to collect and bring back with me is due in large part to the sympathy with which the learned natives received me in these places of worship.[19]

In June, 1928 and June, 1930, Tucci traveled to Ladakh, a largely Buddhist territory. And there he learned that «the truly remarkable success of my travels is, in the end, the fruit of a long preparation. Most importantly, a knowledge of the spoken language, as well as its literature; which is no simple matter [...]». But knowledge of the language alone would not suffice: one had to be capable of recognizing the fundamental aspects of Lamaism, on a religious and iconographic level, and «possess an understanding of the people's beliefs that probed beyond mere surface facts». To overcome the «secular repugnance» held by Tibetans, the reluctance «to speak of their beliefs, to open the doors of their temples, to merely show, let alone part with, their sacred texts», it was necessary to

make it clear that the sacred law was no longer a

mystery to us, to demonstrate genuine sympathy for
their beliefs and religious experiences, and regard
their temples and images with great reverence. My
methods produced such excellent results because
in allowing me to collect these materials, whether
manuscripts, epigraphs, or works of art, the most
vital arguments in the history of Lamaism and of
Tibetan culture would, in part, be resolved, or at least
viewed in a new light and inched toward a solution.[20]

With the years, Tucci would continue to perfect his method
for obtaining these precious treasures. In the diary from his 1933
expedition, he observes that knowledge alone would not suffice
to win the trust of the lamas and pandits, but that one must also
demonstrate a spiritual affinity.

To merely know a language or a dialect is not suffi-
cient: you must learn to win their trust, to give the
impression that, as a visitor, you arebound to them
by a spiritual affinity [...]. I often played the role of
a disciple, even if our conversation on complex matters of theology or metaphysics – when I came across
monks competent enoughto assess my knowledge
accurately – made it clear I was no novice; I bowed
before their statues, I prayed in the austere silence
of their shrines, with devotion I asked the priests to
light votive candles on their altars, all to the increase
of my merit, and before every book and statute I was
offered, I bore the utmost respect.[21]

As we'll see more explicitly in chapter seven, which covers
also the 1933 expedition, Tucci makes it very clear in later pages
of the same diary just how far he was willing to push his method,
resorting even to guile for the sake of obtaining a precious item,

taking advantage of others' good faith. Hoarding treasures at the time was not a criminal offense, and Tucci, as we know, followed a rather personal set of ethics to achieve the goals of his research.

Tucci remained with Tagore until May, when he accompanied the Poet to Dhaka. Tagore spent nearly the entire day of May 10 giving speeches, and

> exhausted himself to the point of aggravating his cardiac troubles. All plans were rendered uncertain and provisional, and for five days the city's entire population was held in suspense, wondering whether one lecture or another would or wouldn't be held. From hour to hour, the reports regarding the Poet's health contradicted one another: Tagore will attend and speak, he will attend but he will not speak, he will not attend. One can imagine the difficult, the unnerving and exasperating, situation in which the members of the Committee in charge of organizing the celebrations found themselves.
>
> The Poet's temper reached its mercurial peak when, according to the schedule, he was to leave the *house-boat* for a night and stay in the home of a History teacher, a man who stood among the most fervent organizers of the grand welcoming ceremonies, and who reserved for himself the right to host the illustrious guest in his own home. Tagore, meanwhile, fell into such a state of nerves that there was no choice but to lead him back to his *house-boat*.
>
> No longer can it be said that caprice is proper only to women: one would be doing the poets an injustice.[22]

The Poet departed for his tour of Europe and arrived in Rome on May 30, 1926. The following day, he went with Formichi to Palazzo Chigi, to see Mussolini. Tucci, meanwhile, remained in India, and traveled to Sikkim with Giulia, his new love interest or, rather, his new wife.

Two Differing Accounts of India

By way of a «rather sluggish» train, Formichi and Tucci traveled to Mymensingh, a small city in modern day Bangladesh that at the time numbered 60,000 inhabitants, only twelve of whom were Europeans. There, at the Anand Mohan College, Formichi delivered a lecture on the *Atharvaveda*. In his book, Formichi also tells of a rather unusual afternoon he spent with Tucci, in pages tinged with subtle humor. Tucci – he writes – was so struck by the beauty of the tigers at a zoological garden in Calcutta, that turning his gaze to a hideous crocodile, he'd exclaimed: «If it was between dying in the jaws of that magnificent tiger and the maw of that deformed crocodile, a thousand times over I'd choose the former».[23] Hearing of their love for tigers, a certain Mr. Guha arranged to photograph them together with three of the gorgeous beasts, two males and a female, Begham. The tamer instructed the males to stretch out at the feet of the two scholars, with the female, the most defiant – with whom Tucci had had a frightful encounter the day before – lying between them. Nevertheless, the photographer, Mr. Guha's brother, after repeatedly shifting the tripod from side to side, suddenly realized that something was missing. He sprinted into the house, followed by Mr. Guha. The tamer, too, had already departed. Formichi and Tucci were left alone with the tigers.

> Fortunately, Tucci and I were equipped with two, hefty walking sticks, with which we were able to keep Begham at bay, for as soon as the two men left, she'd

risen to her feet and seemed gripped with the desire
to sniff us, or, for all we knew, to see how we tasted.
Indeed, a moment of great trepidation. The beast, in
any case, merely clamped her teeth around the end
of my stick, as if wanting to play fletch; the sharp peal
of my voice, meanwhile, sent Guha and his brother
running back. Of course, I was quick to inform them
how prudent they'd been to leave us exposed there
to the dangers of a pouncing feline. God willing, after
a series of failed attempts, if one beast managed to
stay still, another fussed, one of the negatives struck
them as satisfactory, and soon, somehow,we were
rising from our arm chairs, thanking Mr. Guha for
the truly unprecedented experience, and making our
way to the station.[24]

For us, unfortunately, though both scholars wrote to Mr. Guha
on several occasions urging him to send a copy of the photograph,
no response ever came. Formichi would comment on such unre-
liable behavior with his usual verve, recording a fact well-known
to anyone who's spent a bit of time in India:

> Doubtless, Indians are gifted with many excel-
> lent qualities, they're kindhearted, calm, courteous,
> sharp-witted, but when it comes to punctuality, keep-
> ing promises, and the prompt and orderly handling of
> business, experience forbids me to sing their praises.
> Arrange for a car to pick you up from your house
> on a certain date and take you to the station, beg and
> implore that your arrangements are not overlooked,
> come the scheduled date, be certain you'll find no
> car outside your door. Consign a letter to be mailed
> off, and your letter will not reach its destination, for
> the simple fact that it was never mailed.

Woe to whomever entrusts a manuscript in the hands of another Indian: ninety-nine times out of a hundred it will be lost.

Before leaving Calcutta, Consul Pervan and the Italian community kindly offered to hold a banquet in my honor. We were to meet at the restaurant, Peliti, at 8pm, and the Consul informed Tucci and I that he'd pass by in his car at 7:30pm to pick us up. The car, in fact, did come, though Tagore's servants, to save themselves the trouble of climbing up the stairs and informing us that the Consul had arrived, reported instead that we'd already left the house some time ago. And so, we went on waiting. The Consul, meanwhile, seeing that we were not yet at Peliti, phoned, and phoned again, and phoned a third time to see what had happened to us. Each time, he was told we'd already left the house, until, at the end of my nerves, I decided to phone him myself and discovered the blunder. Rather than eight o'clock, we sat down at ten, to the great inconvenience, as might be imagined, of all those present, and the fury of the cooks and waiters.

Nor should one believe that Tagore's household servants had acted in such a way out of ill-will. Behind their actions was nothing but inertia. Out of sheer inertia, an Indian might very well let his house burn down. In evidence, here, quite clearly, is a pathological trait, one which can have grim consequences for all parties involved and obstruct the regular flow of social life.[25]

With his wide-eyed astonishment and spontaneity, Formichi succeeds in transforming the tales even of Indian culture – a culture which at the time remained shrouded in mystery and largely unknown to the general public – into vibrant sketches of daily life and, at times, into a genuine history, unfolded through anecdote. It was the wish of Formichi, for example, who with all probability had in mind the story of *Rikki-Tikki-Tavi* from Kipling's *The Jungle Book*, to acquire a mongoose, for its ability to kill even the largest and most poisonous snakes.[26] "Rathi" Tagore, that is, Rathindranath, the son of the Poet who also served as his secretary, granted Formichi his wish, presenting him with one of «those little beasts». And when it came to his «new companion» nothing was out of bounds: sleeping on his lap, in his pockets or sleeves, on his shoulders or neck. Such affection did he develop for the creature that he would soon find him a wife, Moti. The couple traveled with him back to Italy, along with two birds, a *bhringaraja* and a female *mojna*. Unfortunately, the first was eaten by Rikki, and eight months later, Moti killed the second.

> Rikki and Moti are now Roman citizens, and here they enjoy perfect health. Often in Santiniketan, going out for a walk, I took Rikki on a leash, like a puppy. On one such occasion, one of the many peacocks that roam the streets of Santiniketan caught sight of him, scrutinized him with harmless curiosity, almost as if recognizing an old friend, and began trailing after him. Joining the first peacock came a second, and a third, and a fourth ; and so I returned to my her-mitage in the most absurd of spectacles : a parade of four peacocks, a mongoose, and a professor![27]

In Formichi's book, all that characterizes his student's ac-count is utterly absent: a seriousness, a heaviness, a taste for the dramatic, a supreme indifference to the reality of men and objects around him and to a culture that, in the wake of his famed expeditions, he would come to see as stripped of its individuality, a flattened culture of the masses, with no silence left to plumb, no mystery left to unveil. And such a view of humanity – that was a thing he avoided – would remain with Tucci throughout his life: with the exceptional and uncommon men of the world, he would form the most interesting and advantageous relationships; but when it came to ordinary men, he kept his distance.

Even in his various notes and travelogues, published after his expeditions, completely lacking in Tucci's account are the vivid and often childlike descriptions so common in Formichi's work: minor, everyday occurrences, seen through the eyes of a cultured man of the late 1800s bourgeoisie, a good-natured and well-meaning man (in the best sense of the term), enamored of Indian culture and Nepal. And yet, even into the twenties and thirties the perception of India was marked by the fantastical: India and the Himalayan countries stood as grand repositories for the collective imagination – representations, to the West, of an almost dreamlike world. And in regard to animals, unlike Formichi's warm-hearted but rather simple affection, Tucci demonstrated a profound empathy in consideration of their inescapable *karman*.

The external world, for Tucci, was a reflection of his own personal thoughts and meditations. He was gripped by a thoroughly intellectual anxiety to look within himself, to tell his own story, and often to put his own excellence on display – to show how exceptional he was, how he was able not only to distinguish himself from his equals, surpassing them by great lengths, but also, as no one else could, to integrate with peoples of the most distant and unexplored countries, to speak their language, to eat their food, to pray in their places of worship; Tucci's story is always peppered with a healthy amount of narcissism. Even in the descriptions of his expeditions, one has the sense that Tucci is travelling alone, without the burden or warmth of any companionship with his fellow travelers: it is he alone, in the midst of wide-open nature, he on the march, in the expansive silence, he standing before great discoveries, he who confronts and speaks with the Kashmiris, the Tibetans, the Nepalese. The others serve merely as backdrop, peeking forward now and then, and almost always in cases when they prove to him a burden – lazy caravanners, untrustworthy bearers, and so forth – or, more often, in cases where the person is of exceptional character – yogins, itinerant teachers and ascetics who grasp Tucci at first sight, by a sort of internal affinity. And yet he was constantly surrounded by guides, occasional translators – for each region has its own languages and dialects – by lamas or geshes (*dgeshes*), doctors of Buddhism, who provided him with explanations and aid in buying and selling goods, by bearers and caravanners, and by an entire network of crew members who traveled alongside him day in and day out, an ordered and somewhat militaresque unit of anywhere from fifteen to seventy people. Of course, he couldn't be expected to fill the pages of his books with casual dialogue and petty quarrels: and yet, Fosco Maraini, his travel companion on two expeditions (1937 and 1948), was able to incorporate the stories of "the people" around him and breathe life into his book, *Segreto Tibet [Secret Tibet]* – a stupendous work, which guides the reader through the fascinating world of his expeditions, entertaining and educating along the way.[28]

Tucci, unlike Formichi, is never astonished by the strange customs he describes, never wrapped up in the stories he tells. As it would seem, he never once encounters a difficulty or suffers a moment of awkwardness in the face of cultural or social differences – or, perhaps more accurately, he faces these awkward moments with style, with the detachment of a world traveler and a scientist. Never is he clumsy or out of step, but always the central protagonist of the story, refined and a touch arrogant, for he «stood above the common dealings of man» – as a beloved student of his, and professor of mine, once described him to me many years ago. As a result, while Formichi's account of a journey typically begins in Italy, with the preparations and events leading up to it and all the minor details and problems there involved, with notes on the weather and the kindnesses of his companions, of all those whom he encounters or who lend him a hand, an account penned by Tucci begins always in the place of arrival, with grandiose and impressive descriptions. Tucci is a skilled and enchanting narrator, though he tells his tales as an eagle traces circles in the sky – with full view and control of all below, merely waiting for the right moment to dive down on his helpless prey. Formichi's gift of a benevolent and paternal, perhaps even paternalistic, gaze, is lacking in Tucci's view of the world; as compensation, he possesses a great richness of language and a refined yet fluid style, with an abundance of elegant and unusual adjectives.

And yet, little by little, as Tucci writes his scientific and popular books, his travelogues and reports from the field, such as the article «La città bruciata» («The burned city») – passages of which I've included in chapter eleven – his style begins to take on a poetic quality. As the years pass, the language in Tucci's more popular scientific articles, as well as in his letters with Senator Andreotti, becomes extremely fluid, fecund, and pleasant, filled with nuance, the speech of a man of power, of a scientist in full command of his field, and yet whose thoughts still stir with dreams, fantasies, and future projects. In his first travelogue, on the other hand, written together with Eugenio Ghersi, his tone, as we'll see, is cold, measured, a list of information and events, enlivened with personal flare only in a few, sparse passages – for example, in his brief rant on the filthiness of Kathmandu and Nepal. But this, too, reflects the image Tucci aimed to cultivate of himself: aristocratic, disdainful of the common rules, and different – for the better, of course – than other men. All of which plays a part in the character he presented to others: his audience.

Dhaka, Benares, Calcutta, and Il Duce's Gift

Having concluded their visit to Dhaka, they made for Benares, the most sacred city in the world for Hindu believers, where they encountered a bookseller as learned as a pandit. «The bookseller, in reality a simple shopkeeper, spoke with us in the Sanskrit of an expert scholar and proved himself highly knowledgeable not only in poetic literature, but also in the most specialized philosophy».[29] Having made their rounds of the bookshops, the two rented a large pontoon with a shade top. Each seated in an arm chair, Tucci and Formichi relaxed and took in the view of Benares, or what remained to see of it, enjoying a light morning breeze. They stopped also in Sarnath, nearly 18 miles away: as Buddhists, the site held for them a special significance – home to the famed deer park where Buddha delivered his First Sermon. In Sarnath, as well, they paid a visit to the famous column of the great emperor Aśoka, from 250 BCE, bearing the inscription of one of his edicts against the schismatic tendency of Buddhism: «No one shall cause division in the order of monks». The column's capital, in the form of a lion, stands as a national symbol in India, and is held in the Archaeological Museum of Sarnath, the most ancient museum site of the Archaeological Survey of India.

When they returned to Calcutta, Tagore, who had not been able to bid farewell to Formichi at his departure in Śāntiniketan, invited him to his home.

> In the vast living room of Tagore's home, furnished in the Oriental style, that is, filled with sofas and seats only a few centimeters high, a group convened on the evening of March 9, including representatives of Visvabharatî who lived in Calcutta, a host of friends, and the Italian Consul, Pervan, with his wife. The Poet, still recovering from his last bout of ill health and struggling to stay on his feet, read in a frail and crystalline voice the following message in English, which I've reproduced here in Italian: [...][30]

The lengthy speech was «neatly printed on special, Indian

paper, protected on the outside by a metal foil laminate case, bearing an engraved dedication, and a tablet, and wrapped in a magnificent brocade». It was offered to Formichi along with several other gifts: a musical instrument – a so-called "conch" – used by Indians during battle, a ring, one Shaivite necklace, one Vishnuite necklace, and two bundles of a distinctly scented incense. In addition to the many personal gifts, he received «a complete collection of Tagore's poetry in ten large volumes, printed on lavish paper in Bengali characters» to present as an homage to Mussolini. In his speech, the Poet thanked Formichi for the courses he'd taught at Viśvabhāratī and for his kindness, expressing his full gratitude for the gift of Italian books sent by the Duce, «a gift of staggering magnificence», and for having brought Tucci along with him:

> In this connection I must mention the name of your former pupil, Dr. Tucci, who is still with us and for the loan of whose services I cannot enough thank your government. He has studied with an amazing comprehensiveness, along with most of the other phenomena of Indian culture, the greatest period of India's history; he has pursued the triumphant career of Buddhism in distant countries, following almost obliterated indications across the sand-buried antiquities, among the records of a startled history that has lost the memory of its own language. He can best remind the modern children of India of what has been the most glorious self-revelation in the annals of their ancestors. That was her ideal of universal sympathy [...].[31]

In the Indian press, the gift of books made by Mussolini was remarked upon with unanimous praise. Tagore himself mentioned it to every visitor of his university. Standing as proof of his sincere gratitude is the cablegram he sent to Mussolini and which was reproduced in the December 1925 issue of the monthly English magazine, *The Modern Review*, founded in Calcutta by Ramananda Chatterjee, which quickly became a forum for privileged members of the nationalist and progressive *intelligencija*:[32]

> Allow me to convey to you our gratitude in the name of Visvabharati for sending us, through Prof. Formichi, your cordial appreciation of Indian civilization, and deputing Prof. Tucci of the University of Rome for acquainting our scholars with Italian history and culture and working with us in various departments of Orientalism, and also for the generous gift of books in your name, showing a spirit of magnanimity worthy of the traditions of your great country. I assure you that such an expression of sympathy, coming from You as representative of the Italian people, will open, for the cultural exchange between your country and ours, a channel of communication, which has every possibility of leading to an event of great historical importance.[33]

From Calcutta – while Formichi made preparations for his return to Italy, leaving from Bombay – Tucci departed for Viśvabhāratī. On the evening of March 10, Formichi left on a direct train to Bombay, where he was the guest of R. D. Tata in his splendid villa by the port. With great warmth and hospitality, Tata welcomed the professor, his two mongooses, and his two exotic birds, which he kept in cages, and which, as we know, came to an unfortunate end as mongoose dinner on board the ship bearing the professor and his bizarre foursome back to Genova. As Formichi remarked:

> That he so generously and cordially opened his doors to me, one of the representatives of Western Indol-

ogy and a messenger on behalf of Benito Mussolini,
one can easily understand; but that he received my
Noah's arc with so magisterial a welcome is the highest display of kindness and largesse a host can offer.[34]

TAGORE VISITS ITALY: BETWEEN NATIONALISM AND ORIENTALISM

Formichi was proud of his status as «one of the representatives of
Western Indology and a messenger on behalf of Benito Mussolini».
Il Duce, who through Formichi's actions hoped to intensify and
consolidate diplomatic, political, and commercial relations with
Asia and, as we'll see, open new roads toward colonization, would
send the professor not only to India, but on missions in Japan,
Egypt, and the United States.

Tucci was sent only to Japan: yet, in his explorations and
activities in India he was already a flag bearer for the regime, as
well as its mouthpiece. The entirety of his works and efforts were
marked by a precise cultural policy: the prestige of Italy abroad
– even if his principal aim, in truth, was to satisfy his own need
to stand out among his peers and display his prowess, both as a
scholar and an explorer.

Immediately upon returning to Italy from his first voyage
in India, animated by his time spent with the poet and grateful for his academic year as Visiting Professor at Viśvabhāratī,
Formichi organized a second visit to Rome for Tagore, after his
less-than-favorable experience in 1925. Tagore, in fact, was in
Japan in June of 1924 when Formichi received a letter from the
Bengali scholar, Kalidas Nag, regarding a potential visit. Nag, a
student of Tagore's, filled with enthusiasm and admiration for
the Poet, had earlier traveled to Paris to study with Lévi, during
which time he'd stopped in Italy and had formed an «intimate
and cordial friendship» with Formichi.[35] In the letter, he wrote

that he'd convinced Tagore to pass through Europe as well, and that he, perhaps, would accompany him. On August 20, 1924, Tagore sent a telegram reporting that he'd be able to stop in Italy on his way back from South America, during the winter. After several setbacks, due to the lack of funds to host Tagore and his party, the issue was resolved by Count Guido Cagnola, in Milan, who reached out to his personal friends and to the Philological Circle for financial contributions. His example in Milan was then replicated in Turin and Florence.

Tagore disembarked in Genoa on the morning of January 19, 1925. He would remain there only a short time, though he was immediately received with great enthusiasm by the Genovese people. Only during his train ride from Genoa to Milan, and on no other occasion, as Formichi recounts, did Tagore wish to be informed of the political situation. On the evening of January 21, 1925, after a solemn reception at the home of the Duke Tommaso Gallarati Scotti, President of the Philological Circle, the Poet attended a performance of *La Traviata* at the Teatro alla Scala, under the direction of Arturo Toscanini. All was well, in other words. The following day, however, in the presence of Formichi and the highest ranking Fascist officials, Tagore delivered his first speech, one of disapproval, to a packed audience in a room of the Philological Circle. «Amidst a collective and feverish anticipation» he proclaimed that Europe, with its scientific achievements, had merely come to dominate external nature, but that man was not yet worthy of his own scientific discoveries. As he advocated, men should not serve science, but science should be employed in service of men:

> But discoveries have to be realized by a complete humanity, knowing – Knowing has to be brought under the control of Being – before Truth can be fully honored. [...] Truth when not properly treated turns back on us to destroy us. Your very science is thus

becoming your destroyer.

If you have acquired a thunderbolt for yourself, you must earn the right arm of a god to be safe. You have failed to cultivate those qualities which would give you full sovereign right over science and therefore you have missed peace. You cry for peace, and only build another frightful machine. [...] The powerful are exulting at the number of their victims. They take the name of science to cultivate the schoolboy superstition that they have certain physical signs indicating their eternal right to rule. [...] But they in their turn will be disappointed.

Theirs is the cry of a past that is already exhausted, a past that has thrived upon the exclusive spirit of national individualism which will no longer be able to keep the balance in its perpetual disharmony with its surroundings. Only those races will prosper who, for the sake of their own perfection and permanent safety, are ready to cultivate the spiritual magnanimity of mind that enables the soul of man to be realized in the heart of all races.

[...] We are waiting for the time when the spirit of the age will be incarnated in a complete human truth and the meeting of men will be translated into the Unity of Man.[36]

Tagore's ideas, therefore, were revolutionary for his time, and certainly not fit for an audience of Fascist hierarchs and intellectuals: he proposed equality in human relations and a sustainable development in relation to the surrounding environment. What sense is there anymore, Tagore argued, to a culture of domination based on the belief that certain races, by their very nature, by birth, are destined to take command? Such a view, he held, is nothing but the remnant of an old mentality, founded on nationalistic individualism and a culture of suppression.

The audience, permeated as it was by a Darwinian spirit, according to which the strongest – and so, the most fit to rule – was determined only by a constant struggle, did not quite take to Tagore's words. His speech, published in its entirety in the April, 1975 *Visva-Bharati Quarterly*, alienated him, as Formichi would recall, from the sympathies «of our Fascists», and set off a violent journalistic campaign against him.[37]

The evening of January 23, 1925, after a grand and moving ceremony held at the People's Theater, before all the school children of Milan, Tagore felt slightly ill. The following morning he woke with a fever, a cough, and a faintness of heart, leaving him in need of medical care. Though not particularly grave, his illness «so depressed his spirits that to continue his tour of conferences around the peninsula was no longer possible».[38] The poet left the country ahead of schedule. Drawing him away, as well, were the cold winter temperatures in Italy, which proved adverse to his health; and yet, constrained to his bed, he would compose in Bangla – the language, that is, referred to also as Bengalese, Bengali, or Bengoli – the poem *All'Italia [To Italy]*, which Formichi translated and which was published in every major Italian newspaper. Though the poem was purely lyrical and centered on his return that coming spring, there were those wont to detect a «malign allusion to the elections to be held that spring, in which the parties opposed to Fascism were promising an unfavorable outcome for the Government».[39] Tagore's first visit was therefore exploited by the Fascists, who, after the gaffe of his speech at the Philological Circle, began to interpret all he said and did in political terms.

On his second visit to Italy, Tagore disembarked at Naples on May 31, 1926. In Rome, he met with Mussolini on two separate occasions, with Formichi serving as interpreter, and on June 5 he made the acquaintance of King Victor Emmanuel III. One can readily imagine that Mussolini's speeches had been slightly adjusted in translation, in order to prove more appealing to Tagore. Reading through *India and Indians*, it is quite clear that all was presented to the Poet in the most favorable manner, through the eyes with which Formichi himself viewed the Duce. Tagore admired the charisma and personality of Mussolini and was excellently received, given that he presented himself as a poet, with no bearing on political matters. Tagore and Mussolini spoke also of a project that was dear to Formichi's heart, and which would be carried ahead by Tucci: that of establishing lasting cultural ties between Italy and India. To this aim, they discussed the possibility of «creating scholarships to promote an exchange of young Indian and Italian students».[40]

As witnessed before, in discussing Formichi's farewell ceremony in India, Tagore once again expressed his gratitude to the Duce for his generous gift of Italian books for the Viśvabhāratī library and for sending the two Italian professors. Nevertheless, upon departing from Italy Tagore demonstrated himself contrary to the regime; and in response to his declarations of anti-Fascism – as we'll see in greater depth in the following chapter – Formichi would react harshly, dashing the poets hopes of salvaging their friendship. Formichi criticized him not only for having betrayed his friends in Italy, but for having betrayed his own choice to refrain from taking any direct involvement in political matters.

In 1928, Formichi declined an offer to represent the Ministry of Public Education at the Congress of Orientalists at Oxford, in order to prepare for his upcoming trip to California. Indeed, as he wrote to the minister of Public Education on June 9, he'd been invited by the president of the University of Berkeley to inaugurate the newly founded professorship in Italian Culture, and to teach a course from August to December, 1928. His request for leave during this period was granted, «given the high cultural value and the expressly Italian nature of the mission». On October 6, 1928 the newspaper, *L'Italia*, run by San Francisco's Italian community, published a full-page article on the new professorship of Italian Culture inaugurated the day prior, along with a passport photo of Formichi, the first to hold the position. Upon visiting the library of the University of California-Berkeley, I even came across works of Formichi that in Italy are now almost impossible to track down.

Formichi's inauguration speech was entitled «Grandi vecchi maestri del Fascismo» («Great old masters of Fascism»). In it, he read a small collection of quotes from past figures whom the Fascist party held as its forbearers – without, however, citing their names. One much-celebrated quote read: «Never will a man be faulted for using violence to better the world around him». And who other than Mussolini, Italy's exemplary leader, Formichi declared, had used violence to achieve a positive end – to bring order back to a discouraged Italian peninsula, gripped by a constant political struggle between right and left, and weighted down by an inefficient, incapable government? And who other than Mussolini had so foolishly been criticized for such behavior? Formichi spoke out, as well, against critics of the Fascist political stance, borrowing the words of the Dante scholar and historian, Isidoro Del Lungo: «The love of dissent so inherent to the Italic peninsula, our sin, an unnatural love». If, in science, criticism is productive, Formichi went on, in politics it can only do harm.

In California, Formichi published an essay in Italian, «Il simbolismo nella Vita Nuova e nel Canzoniere di Dante Alighieri» («Symbolism in La Vita Nuova and the Canzoniere of Dante Alighieri»).[41] In order to promote cultural relations with the United States and to aid American students who wished to enroll in Italian universities, Formichi also proposed to the Ministry of Public Education, in February 1929, that a new branch of the Ministry be established in New York, «made up of Italian and American representatives, well practiced in the scholastic laws of both countries». In 1930, he was sent to New York for a month by the Royal Academy of Italy, in accordance with the Ministry of Foreign Affairs. During his visit he ran into Tagore, on his way back from the Soviet Union. And when the poet expressed a desire to resolve any misunderstandings that had arisen between him and Il Duce, Formichi convinced him to write to Mussolini himself. Tagore's letter, dated November 21, 1930, would, however, do nothing to reestablish relations between the Italian government and Śāntiniketan:[42]

1172 Park Avenue

New York, Nov. 21, 1930

Your Excellency:

It often comes to my memory how we were startled by the magnanimous token of Your sympathy reaching us through my very dear friend Prof. Formichi. The precious gift, the library of Italian literature, is a treasure to us highly prized by our institution and for which we are deeply grateful to Your Excellency.

I am also personally indebted to You for the lavish generosity You showed to me in your hospitality when I was your guest in Italy and I earnestly hope that the misunderstanding which has unfortunately caused a barrier between me and the great people You represent, the people for whom I have genuine love, will not remain permanent, and that this expression of my gratitude to You and Your nation will be accepted. The politics of a country is its own; its culture belongs to all humanity. My mission is to acknowledge all that has eternal value in the self-expression of any country.

Your Excellency has nobly offered to our institution on behalf of Italy the opportunity of a festival of Spirit which will remain inexhaustible and ever claim our homage of a cordial admiration.

I am, Your Excellency,
Gratefully Yours
Rabindranath Tagore.

Formichi's American sojourn proved a triumph, crowned by an honorary Doctor of Law degree from Berkeley. He was beloved and admired by his students – so much so that, as he himself wrote in his *Relazione sull'opera di propaganda culturale svolta dal prof. Formichi negli Stati Uniti d'America [Report on the cultural propaganda carried out by Prof. Formichi in the United States of America]*, though his course in Italian at Berkeley began «in a narrow lecture hall» with a twenty-person capacity, it would soon become «the most popular [course] at the university, where nearly 15,000 students were enrolled»! Among the many invitations he received from universities around the country to speak as a guest lecturer, questions of time permitted him to accept only those from the most important universities: Stanford, Harvard, and Columbia. Toward the end of the trip, given his constant economic limitations, he appealed to the government to cover his boat fare back to Italy, as recognition of his «distinguished work of Italian propaganda».

In the United States, meanwhile, an extremely active, if rather marginal, antifascist propaganda was developing. In the mid 1930s, in fact, the American League Against War and Fascism, later renamed the American League for Peace and Democracy, began publishing pamphlets such as *The Fascist Road to Ruin* and *Young People Against War and Fascism*. Distinctly anti-fascist opinions were therefore present in the United States. All of which, in Formichi's view, did nothing but bring harm to Italian social and political life and to their long sought, and at last achieved, stability.[43]

Formichi was inducted as a member of the Royal Academy of Italy, the prestigious cultural institute founded by Mussolini, on January 18, 1929, serving as the organization's Senior Vice-President until his death. Wielding the influence of his position, he proposed immediately that Tucci be named a member of the academy. Tucci's merit as a scholar, along with his kind and amicable nature, was widely recognized by the official cultural bastions of his day: he was a national member of the Lincean Academy, an honorary member of Arcadia, a corresponding member of the Association Française des Amis de L'Orient, and an honorary member of the New Orient Society of America.

In 1931, «for the purpose of forming productive and principled citizens, devoted to the motherland» Formichi gave the «Processo verbale di prestazione di giuramento al Rettorato della R. Università di Roma» («A sworn testament of allegiance to the President of the Royal University of Rome»), pledging faithfulness to the king, his royal successors, and the Fascist regime, and denying involvement, present or future, with any association or party whose activity did not accord with his official duty. In other words, he declared his faith to Fascism. In that period, however, all professors were called upon to swear an oath, and all of them, with the exception of twelve, said the words – including Tucci.

On October 31, 1932, the Ministry of National Education, in conjunction with the Ministry of Finance, nominated Carlo Formichi, Full Professor of Sanskrit at the Royal University of Rome, and Giuseppe Tucci, Full Professor of Religions and Philosophies of India and the Far East at the same university, to carry out scientific research in Tibet and Nepal, from November 1, 1933 until January 31, 1934.[44] Formichi was then sixty-one years old, Tucci thirty-eight. For both, accompanied by the Royal Navy's medical captain, Eugenio Ghersi, it would be their first official mission in Nepal and Tibet – even if, in the end, Formichi would never step foot in Tibet. The two men were relieved of their professorial duties, maintaining their salary, though with no additional wages to be garnered from the mission itself. Before leaving for Nepal, in 1931, Formichi, together with Vittore Pisani, edited the Italian translation in *ottava rima* of several episodes from the *Mahābhārata*, done by his teacher, Michele Kerbaker.[45]

WITH CAPTAIN GHERSI: FORMICHI'S EXPEDITION IN NEPAL

Formichi leaves account of his voyage in the brief volume, *Il Nepal. Conferenza tenuta all'«Augusteo» di Roma il 26 febbraio 1934-XII [Nepal. A Presentation Given at the «Mausoleum of Augustus» in Rome, on February 26, 1934-XII].*[46] At the time, its doors closed to all foreigners, Nepal was forbidden fruit, and Formichi explains the reasoning behind their precaution:

> The Nepalese, in their blessed valley at the foot of the divine Himâlaya, just as Italy's sons and daughters in Piedmont once stood at the base of the Alps, in the sorrowful days before independence and the unification of Italy, look out on India and see her lands almost entirely subjected to outside rule, with a distressing past of invasions by civilized and barbarous peoples alike, by Greeks, Shiites, Huns, Muslims, Europeans, and meanwhile, there they are, a most conspicuous and felicitous exception, free and independent, jealous guards of a magnificent cultural patrimony thousands of years in the making, pure, intact, untouched by exotic populations who practice different customs, obey different laws, and profess

different beliefs. If I were a Nepalese, I too would lock
the doors of my homeland and turn the deadbolt.[47]

The true reason, however, for which the Rana family denied
access to all foreigners but Indians, Sinhalese, and Tibetans was
not to keep their cultural patrimony intact, as Formichi naively
assumed, but to isolate the Nepalese people, to keep them in
ignorance, and therefore to govern them with greater ease. In
the Nepalese people, that is, Formichi seemed to sense a certain
pride and nationalism – characteristically Fascist and conservative values – while of the Prime Minister's despotism he seemed
to take no note at all.

One other reason Formichi points to as a cause of Nepal's logis-
tical and political isolation is the fear that the caste system would
be contaminated – a phenomenon which, in realty, concerns almost exclusively the two highest ranking castes of Hindu society –
the Brahmins, and just beneath them, the *cchetris*, who represent
a relative minority and who live principally in the Kathmandu
Valley. Buddhists make no distinction in regard to ethnicity or
caste, though they themselves are divided into dozens of sects and
schools. The majority of the population, composed of a mix of
different ethnicities, from Muslims to believers of other minor
religions, is now no longer driven by any strict law regarding
the preservation and purity of the caste system, but rather by
well-defined social laws.

In Formichi's time, the situation was different:

In British India, while the Brahmans go about shaking
the hands of Europeans, eating, perhaps, at the same
table, and sending their children to work or study
in Europe, still widely held in Nepal is the idea that
any contact with a foreigner is of impure origin, may
bring about one's removal to a lower caste, and is

cause for repentance and ablution to clean oneself of the impurity.[48]

While considering this fear of contamination held by the Brahmins, I'd like to recount an experience of mine in Kathmandu. Only a few days after my arrival in February, 2000, I asked Kesari, Hem Raj's oldest son, who at the time was serving as Vice Royal Preceptor, if his father loved being in contact with so many scholars, who came from every corner of the world to consult the texts in his immense library and to request his enlightened opinion on subjects of all sorts and on doctrinal matters of extreme detail and complexity. Kesari responded candidly, but with some reserve:

– My father was a lover of culture, in whichever language it expressed itself, and that was why he invited the most sophisticated minds of his time to visit his home. But contact? Once, he shook the hand of a foreign scholar who'd mailed a book back to him from France. That man may have been Sylvain Lévi. Afterwards, however – Kesari added, turning his gaze from mine – it appears he went immediately to wash off his hand.

Kesari's lips curled into an eloquent grin of distaste, in which he resembled his father.

– Most assuredly – he concluded – my father never shook the hands of foreigners, nor dined at the same table.

As Formichi recounts, Nepal's doors stood open to Tibetan devotees making pilgrimages to Buddhist temples – shepherds, monks, and lamas, for the most part, wrapped in yellow or red cloaks. Quickly, devoutly, they climbed up the narrow paths that led to the sanctuaries, in silence, their robes fluttering behind them. For a true taste of Tibet, without actually traveling there, one need only visit Nepal. There, still widely spread, as we've seen, was the idea that contact with foreigners was of impure origin and potentially contaminative. Nevertheless:

> Before the majesty of religion and science, before that which we regard with the highest reverence in the world, that is, all strict decorum dissolves into a generous liberality. [...]
>
> Another effective passport is science, not our own, naturally, but that of Indology, which presupposes a knowledge of Sanskrit and of India's philosophical-religious and literary texts. Such a passport served Sylvain Lévi of the Collège de France, F. W. Thomas of Oxford University, and Giuseppe Tucci, of the Royal Academy of Italy, allowing them to travel deep into Nepal's interior and to remain there for more or less extended periods of time and to examine and collect manuscripts from the famous Durbar Library – a true mine of rare and precious ancient codices, containing all that India has produced over the course of three millennia, in every branch of science, sacred and profane.[49]

Thanks to Tucci's resourcefulness and the fame he enjoyed among the court and Nepalese intellectuals, in fact, the Prime Minister would lend several of these precious manuscripts to the Royal Academy of Italy.

> Only when Giuseppe Tucci, a then student of mine, now a most deserved colleague at the University and the Academy, having won the admiration of Nepal's learned men, thanks to his mastery of Sanskrit and the depth and breadth of his knowledge as a scholar of Indology, only when he fell into the good graces

of the Nepalese Court did a profound sympathy arise in relations between Italy and Nepal.[50]

Judging from Formichi's account, his voyage to Khatmandu with Ghersi and Tucci proved as dangerous as one could possibly imagine, though both he and Tucci, as official envoys of the Ministry of National Education (as the Ministry of Public Education was renamed in 1929) had been furnished with every possible comfort. Formichi boarded the *Conte Rosso* in Brindisi on November 11, 1933 and arrived, «after a most fortunate crossing», in Bombay on the morning of the 22nd. That same evening, he boarded the Bombay-Lucknow direct and, after nearly thirty hours of travel, arrived at his destination, crossing through regions stricken with bubonic plague and cholera. Once in Lucknow, he left behind the great rapid lines of communication and passed two more days and nights of sluggish travel,

> eating poorly, sleeping worse, constantly on the watch, with luggage in hand, for frequent changeovers. At last, on the morning of November 25, I crossed the border of British India and stepped off the train at the Raxaul station, to meet up with my colleague, Tucci, and Doctor Ghersi, who were awaiting my arrival in the bungalow of the Mahârâja.[51]

Formichi knew he'd entered Nepal when he could no longer tell if the men he encountered were «Tatar, Chinese, or Japanese». Raxaul stood nearly 75 English miles outside of Kathmandu, or more than 120 kilometers. The first 25 miles stretched through a jungle, populated by tigers, rhinoceroses, elephants, and wild beasts of every kind, and across an alluvial plain, which itself became a jungle in September. The plain was known for its vaporous emissions, particularly after the annual monsoon, from June until September, «a miasma that could kill within only a few hours,

and without hope for cure, to which they'd given the name *aoul*».
The peoples who lived there, the Kumhas, the Tharus, and the
Mangis, were healthy carriers of the terrible disease – none other
than malaria. For entire generations their populations had been
decimated, and now they were immune. These peoples referred
to themselves as *aoulia*, after the name of the disease itself, and
were skilled hunters of elephants, or else *mahuts*, elephant guides.
Behind Formichi's words, however, one can sense his great terror:
the natives there may have been immune, but he was not!

In Tucci's accounts, on the other hand, the reader finds no
trace of worry in the face of diseases or other obstacles, though
the scientific missions he would carry out in western Nepal,
nearly twenty years later, were as hazardous and perilous as
could be imagined.

In Nepal of 1927, the train connecting Raxaul and Amlekhganj
was up and running. Together, the three left Raxaul on the morning of November 27. Nearly four hours later, they stepped off
the train. They'd arrived in Amlekhganj: «Four hours to travel
only 25 miles!» Formichi remarks. The train's engine resembled
that of the first to run in America – a tiny contraption, at the
time on display in New York's Grand Central Terminal. Formichi
remained throughout the journey with his head peeking out of
the train, hoping to catch a glimpse of a tiger, or an elephant, or
any of the jungle's many beasts; frightened by the clatter of the
train, however, the animals kept their distance. To travel from
Amlekhganj to Bhimpedi, their luggage was loaded onto a truck
and they piled into an automobile;in just over three hours they'd
reached their destination, driving past the dry branches of Sal
trees and footbridges still half-destroyed by the previous year's
monsoon rains.[52] From there, they had to traverse the mountains.
There were many ways to cross: on horseback, by the strength
of their own legs, or «by the strength of the legs and shoulders
of others, I mean to say, by palanquin», that is, a covered seat,
propped on two poles and borne by eight men, four up front

and four behind, who «haul the weight forward like donkeys and mules under the yoke».

His «two bold young companions» – that is, the thirty-nine-year-old Tucci and the twenty-nine-year-old Ghersi – as seasoned mountaineers well used to the long treks, having just completed a mission from June to October in western Tibet, «spurned the extra convenience of a palanquin, a lady's mode of travel», while Formichi, «a painfully mediocre mountain climber, with more gray hairs than black» – indeed, he was sixty-two at the time – allowed himself the luxury. And yet, alas, his ride proved an uncomfortable one: he was «forced to keep head down and feet up every time the incline steepened, which was quite often». Moreover, whenever exhaustion set in and the bearers came to a halt, Formichi could hear the sound, muffled by their turbans, of moaning and invocations to the god of grace, Viṣṇu, – the four up front wailing the loudest, the four in back more quietly, more solemnly. And so, as if by the force of magic, Formichi floated in his sedan to their destination, «reachable only by excruciating effort»:

> Though I be of meager weight, what weight I do carry brought me ever more shame as the bearers, chatting amongst themselves, began finishing every sentence with a kind of moan, which I came to interpret as the Dantean *più non posso [I can bear no more]* of the sinners who *più o meno eran contratti secondo ch'avean più e meno addosso [the greater or lesser the burden they bore, the more or less they hunched their backs]*, who make their plaint in the tenth Canto of his *Purgatorio*. As I would come to discover, to the great relief of my conscience, such lament was not the result of their intolerable struggle of bearing my weight on their shoulders, but was, rather, a common occurrence among their people: the final words of a sentence, as

they're accustomed, must always be pronounced as quietly as possible and with a concluding moan.[53]

After a steep, four hour climb, the group reached Sisagarhi, a fortified town of sorts, at more than 2,625 feet above sea level. There, they passed the night in another bungalow, one of the many large structures constructed throughout the country by the Rana family, which they used as hotels when traveling. And for Formichi,

> the impressions and sights we encountered during the day were of such effect that, in my journal, I was given to write the following words: «all seems new here, even the sun and moon, even the earth and sky».[54]

In all, their caravan was comprised of seventy men, escorted by two police guards. With them the guards carried Nepal's national weapon, the *kukkuri* – an enormous steel blade, curved like a scythe but shorter and much broader, with which all soldiers in the army were equipped. For ten hours, the group crossed mountains and traversed valleys. They passed through the villages of Kulikhani, Palampur, Citlang, and Chandragiri, and arrived in Thanakot after sunset. In under an hour, the Maharaja's car had whisked them to Kathmandu.

Above all else, it was the landscape that most struck Formichi. Having passed through Chandragiri, the Himalayas appeared of a sudden in all their majesty, with Nepal at their foot, with their «glaciers and perpetual snows, inaccessible up at the peaks, which seemed to belong more to the sky than to the earth». For him, the unbounded green of the jungle and

> the colors of heaven's vault, overlapping almost as if to reveal the purest, the most intense blue, the

most enflamed red, the sweetest flush of pink, a
white so vibrant and ethereal it seemed a worthier
fount of light than the sun itself; an unfathomable
silence, as wide as the sprawling landscape; all of
it moved one to tears, inebriated the spirit, overwhelmed.[55]

THE SKIES OF THE HIMALAYAS
AND THE KATHMANDU VALLEY

In early March of 2000, having just passed through the Kathmandu Valley and slowly ascending the hills of Hāttiban, the
string of the Annapurna to the east, the Himalayas to the west,
and the peak of Ganesh mountain on my left, my stomach coils
in a knot and I'm nearly struck with vertigo. The halo of clouds
above leave me with an almost reverential sense of fear, a profound, unbridled joy: the very lift, the elation felt by all who
look out on this majestic landscape, all but impossible to witness
up close. An inhaling and an exhaling, almost, of something far
greater than us, something understood only at great pains, becomes perceptible. I feel lifted above pettiness and labor. At last
I feel light, weightless, my body unchained from daily life and
gravity.

My days I pass reflecting on the white of the snow, almost
phosphorescent at sunset and in the first light of dawn, delighting
in the permutations of color on the ice, in the altitude, in the
peaks which, though themselves unchanging, hourly change their
garments – veiled during the day, at dawn and dusk they project
themselves clear against the turquoise sky.

I must, I decide, capture it in endless photographs, freeze it
in space and time and bring it back with me, back home, intact
forever. I wake at dawn and, climbing the Sarasvati hill, spend
three rolls. At sunset I climb again. After the monsoon, they

say, the air turns so clear that the mountains, ringing around you in a massive wall, seem almost cloistering. My prints will be extraordinary, I imagine, at home the scene will stretch again before me, pure and untouched. I'll need only close my eyes and the same air will fill my lungs, just as crisp and clean, just as silent.

At home in Milan I looked back over my photos. Nothing, I realized with bitterness, nothing of the mountains' splendor or majesty remained. Not a thing to see but the green of the Kathmandu Valley and bluish blurs at the horizon, climbing up into a few wisps of white crests that seem to rise from nothingness, so distant are they from the land below. All the rest was opaque, as if veiled by a fog – flat and unremarkable.

Only in Nepal can one get a true sense of the magnitude and imposing grandeur of its mountains, of the crystalline clarity of its skies. Only there does such silence prevail, leaving only the wonder and intense pleasure of standing before one of nature's miracles.

The group crossed through the jungle and reached the Kathmandu Valley – the soil of which was of a particular richness, for according to tradition it had once been a lake. There, Formichi, Tucci, and Ghersi suddenly found themselves standing before every type of cultivated plant: cotton, rice, wheat, barley, oats, ginger, potato, sugar cane, as well as the entire array of Mediterranean vegetables and fruits, and even pineapples and bananas. Meanwhile palms, cactus, and bamboo were there flourishing alongside of them. In the ring of hills that encircle the valley, tobacco, tea, and opium were grown. Digging into the earth, one could find silver, gold, fine marble and precious stones. As Formichi saw it, the jungle of Terai and the numerous others that cloaked the hills leading up to the Himalayas in green, were a hunter's paradise: home to elephants, tigers, leopards, panthers, rhinoceroses, bears, wolves, jackals, deer, fallow deer, chamoix, gazelles, musk deer – a small deer typical of the Himalayan region – hares, and a staggering variety of birds of every shape, size, and color.

All of the land surrounding Kathmandu – that for many years was second only to Mexico City in its level of pollution – is referred to as a jungle, though nothing remains of the flora and fauna that only eighty years before filled the landscape. Today the land is a barren, steppe-like region, run through with vast, intensely cultivated plots of land, rescued from the arid climate by a thousand-year-old irrigation system, one of the most sophisticated ever achieved by man.

The bloodthirsty Tantric goddess, Dakhinakālī, is appeased only by living sacrifice; and so, every year on the fifteenth of February, buffalo, goats, or other small animals – depending on what the devotee could afford – are slaughtered at her altar. In my amblings in search of her temple, I was accompanied by Balarām, a retired soldier and father of three. He was born in Terai, the stretch of wooded land that covers 40% of the country and separates Nepal from India, to an extremely poor family of farmers, but an atavistic hunger had driven him to abandon his family's traditional occupation. He, his wife, his three children, two nanny goats, a sheep, and numerous hens lived together in a small, mud and brick house with a straw and metal roof and no windows. The ground floor had been arranged around a chimney in the corner, whose flue ran straight up through the flat roof. On the second floor was the master bedroom, with its sparse furnishings: the family assets. Children and animals lived on the ground floor. The toilet – a fetid hole in the ground shared by four or five families, guarded by sheet of metal and a crooked door that wouldn't close all the way – was outside, in the midst of the village.

Here is where Balarām's family lived, in this village whose name I cannot remember, a small cluster of simple houses much like his own, of straw and mud huts at the edge of the Kathmandu Valley, at the foot of the hills, along a red dirt road. Lining the sides of the path, and occasionally smack in the middle of it, was now and then a restorative and providential tree, the road swerving around it. Where the road widened was a single bazaar, five or six pieces of clothing laid out over the ground, a few well-arranged pieces of merchandise, and nothing else; no school, no small temple, no gathering post to speak of – not even, say, a simple kiosk for *chai*. On the path to the temple, the hills and escarpments were filled with snakes and "luck-bearing" lizards, fire red with a pointed crest, as big as kittens. Balarām warned me repeatedly: «In the jungle you must stay alert». He was forty-nine and already considered himself old – he could quite easily, in fact, have been mistaken for a man in his late sixties, for as wizened as he was. I asked him why they called it a jungle. When he was young, he replied, the entire region just outside of Kathmandu was decked in a lush green, filled with tigers, buffalo, all types of snakes, monkeys, and every species of animal.
– My grandfather was a *mahut*, for then there were elephants, too – Balarām told me with an expression of deep-felt sadness. After a long pause, he went on: – But now, Ma'm, the earth is barren, scorched. Nothing crawls here but lizards and poisonous snakes. And do you know why? Deforestation. Every day they chop it down and haul it off, under the sun and under the stars, in secret, hundreds of great trunks. The oldest of them were here even before my grandfather. The manufacturing and exporting of wood are the country's largest industries. Before long, only shrubs remain, and shrubs cannot survive in the spring and summer sun. Before the monsoon arrives, all is dry here. The jungle is becoming a desert. The people here are poorer every day, and so they go on chopping it down. What animals, Ma'm, would you expect to find in a place like this?

In 1933, the population of Nepal numbered no more than five and a half million inhabitants, in comparison to the nineteen million counted in 1994. The country was traversable by train. In Kathmandu was the occasional car, but there were no roads; Formichi speaks of a line of transport for merchandise, luggage and other materials from Bhimphedi – a city that lies some 62 miles to the south of Kathmadu, in the region of Narayani. There, in 2011, no more than 6,000 inhabitants could be counted, many of whom had come from the surrounding mountains, though up until the 1950s the population had grown to more than 50,000; it stood as the region's capital, and an important hub along the trade route connecting India and Kathmandu. In the following years, the construction of other trade routes impoverished the city. Despite its great size, no hotels were built in Bhimphedi, for no foreigners ever visited; Formichi, Tucci, and Ghersi, therefore, took up lodgings in the only existent bungalow, a branch of the royal house itself, used by the Maharaja to host the occasional visitor.

The three principal cities of Nepal were Kathmandu – a corruption of the name Kāṣṭhamandapa, meaning «temple of wood», many of which fill the city center – which in 1933 numbered some 90,000 inhabitants, as opposed to the 1,744,240 and counting there as of 2012; Patan, an abbreviation of Lalitapaṭṭana; and Bhaṭgaon, or Bhaṭṭagrāma, which today goes by the name Bhaktapur. Patan and Bhaktapur are neighboring cities to the capital, and each held a population of around 30,000; Patan boasts somewhere around 226,720 inhabitants and Bhaktapur 81,748. All together, the district of Kathmandu now holds a population of more than two million, and is in a state of constant and rapid expansion. Faced with a devastated economy, men and women flock to the district from the mountains and fields in search of a better life – water, electricity, schools, hospitals – often constrained to take up residence in a shack or a tent in the slums, where filth and misery reign.

Formichi, Tucci, and Ghersi made careful visit of the temples in all three cities and the surrounding areas, including the Harasiddhi Temple, dedicated to Kālī, located a few miles south of Kathmandu, on the road to the Maharaja's summer residence. There, according to Formichi, «in temples not far from us, human beings, and predominately babies» were immolated. Today, the goddess is content with animal sacrifices and dramatic dances, with the priests wearing masks that weigh sometimes as much as 22 pounds. In his lecture, Formichi observes that, though the city's population lives in scant two-story houses – one floor stacked on top of the other, laid out in rows with no more than a car's length between them, just as in India – the Nepalese, «unlike the Indians», give evidence of «cleanliness, health, and hardiness».[56] He notes also that each and every house, even the most humble, is decorated with fine windows, their wooden frames carved with the figures of monsters, demons, divinities, and religious symbols. The Nepalese soldiers he describes as magnificent – tall, robust, proud young men, unrivaled in their precision in firing weapons, and accustomed to even the most exhausting labor; no secret of the military art is unknown to them, for the Maharaja, both then and in the past, called upon officers of the British army to instruct their troops. Together, the soldiers formed the troops of the much-feared Gorkhas or Gurkhas – from the ancient name for Nepal, which was, in fact, Gorkha – who leant their services to the British Indian Army. Up until recent years, the Nepalese army reserved officer positions solely for Englishmen, and soldiers were required to learn the language, while the highest ranking officers, such as the Supreme General of the Army, were under the control of the Rana family. Today, the Nepalese can rise to any military rank, but pay is severely low and they are frequently sent to the most dangerous and impenetrable regions, up in the mountains and along the borders.

LETTER TO THE ROYAL PRECEPTOR

In Kathmandu, the Italians were welcomed by the Maharaja, while a band showered them with music from a park neighboring the Royal Palace. They participated as well in the reception ceremony held in honor of the former British resident in Nepal, Sir Frederick O'Connor. Formichi marveled at the sight of the thirty-two army generals circling the Maharaja in an ornate marble hall, the very finest tiger furs draped over the floor, as a symbol of earthly and spiritual grandeur. But what most impressed him were the helmets worn by the dignitaries, studded with precious stones, the lower end ringed with «marvelous emerald pendants. A general's helmet was worth millions of lire, and the Mahârâja's, many millions more».

They returned to the palace the following day and, after witnessing acrobatic games, fencing matches, and a «strange and amusing duel between two men made-up to look like roosters», they themselves joined in on a shootingcontest. To be a fine shot, Formichi notes, has always been held as the most prized virtue among the warrior caste, and in Indian tales the most beautiful princesses marry the best archer among them. At the time, the bow and arrow had been replaced by the air rifle. The Maharaja opened the ceremonies and struck the moving target – a cardboard buffalo. One after the other, the generals took their shots, striking now a tiger, now a rhinoceros, now a leopard, and now – a *ghazi*, an Afghan bandit! Of the three Italians, only Captain Ghersi accepted the challenge: on his turn, the target was a balloon floating from the head of a flying falcon. Formichi's heart, he confesses, was pounding in his chest, «though it was all merely for sport», as Ghersi drew back the string. The Captain fired. The balloon burst, sending the falcon to the floor. And in the true Fascist spirit, Formichi notes, «Even in games, Italy upheld its honor!»

At the time, the government of Nepal was in the hands of the Maharaja, Juddha Shamsher Rana, the Prime Minister from

1932 until 1945, endowed with full political and military power. The position was hereditary, and the *adhirāja*, or the true king, functioned merely as a religious representative, the incarnation of Viṣṇu. The Grand Council, which the Maharaja assembled to make his most important decisions, was made up of the king's relatives, generals, high dignitaries known as Kaji, Sirdar, Bhardar, and lastly, the Guruju, Hem Raj Sharma, who signed his name, however, with the Sanskrit title Rājaguru, «Royal Preceptor». On December 8, 1933, just before departing, Formichi wrote a brief letter to Hem Raj in Sanskrit, on letterhead from the Royal Academy of Italy.

Royal Preceptor,

My mind took great pleasure in the subject of the Mahābhārata, the text which Your Honor now teaches and which, over and again, at the first light of day, I studied [with You].

Nonetheless, with all of the work brought on by the approach of my departure, my mind was not properly concentrated; or perhaps, knowing my mind incapable of reflecting upon a subject of such profundity, I ask, Royal Preceptor, as Your Honor so promised, if you could send a written commentary to me in Italy. It would be of tremendous help.

Such is my communication.

With pleasant memories, Your Holiness, of our encounter – respectfully and with great esteem,

Yours,
Carlo Formichi

On January 15, 1934, after the trio's departure, a violent earthquake shook Bihar and the Kathmandu Valley, leaving 10,700 victims in its wake, 8,519 of which from Nepal, and destroying 207,740 buildings in the capital. Formichi wrote:

> A sense of humanity, the friendship which we so dutifully and willfully return to a country that loves Italy and truly admires its Duce, the ardent wish that its inestimable treasures of art have not been irreparably lost, all concurs to inform us that the newspapers haveexaggerated in their reports and that the fury of its devastating scourge has spared the rich, golden temples of Kathmandu, Patan, and Bhaṭgaon. With his wild dance, Çiva brought terror and destruction to the fertile and peaceful valley, over which he watches and rules from the peak of Kailâsa. May the merciful Vishṇu speed his graces to that strong and beautiful land, repayeach death with a thousand lives, and compensate for this mournful hour with the most lasting prosperity.
>
> Such is Italy's wish for its dear friend Nepal.[57]

Following their departure from Nepal, Formichi, Tucci, and Ghersi traveled to several cities in India: Lucknow, the capital of the northern state, Uttar Pradesh; Kanpur, whose name, prior to independence, had been anglicized to Cawnpore, and Agra, where they visited the mausoleum of Taj Mahal; and Delhi, the capital city of the like-named state. Cutting sharply to the southwest, they went on to visit the Ajanta Caves, considered a masterpiece of Buddhist art, and those of Ellora, both in the state of Maharashtra; they then traveled to Pune, to the east of Bombay, the capital city, which in 1995 readopted its ancient name, Mumbai. Formichi would describe Pune, or Poona, as the name had come to be anglicized, as «the Leipzig of India»; and Leipzig in fact, at the time, stood as the European center of Buddhist and Indological studies. To Pune, scholars would travel with the intent of stocking up on texts that could not be found in Europe – and to this day the city houses numerous bookstores and libraries, abounding with wonders, along with one of the most important Sanskrit grammar schools in the world.

Formichi, at last, set sail from Bombay aboard the *Conte Rosso*, making the trip back to Italy, to his great joy, in the company of the president of the Royal Academy of Italy, Marquis Guglielmo Marconi, on return from his triumphant tour of the United States, China, and Japan. Tucci and Ghersi, meanwhile, remained in India.

«Benito Mussolini's Message Bearer»

In 1937 Formichi was awarded with the class of Knight by the Order of Saints Maurice and Lazarus of the Ministry of National Education. In March 1939 IsMEO, in cooperation with Mussolini and the Ministry of Foreign Affairs, elected Formichi to hold a series of lectures in Tokyo for a period of two months, as a representative of the Royal Academy of Italy – an assignment in which Tucci had preceded him, in October,1936. The missions were designed to spread and increase the awareness and prestige of Italian culture abroad. That Formichi was Italian by race and a member of the National Fascist Party was made explicit in the agreement. In a letter to the President of the University of Rome, Formichi pointed out that, beyond travel and lodging expenses in Japan, he would be receiving no additional compensation. He therefore requested the means by which he could avoid being perceived as «an invalid, or worse, some loafer on leave as a mode of dodging hard work». He asked, as well, that his salary be maintained.

In his report submitted to King Victor Emmanuel III in year XVIII of the Fascist Era, recounting the previous year, the President of the Royal Academy of Italy spoke in the following terms of Formichi's mission in Japan and Tucci's in Tibet, which bore «new and precious fruit»:

> In the year XVII, the organization of scientific mis-
> sions either initiated or carried out on behalf of
> the Academy continued unimpeded: from Carlo
> Formichi's voyage to Japan, where our eminent
> comrade, by way of his brilliant personal activity,
> strengthened the bonds of cultural cooperation be-
> tween our two countries, to a recent expedition
> in Tibet by Giuseppe Tucci, who has carried back
> with him the new, precious fruits of his brave and
> ingenious explorations.[58]

In October 1941, year XX of the Fascist Era, Carlo Formichi was decorated as Commander by the Order of the Crown of Italy and Grand Officer of the Order of Saints Maurice and Lazarus. That same year, on October 29, he was placed in retirement on account of his age, with the sincere gratitude of the Undersecretary and Secretary of the Ministry of National Education. The Directorate-General of the Order of Universities proposed his election as Professor Emeritus – a title conferred upon him in a royal decree by Victor Emmanuel III, by the Grace of God, King of Italy, King of Albania, and Emperor of Ethiopia. The date was January 12, 1942. Formichi, nonetheless, remained poor, so much so that on December 10, 1943, Tucci wrote to Gentile requesting aid on his behalf. But he was too late: on December 13, 1943, year XXII of the Fascist Era, the university offered its official condolences for the death of Carlo Formichi, in Rome. In the meantime, Formichi had legalized his union with Luisa Aloisi, making her his wife.

Much of Formichi's scientific and literary output bears the stamp of the glorified culture of the regime, reflecting his role as the Duce's representative abroad; above all, however, Formichi was a scholar and an impassioned admirer of India. In his eyes, the link between regime and culture was clear: he was an Indologist faithful to the constituted order, whatever that may be. Social order, for Formichi – even a Fascist social order – was an indispensable element, an indication of composure, precision, loyalty, and sense of duty. He would come also to defend violence, with which Fascism had established itself, as a necessary element to end the state of chaos, disorder, and labor strikes into which Italy had plunged. During Tagore's first visit to Italy, in January 1925, when requested by the poet to speak on the political conditions in Italy, Formichi replied as such:

> One must first have suffered the anguish of anarchic danger, I added, to understand the gratitude which the Italian people owe to Fascism and the obligation we have to pardon it for acts of violence that were necessary to bridle the wild horse.[59]

According to Formichi, the Poet leant full attention to his words, nodding along in agreement.

The fact remains, as well, that European Indological culture, up even until the last generation of scholars, has long favored the political right, which allowed for the coexistence of a contempt for the colonial and an admiration for all that was elitist and purist in Indian culture. And for thousands of years, this culture – or to be more precise, India's dominant culture, Hindu, which represents over 80% of all religions on the subcontinent – has founded itself on the division of labor and the purity of its caste system, and is therefore hierarchically ordered on the basis of such supposed purity. «A place for everything and everything in its place», as the Fascist proverb dictated. And Formichi, even before the advent of Fascism, demonstrated himself as highly respectful of authority and established social position: teachers are to teach and keep out of politics, students are to study and respect their teachers.

In an unpublished letter to his friend and colleague, Uberto
Pestalozza, the first professor of History of Religions at the State
University of Milan, written on February 12, 1910 – a full nine
years before the rise of the Fasci italiani di combattimento (Italian
Fasci of Combat) – he claimed to have voted against the transfer of
Gaetano Salvemini from the University of Bari to the University
of Pisa, where Formichi was teaching at the time, objecting to his
abrasive methods and lack of respect for others' freedom. Moreover, rather than teach his students in class, he'd have wearied
them with politics:

> That was all the evidence I needed. Not only would
> I have refused the zealous apostle my vote, but I'd
> have waged war, incapable [...] as I am by nature of
> such lukewarm behavior or of taking the middle road.
> I am always one for extreme measures.

Formichi was a bourgeois who defined himself as apolitical
and an admirer of authority and the constituted order, just as
Tucci was – if, perhaps, for different motives: Formichi because
he believed it with all his heart, Tucci, at least to a certain extent,
for convenience. As we shall see, Tucci's nationalism was an
extension of his belief that Italy, in the eyes of the world, must be
seen as a nation of the first order, at least in regard to Oriental
studies. But might not such a belief be founded on the fact that
he himself was the foremost representative in that very field of
study?

In the same letter to Pestalozza, Formichi continued his argument:

> Political passion played no role whatsoever in my de-
> termination. I belong to no party, no secret society,
> and the independence of my vote and judgment re-
> mains uncompromised. I am, indeed, a partisan of or-
> der and I hold the utmost respect for the constituted

authorities and hate wholeheartedly the claimants
and defendants of rights the people do not have; and
as my actions have revealed in regard to the transfer
of the Republican militant, Mancini, who speaks reg-
ularly at public rallies and is therefore more devoted
to politics than to science, I hold justice above all
other causes.[60]

Sharp-witted, Perspicacious, and *Greedy*

To learn more of Tucci, Formichi, and of the relationship between
them, on November 28, 1998, I met with Professor Pio Filippani-
Ronconi, who passed away in 2010. I'd spoken to him already the
day before, when he'd been the first and most brilliant lecturer
at a conference held in Milan, entitled *1898-1998: Julius Evola: Un
pensiero di fine milennio [1898-1998: Julius Evola: A Thought at the Close
of the Millennium].*[61] Evola had been a friend of Filippani's, and had
kept in close contact with Tucci as well. As it would appear, in
fact, the two first met in the 1920s, when Tucci was frequenting
the Rome branch of the Italian Theosophical Society, the Indepen-
dent Theosophical League, which drew its principles from Rudolf
Steiner – and which, as an anthroposophical school, «provided
Ur group with the most direction and the most collaborators».[62]
In 1939, however, the group was disbanded by the Fascist regime
for having refused to accept its doctrine and adhere to the racial
laws then in effect. Nevertheless, the group continued to meet in
secret and would resurface in the immediate postwar period.

At the conference of November 27, Filippani wears a blue
jacket and a black Fascist beret, which gives off the faint odor of
naphthalene. Afterward, we speak at length of his experience
with the Ur Group, the esoteric group of intellectuals in which
Evola took part, and of their artistic and political activities. In
truth, the Ur-Krur group, though well-renowned, was short-lived,

lasting from 1927 to 1929, when Filippani was still just a child. His intention, in all likelihood, was to indicate that he had followed in the "Tradition" spread by the group. Filippani was, in 1998 – together with the Tibetologist, Luciano Petech – the oldest living student of Tucci's and had collaborated in the early stages ofIsMEO, despite his coy attempts to conceal his age: when I met with him in Milan and in the years afterward he claimed to be just over sixty. I'd crossed paths with him several times in Rome and once in Assisi as well, and as soon as I mentioned the name Tucci he agreed enthusiastically to speak with me. Not that Filippani has ever been one to hold his tongue. Any chance to speak of himself is an opportune occasion, even in the midst of his extraordinarily busy schedule as a professor at the University of Naples "L'Orientale", taking the train in two or three times a week to teach his courses. And of such discipline he boasted repeatedly – not once had he missed a lecture, not like those «vermin», as he referred to Tucci and his followers, who «forget to hold lectures for which, I'll mind you, they're being paid».

To hear him speak is always a great pleasure. Filippani has an encyclopedic mind and a knack for quick characterizations – in just a few, carefully-chosen words he can capture a fact, an environment, a situation, a person, a historical period, a philosophical concept, a political event, or a study on alchemy. Words, as he uses them, are not a means of describing, but like quick flashes of light that suddenly strike an argument or a discipline, even the most intricate and obscure, and lay it out in plain sight. During one of our meetings, in Rome, he showed me his war medals, well kept in a velvet lined case: two for the injuries he'd suffered, and two Iron Crosses, 1st Class and 2nd Class, for his two years of service in the Nazi SS, which he spoke of with a certain haughtiness. When I asked him if he'd ever been a Nazi, his natural response was that no, never – he'd respected the loyalty and the faithfulness of the epoch and of the «group», as he called it, as well as the ideal of *aristos*, to strive to be the best, the wisest, the most courageous, the most just. Above all, he considered the Italians' repudiation of the alliance between Mussolini and Hitler to be an act of betrayal. Strangely enough, Filippani was an Orthodox Christian, and had become so, together with his family, when the Roman Rota began «issuing marriage annulments left and right for the most bizarre reasons». Orthodox practice, after all, is so rich, so beautiful, so over-the-top! Perfect for Filippani, who came off like the reincarnation of an 1800s Tsarist Baron, once devoted to Gnostic rituals, who'd been slain in battle.

Filippani lived with his wife in a beautiful, slightly decaying home, done in the Fascist architectural style of the EUR district in Rome, on a street whose name matched his profession, in an apartment with an enormous living room, its walls blackened with age and decked with objects and souvenirs: a photograph of Filippani shaking hands with the former Shah of Iran, Reza Pahlavi; another of him as a young Nazi; him with the Pope; him together with ambassadors in various Asian countries; a *katana,* there to protect him, hanging above the dresser – his favorite sword, the kind which a samurai will defend with his life; medals, diaries, strange and precious objects scattered all about. His bedroom library was vast, and his bookshelves, which surrounded the room from floor to ceiling, were crammed with books, photographs, and loose papers. Everything about him spoke of a once magnificent past now in decline, of noble origins, of values fought for to the death, and at the same time, a certain nonchalance, an ease: though even in Milan he was extremely attentive, informed of all the happenings at universities, as up-to-date on political events as the finest journalist, and as biting as ever in his judgments. Even the most maddening truths he can utter with detachment and irony.

In 2000, a controversy broke out over Filippani and his political past, just after he'd begun writing for the national newspaper, the *Corriere della Sera [The Evening Courier]*, spurred by his involvement with the Nazi party, which not only had he not concealed, but rather had flouted. While in the ranks of the Waffen-SS, he boasted, he'd slit the throats of his enemies and false friends, and claimed to be better with a knife than with a fork. Odin and Hermes, he affirmed, had been his protectors – furnishing him with the power to destroy and the ability to avoid enemy fire – as well as, and above all, Śakti, power in the form a goddess: he took spiritual refuge in her when paralyzed by the blood of his slain enemies, he looked to her for courage and as an ideal worth fighting for, and when he felt his own energy waning, he relied on her for strength. In the name of this archetypal feminine figure, he worshipped woman and the ideal of femininity, the creative force, even when Śakti was transformed into the terrifying Kālī, the bloodthirsty divinity: an aesthetic of *eros* and *thanatos*.

And he too, like my father, was a fascist of a certain type – those faithful to the values set forth by Fascism as it was originally conceived, not that of the Blackshirts, but the aristocratic and elitist Fascism of Gentile, Fascism as they themselves had experienced it: values which are, at heart, conservative but universal: love for one's native land and family, respect for the weak, defense of the defenseless. He too declared himself a non-Racist, non-Blackshirt Fascist. A man is inferior, as he expressed, when he behaves like a vermin, not because he's born of another color. These were the ideals to which the young men and women of 1921 prescribed – many of whom, after the 1930s, would come to feel betrayed by Fascism. But can one embrace political ideals in theory alone, if those very ideals lead to such distortions and perversions as those willed by the regime?

As Filippani repeatedly expressed to me, he wanted nothing to do with such «imbeciles» and «vermin» – that is, with the men and women who prostrate themselves before whomever or whatever they must in order to secure their patch of grass. Those, he described, who are born with a servile spirit, who bow to the powerful and snicker at men beneath them; not servants, but the men and women who betray themselves. Those who, for material gain, allow themselves to be used by those in power. Men and women who distort and manipulate reality, who trample others to raise themselves up.The vermin – as he said again and again – they are the ones responsible for evil, the ones who flee the light.

In describing his own achievements, he was fond of saying he'd made it to heaven «in spite of the saints» – of having obtained a professorship in Chinese Language and Literature in Naples, which Tucci had once held, as well as Ottoman Turkish Language and Literature and, later, Sanskrit Language and Literature, despite being disliked and envied by his peers, in particular by the all-powerful Tucci, and therefore "by his acolytes and by all those in the highest spheres of politics». The so-called «vermin», that is. He'd worked initially as a reader and official translator for the Ente Italiano per le Audizioni Radiofoniche, or the EIAR – Italy's public broadcasting service during the Fascist period; and in the 1960s, as it would appear, he worked with the secret services in both Italy and Guatemala.

Filippani has been described by many as a *tombeur de femmes*, to a greater extent even than Tucci, who abounded with vigor: he himself has given accounts, and with great satisfaction, of having challenged colleagues and acquaintances to duel for the affection of one or another beautiful woman. Filippani loved to shock and scandalize, he built a myth around himself; but he was also a man of extraordinary culture and uncommon intelligence. During our talk on November 28, 1998, he would, after more than fifty years, give the following account with clear astonishment and displeasure:[63]

– Tucci, after an initial period of great sympathy, began to despise me for my superior ways with women. He was immensely jealous and competitive toward those more fortunate than him, and better scholars. I'm no great beauty myself, but I love women and in my eyes they're all queens, they all have that inherent feminine trace of the ineffable: he disrespected them.

– Formichi – he says, his tone more mellow now – was an extremely kind and even-tempered man. With his students, too, he was greatly generous, with his time and with his knowledge, helping them in their studies and in their lives. He was a just man, and never let himself be taken by any rash or sudden enthusiasm, or by that profound dislike of another inferior to himself, as Tucci often did. Peppino – the nickname by which he referred to Tucci, and with a certain disrespect – was completely untrustworthy, now charming and fascinating, now petty and cruel, sometimes even toward the same person, and with no apparent motive but for his own capricious and narcissistic nature. –

In Filippani's view, Tucci was a cold, calculating man, who at first glimpse judged whomever was before him to see if he might be of use or not. – That was the problem for all of us – he tells me – everyone had to be useful, everyone had to fit *in the perfect little box that he'd assigned you to.* And God forbid you didn't fit in the box! He would eliminate you, mercilessly, and leave you standing in a vacuum.

To assign roles to particular groups and persons, to set them in fixed boundaries, is a characteristic common of all totalitarian regimes: the *Balilla,* the Avant-gardists, the *Corporazioni,* the orders and professional guilds, the Woman's Leagues, the Rural Housewives branch of the Woman's League and so on and so forth. In Fascism, all, even the recreational club, was regulated and tabulated and stuffed in its little box, and acting outside of one's role was out of the question.

For dinner, though he knows I'm a vegetarian, Filippani orders a risotto with pork shank and downs it greedily, staring me directly in the eye: and yet, his humor, his memories, and his stories hold me in their sway until midnight. When I later ask if he wouldn't mind responding to a few more questions regarding Tucci he seems perturbed: all of his attention-seeking, his theatrical spirit, his almost infinite capacity to string together memories and stories, passing from the Shah – a friend of his from his days at the luxurious University of Tehran, where he taught and from which he received an honorary degree – to nostalgic accounts of famous intellectuals and long lost regrets for beautiful women he'd met in the mid-nineteenth century, all such showmanship retreats behind a wall of rigid hostility. And I can sense this time that he isn't merely acting, feigning in order to shock or scandalize.

– Yes, Formichi was a true gentleman. A good man, courteous with everyone he met and profoundly attentive to the fate not only of his own studies, but of his students, of mankind. – He smiles. – To study with him, to attend his lectures was always a pleasure. I was just a young man and there he was, famous and with such influence, and he always asked me if there was anything I needed, he was always kind to me and genuinely interested in my well-being.

– But what about Tucci, Professor? Do you remember anything else about him?

– To forget a man like him would be impossible. Though you'd be happy to, if you could. At first he was attached at Formichi's hip, he was his shadow, his doting servant. Always kind, so kind with him, almost too kind. Once he became a professor, on the few occasions when he showed up at the university, Tucci would pace up and down directing and giving orders, a trail of teachers, students, and secretaries at his heels, all hanging on his every word and terrified of his outbursts. Only now and then did he greet Formichi. Even as an old man, when he'd long ago stopped teaching, he would act as if the university was his personal property. His moods and judgments oscillated wildly. One minute he was overflowing with words and almost helpful, the next he was staring you down like he wanted your head. We didn't know how to act around him. He had everyone on a string, and so everyone feared him. He was filled with gripes and insults of every sort and we could do nothing but step aside and let it go. Take my word for it, there's no use talking about him. It's a waste of time.

What's important are the writings he left us, if anything good of him remains.

He stops speaking, makes a joke or two, then, without my asking, picks up where he left off, with evident discomfort.

– Mario Carelli was a student of his, an exceptional student. When Tucci was in Bengal, he mailed him his translation and an annotated manuscript of a commentary on the *Sekoddeśa*, a section of the *Kālacakratantra*, a Buddhist text that was later published by, wouldn't you know it, Tucci's favorite student.[64] Tucci never mailed back the manuscript, nor the work. In fact, he never responded at all. As soon as Tucci came back to Italy, Carelli asked for the manuscript: he was nice enough about it, but claimed he'd never received the texts. Carelli was the best student of all of us, a group which included myself. Luckily he had another copy of the manuscript, and in the forties he published a critical edition with the Baroda Oriental Institute.[65]

He fidgets, as if to stand, then settles again. And when he speaks this time it seems he's acting against his will, as if combating a desire to turn away from the unpleasant memories.

– When Tucci came back, I remember, he began to prey on Carelli's fiancé, a simple girl from a small town in Lazio. Maria X, let's call her, a fellow student of mine. Here he was, a notorious professor and she a country girl, not a deceptive bone in her body, absolutely honest. That a man of his stature was suddenly claiming his love for her, of course, she found flattering. And she didn't know he was married. Every once in a while I went to study in her room. I remember that tiny, dim little bedroom, with her little shoes all in a row, toes facing the wall. I still remember her little shoes and that small, tidy room.

– But why would he have done it? He was already a famous professor at the time and Carelli was just a student. And the girl – was it that she was particularly beautiful or intriguing in some way?

– No, she wasn't beautiful, but she had a certain freshness about her. She was graceful. Carelli, though, was too well-behaved to say anything, and he trusted his teacher. The only reason Tucci did it was because he was *greedy*. He couldn't bear having someone else around that was better than he was. He had to punish him, to humiliate him. Yes, Tucci was *greedy* – he says, using the English adjective.

– She was innocent, and he far too experienced. Giuseppe, yes, he was rather on the short side, with a pointed face, a high, wide forehead, and a sharp nose. And with that nose of his he wedged himself into other peoples' business. Yes, he was extremely sharp-witted and perspicacious, but he was *greedy*. And then, with some he could be extremely conceited and arrogant, with others, those with authority, almost embarrassingly humble. – With a touch of melancholy, he continues: – After that, Carelli quit studying with Tucci and went to Holland. He was sad and embittered. There, he went on to teach a few modern languages, among them, Dutch. Tucci was ajealous man, no one else was allowed to be great, and certainly not better than him. And Carelli, though he was young and naïve, he had more talent than Tucci did, he was more intelligent. Moreover, Tucci was a turncoat. Later he sparked a friendship with Andreotti that lasted for years. But was it really friendship? No, he was only doing what was most convenient for himself. He knew Andreotti had a soft spot for culture and Tucci was an avid opportunist. Then Carelli took his own life and his family started accusing me of having led him to suicide with my powers – Filippani refers often to his mystic powers, or more precisely, his gnostic magic. – It's a tragic story no matter how you look at it, but the truth is he killed himself out of bitterness, because he felt betrayed by his teacher, and by his fiancé. –

I don't know if Carelli took his own life, but I remind him that other renowned professors, some of them Tucci's students, were friends with Andreotti. I see nothing particularly strange in court-ing his friendship, or for that matter, his protection, especially for an ambitious professor between the fifties and eighties.

Toward the end, I ask him of P2 (Propaganda Due) and of Tucci's, or any of his students', ties to the famous Masonic lodge. He hesitates, as if he can't push beyond the personal, the unpleasant memories, his relationship with his former teacher. Or perhaps, more simply, he avoids the question, seeing that I was transcribing the conversation word for word.

– Tucci did only that which was most beneficial to himself. I still have some of Carelli's letters. I know the whole story. I knew his disappointment. I knew his struggle with the thought that a man whom he'd considered to be great, a truly special man, had betrayed and scarred him. Tucci couldn't bear the idea of his image being marred by someone better than him.

He pauses for a long while with a saddened expression, and then, in an instant, the witty play-actor, the dramatist bent on enchanting and entertaining retreats, and again the old sage surfaces, filled with good will and good sense, as he so often was. Not only are Filippani's judgments of others always cutting, but they're exact.

– Tucci hated me. He couldn't believe how quickly I was able to pick up the Tibetan of the *Guhyasamājatantra*, which we read together and on which I would later publish...[66] But do you want to know how he taught me Tibetan? He placed the book in front of us, opened it up, read a passage himself and then said: now you read. I had fifteen days to learn how to translate it! I did it, laboring night and day with my head in a book, but immediately afterward he turned against me, for no good reason: he was jealous. He was constantly sending me off in a hurry to grab this or that manuscript or xylograph in the IsMEO archives, which he was always moving around from place to place. I marked up the "Livorno paper", you know, the paper that Tucci had the librarians wrap the books in, to protect them, to make them easily recognizable. I shouldn't have done it. I too have committed my share of sins. But most of those books he robbed. Yes, he robbed them, because he was *greedy*, filled with avidity for everything around him. He wanted all of it, even that which didn't belong to him. He didn't just want to be the best, he wanted to be the only one at all. Only he existed, no one else.

Such is the portrait Fillipani-Ronconi left me with of Tucci. Five years later, Fosco Maraini would paint me a nearly identical image, though his in a tone of warmth and good nature, veiled ever slightly with bitterness.

Mario Carelli was "rewarded" by Tucci for his discretion and became secretary and librarian of IsMEO. In 1935, he published several brief articles on India and Tibet, first in the *Bulletin of the Italian Institute for the Middle and Far East* (B.I.M.E.O), and later in *Asiatica*, both founded by Tucci. In 1937 he coedited a catalogue on the ethnographic museum Pigorini (Pigorini National Museum of Prehistory and Ethnography), in Rome, and published the article, «Esplorazioni tibetane» («Tibetan Explorations») in *Asiatica*, a detailed presentation of *Santi e briganti nel Tibet ignoto* (*Saints and Brigands in Unknown Tibet*), Tucci's account of his 1935 expedition in Ladakh and western Tibet with Eugenio Ghersi.[67]

In 1938 Carelli was sent to Bombay, where the consulate had initiated a series of Italian courses for Indian students, aiming to spread the good word of Fascism.[68] He was given the task of managing relations with Italy and supervising all activity. In 1939 he organized at the Casa d'Italia (House of Italy), where he lived, a successful welcoming party with music, dance and an art exhibition for Tucci's visit. According to Carelli, Tucci arrived in Bombay on January 16 and stayed there for two months; in April he would go back to Rome to organize the expedition in Tibet.

Had Filippani mixed up Holland and India? Or had his stint in Holland merely preceded or followed his trip to India? What we know for certain was that Carelli seemed to be "at the service" of and rather close with Tucci, welcoming him in his home as well as with Gentile, and was active in the regime's propaganda efforts:

he published articles, in fact, on the Fascist municipal building, *Casa dei Fasci,* and on the *Corporazioni.* Had he perhaps been sent on his mission in Bombay, far from academic life in Rome, because Tucci found his presence undesirable? Carelli, without doubt, in 1940 was eager to go back to Rome to participate in the national competition for a chair in Sanskrit held in 1942 by Formichi, as he headed into retirement, though the hiring committee, or «constellation», was not favorable to him. By the constellation, of course, he meant Tucci. Formichi, on the other hand, was «quite favorable».[69] He did not get the position.

We find Carelli's name listed as the translator of *To Lhasa and Beyond*, a translation of Tucci's *A Lhasa e oltre* published by the State Polygraphic Institute – his journal, that is, of the 1948 expedition with an appendix by Regolo Moise on medicine and hygiene in Tibet.[70] In terms of their student-teacher relationship – as is typical in the field of Oriental studies throughout the world, and in particular with Italians and Asians – it is not surprising that Carelli would remain faithful to Tucci, even if he had indeed been hindered by him. Such behavior is considered an act of loyalty to the school.

As portrayed to me by Filippani, Tucci was a detestable man. And yet, other students of his admire him and speak of him with great respect. I'm beginning, I think, to get an idea of this man's character: he was both of these things, both hateful and admirable, petty and generous, humble and arrogant. Of all his sins, mediocrity was not one.

INDEX OF EPIGRAPHS

This list includes the bibliographic references of the epigraphs written at the beginning of each chapter. You can find the complete bibliographic information in the bibliography, in volume 9.

CHRONOLOGY OF GIUSEPPE TUCCI

June 5, 1894 Born in Macerata (Marche, Italy).

1912 Obtains high shool diploma at the "Liceo Classico" in Macerata.

1913 Registers at the Royal University of Rome, Faculty of Letters and Philosophy.

1916–1918 Serves as lieutenant in the First World War.

1919 Graduates in Letters.

1919–21 Serves as temporary teacher in the secondary school, F. Stabili of Ascoli Piceno (Marche, Italy).

1920 Marries Rosa De Benedetto.

1921 Appointed administrative secretary at the Library of the Chamber of Deputies.

1923 His son, Ananda Maria, is born.

January 1925–October 1926 Appointed Temporary Professor of Religions and Philosophies of India and the Far East at the Royal University of Rome (known today as La Sapienza University of Rome)

November 1925 Travels to Śāntiniketan as Visiting Professor of Italian Language, Literature, and Art.

1926 Leaves Śāntiniketan.

1926–1931 Lives in India; begins his travels in Nepal and the Himalayan region.

1927 Marriage with Rosa De Benedetto annulled; marries in India Giulia Nuvoloni.

1927 Relieved of his duties and assigned indefinitely to the Ministry of Foreign Affairs, General Direction of Italian Schools Abroad.

1929 Appointed Academician at the Royal Academy of Italy.

November 1930 Obtains a permanent professorship of Chinese at the Institute of Oriental Studies of Naples (known today as the University of Naples "L'Orientale").

January 1931 Returns to Italy.

July 1931 Third well-equipped expedition in Tibet; November: Second trip to Nepal.

1932 Appointed Full Professor of Religions and Philosophies of India and the Far East at the Royal University of Rome.

June 1933 Fourth expedition in Tibet.

October 1933 Third trip to Nepal.

1933 Founding of IsMEO: Giovanni Gentile serves as President, Giuseppe Volpi di Misurata as Vice-President, Tucci as Managing Vice-President.

1935 Fifth expedition in Tibet (possibile fourth trip to Nepal).

1936–37 Sent as a governmental representative on an official mission in Japan.

1937 Sixth expedition in Tibet.

1939 Seventh expedition in Tibet.

1943 IsMEO is placed under temporary receivership.

August 1, 1944 Tucci is relieved from service (purge).

January 8, 1946 Readmitted at university as Full Professor.

1947 IsMEO is reopened; Tucci serves as President.

1948 Eighth expedition in Tibet.

1952 First well-equipped expedition in Nepal.

1954 Second well-equipped expedition in Nepal.

1955 Survey of the Swat Valley (Pakistan).

1956 Archaeological excavations in the Swat Valley begin.

1957 The National Museum of Oriental Arts is founded.

1957 Archaeological excavations in Afghanistan begin.

1959 Tucci donates his library to IsMEO.

1959 Archaeological excavations in Iran begin.

1968 Tucci retires.

June 20, 1968 After divorcing Giulia Nuvoloni, Tucci marries Francesca Bonardi in the Catholic parish of San Roberto Bellarmino, Rome.

1970 Appointed Professor Emeritus.

1978 Appointed Honorary President of IsMEO.

April 5, 1984 Dies in San Polo dei Cavalieri (Rome).

Figure 29: Giuseppe Tucci, *Tra giungle e pagode*, front cover, 1953.

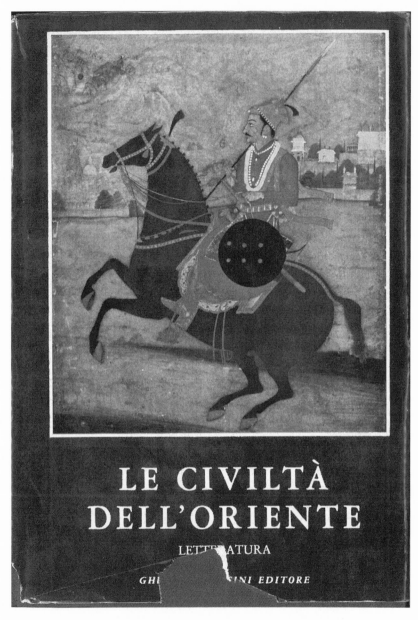

Figure 30: Giuseppe Tucci, *Le civiltà dell'Oriente*,
vol. 1, front cover, 1956-1962.

Alcune di queste biografie contengono informazioni preziose sui viaggi compiuti dai personaggi di cui si racconta e quindi rappresentano una fonte storica notevole; tale, per esempio, è la biografia di Urgyan pa, che nel XIII secolo si recò nella valle dello Swat, lasciando un suo itinerario di grande interesse. Il suo esempio venne poi imitato da sTag ts'an ras pa, fondatore del monastero di Hemis nel Ladakh, recatosi anche lui nello stesso paese considerato nel Tibet come sacro perché patria del taumaturgo Padmasaṃbhava.

La letteratura tibetana è indifferentemente in prosa od in versi perché, anche nel Tibet, secondo gli schemi indiani, le opere filosofiche vennero scritte molto spesso in versi, lasciando alla prosa il vero e proprio commento. Ma anche le opere interamente in prosa si aprono con

Foglio miniato di un manoscritto di un'opera medica tibetana.

una invocazione o una formula augurale (*maṅgalācaraṇa*) in versi e quasi sempre in versi è la conclusione nella quale si esprime il voto che, quale che sia merito l'autore si sia procacciato scrivendo, questo possa essere devoluto al beneficio spirituale delle creature tutte, e cose simili nobilissime.

Quanto alla parte poetica, i versi tibetani non hanno la grande varietà di quelli indiani sebbene i maggiori scrittori non fossero ignari della metrica indiana, ad essi accessibile attraverso il trattato di Ratnākaraśānti intitolato *Chandoratnākara:* essendo le due lingue diversissime, gli schemi della metrica indiana si mostrarono difficilmente applicabili alla poesia tibetana la quale non conosce la quantità delle sillabe. I versi sono regolarmente di sette, nove, undici, tredici, quindici, diciannove, ventuno sillabe: ma, specialmente nella letteratura popolare, sono usati soprattutto versi di un numero pari di sillabe.

Di vera poesia profana non c'è abbondanza nel Tibet, perché non raggiunsero mai altissime vette i canti del VI Dalai Lama (morto nel 1706) che si ritrovò contro sua voglia ad essere capo dello stato in uno dei momenti più difficili della storia tibetana, mentre a lui

Figure 31: Giuseppe Tucci, «Letteratura tibetana», in
Le civiltà dell'Oriente, vol. 1, 1956-1962, p. 787.

Tsoṅ k'a pa. (*Dipinto su rotolo, o t'aṅ ka*)

I primi abati Sa skya pa, dei quali aP'ags pa doveva ricevere da Qubilai (1215-1294) una investitura nominale sul Tibet, furono grandi poligrafi; ma non si trova, in questa loro opera vastissima, nulla che non risenta l'influsso dell'India: neppure le lettere che essi scrivono agli imperatori mongoli e che contengono istruzioni religiose ed epitomi della dottrina possono dirsi originali, perché è chiaro che componendole essi si ispiravano all'esempio delle famose epistole di Nāgārjuna o Candragomin. Questa attività letteraria ha tuttavia un grande valore perché dà forma e veste tibetane ad uno dei pensieri più complessi e

Figure 32: Giuseppe Tucci (ed.), «Letteratura tibetana», in
Le civiltà dell'Oriente, 1956-1962, p. 783.

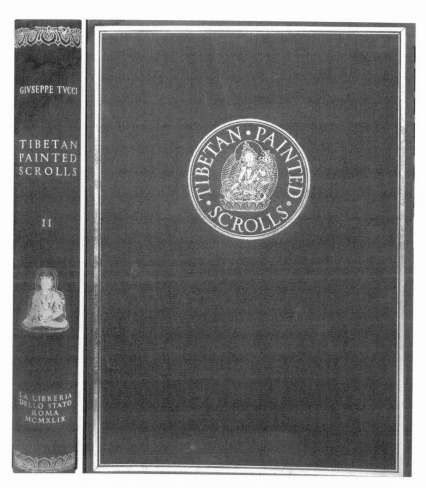

Figure 33: Giuseppe Tucci, *Tibetan Painted Scrolls*,
spine and front cover, vol. 2, 1949.

Giuseppe Tucci

Storia
della
filosofia indiana

Editori Laterza ~ Bari 1957

Figure 34: Giuseppe Tucci, *Storia della filosofia indiana*,
front cover, 1957.

L'ILLUSTRAZIONE ITALIANA

BRAMANTE EDITRICE   AUTUNNO 1974

Figure 35: *L'Illustrazione Italiana*, front cover, Autunno 1974.

L'«incompiuta»
divinità Khmer
di Ca'Pesaro

La grande «incompiuta» Khmer (Cambogia) del Museo Orientale di Venezia, scolpita non in basalto ma in arenaria sulla quale la volubilità della luce disegna improvvisi giochi d'ombre e di rilievi, parla con il silenzio dei suoi occhi non ancora aperti. Un torso di provenienza sconosciuta (da attribuirsi alla fine del X o al principio dell'XI secolo) riesce a risvegliare in noi, per suo magico incantamento e per una sua divina ambiguità, il mistero del suo inespresso messaggio: che è di ammonimento e di pietà. Avvenimenti ignoti non ne hanno permesso il compimento; i lobi delle orecchie non toccano le spalle, ma soprattutto manca l'apertura degli occhi, che durante la consacrazione delle statue, inseriva in esse la divina dimensione, quasi dissolvendo la caduca gravità della natura, aboliva lo sbarramento fra il mondo esteriore e l'interiore e apriva uno sguardo sottile e indifferente all'esterno perché non fossero turbati la serenità e il raccoglimento assorti dello spirito. L'immagine non rappresenta un Bodhisattva come è stato detto, ma una non identificabile divinità Hindu; le divinità indiane rivelano il proprio nome mediante gli atteggiamenti delle mani o gli strumenti che queste impugnano. E in questo caso il mutilamento rende vana ogni ipotesi.

La incompiutezza e la dolorosa amputazione non offendono tuttavia la bellezza di questo capolavoro dell'arte Khmer: anzi sembrano accrescere le vibrazioni di una vitalità interiore, come una corda colta nell'atto del suo tendersi: che già dal lieve procedere della gamba destra sembra pronta a prendere lo slancio dal vuoto di una invisibile crisalide che la racchiude per ascendere il cielo. Una creatura divina sorpresa nell'attimo del suo farsi e per capriccio delle vicende restata mozza perché lasciasse vagare la fantasia nei liberi spazi delle visioni che hanno l'incomparabile pregio di insinuare immortalità a ciò che è morto.

GIUSEPPE TUCCI

Figure 36: Giuseppe Tucci, «L'"incompiuta" divinità Khmer di Ca' Pesaro», in *L'Illustrazione Italiana*, Autunno 1974, p. 4.

Figure 37: Giuseppe Tucci, «L'"incompiuta" divinità Khmer di Ca' Pesaro»,
in *L'Illustrazione Italiana*, Autunno 1974, p. 5.

BIBLIOGRAPHY OF GIUSEPPE TUCCI

This bibliography includes all the works by Giuseppe Tucci in chronological order.

The titles followed by an asterisk were never listed in the available bibliographies (with the exception of Enrica Garzilli, *L'esploratore del Duce: le avventure di Giuseppe Tucci e la politica italiana in Oriente da Mussolini a Andreotti. Con il carteggio di Giulio Andreotti*, Asiatica Association, 3rd rev. ed. 2014, pp. 479–512).

I did not list the journalistic articles; some of them, which were published in *Il Popolo d'Italia* (1931), *La Stampa* (1935–36), *Yamato* (1941–43), *Epoca* (1951 and 1952), *Il Messaggero* (1970), and others, have been listed in the biography.[1] I did not list Tucci's letter published in *Il Tempo* as an answer to the article by Guglielmo Rospigliosi.[2]

I did not mention Tucci's commentaries, sometimes of high scientific quality, such as his commentary in the documentary film *Nelle steppe della Mongolia. Con commento dell'Eccellenza Giuseppe Tucci Accademico d'Italia* [*In the Mongolian Steppes. With a Comment of his Excellency Giuseppe Tucci, Academic of Italy*] (undated, but before 1937), of the Istituto Nazionale Luce, and the comments to the three films of the expeditions listed in the general bibliography.

I did not list all the translations in Russian, Chinese and Japanese of Tucci's books, expecially his travel accounts of Tibet and Nepal.

1911

«Inscriptiones in agro Maceratensi nuper repertae neque iam vulgatae», in *Mitteilungen des Deutschen Archäologischen Instituts,*

Römische Abteilung, XXVI, pp. 284–287.

1912

«Ricerche sul nome personale romano nel Piceno», in *Atti e Memorie della Regia Deputazione di Storia Patria per le Marche*, n.s., VII, 1911–12, pp. 301–369.

1913

«Totemismo ed esogamia», in *Rivista Italiana di Sociologia*, XVII, pp.617–630.

1914

«Osservazioni sul Fargard II del Vendidad», in *Giornale della Società Asiatica Italiana*, XXVI, 1913–14, pp. 243–251.
«Nota sul rito di seppellimento degli antichi persiani», in *Rivista di Antropologia*, XIX, pp. 315–319.
«Note sull'Asia preistorica», in *Rivista di Antropologia*, XIX, pp. 689–694.
«Il Tao e il Wu-wei di Lao-tzu», in *Coenobium*, VIII, fasc. 10, pp. 25–29.

1915

«Dispute filosofiche nella Cina antica», in *Rivista Italiana di Sociologia*, XIX, pp. 49–69.
«Un filosofo apologista cinese del sec. IX», in *Rivista di Filosofia*, VII, pp. 351–355.
Review of Pietro Tacchi Venturi, *Opere storiche del P. Matteo Ricci, S. I.; edite a cura del Comitato per le onoranze nazionali, con prolegomeni, note e tavole dal P. Pietro Tacchi Venturi*, in *Atti e Memorie della Regia Deputazione di Storia Patria per le Marche*, n.s., X, pp. 193–196.

1916

«I mistici dell'Oriente», in *Rivista Italiana di Sociologia*, XX, pp. 173–191.
Review of Ferdinando Belloni-Filippi, *I primi sistemi filosofici indiani*, in *Rivista Italiana di Sociologia*, XX, pp. 86–90.

1917

«Note cinesi, I (I: Come Sse-ma Ts'ien concepì la storia; II: Han-fei-tzu e le sue critiche al confucianesimo)», in *Giornale della Società Asiatica Italiana*, XXVIII, 1916–17, pp. 41–63.
Review of F. Alexander von Staël-Holstein, *Gaṇḍistotragāthā*, in *Giornale della Società Asiatica Italiana*, XXVIII, 1916–17, pp. 202–207.
«Aspirazioni di pace e necessità di guerra nell'Estremo Oriente», in *La Rassegna Nazionale*, XXXIX, fasc. 2, pp. 125–132.

1920

«Note cinesi, II (I: Le biografie 2–7 di Sse-ma Ts'ien; II: Kuan Chung)», in *Giornale della Società Asiatica Italiana*, XXIX, 1919–20, pp. 29–60.
«Dei rapporti tra la filosofia greca e l'orientale», in *Giornale Critico della Filosofia Italiana*, I, pp. 38–59.
«A proposito dei rapporti tra cristianesimo e buddhismo», in *Bilychnis*, XV, pp. 332–341.
Review of Berthold Laufer, *Dokumente der Indischen Kunst: das Citralakshaṇa nach dem Tibetischen Tanjur Herausgegeben und Übersetzt*, in *Rivista degli Studi Orientali*, VIII, 1919–20, pp. 851–856.

1921

Scritti di Mencio, Lanciano: Carabba, 1921.
«L'influsso del buddhismo sulla civiltà dell'Estremo Oriente», in *Bilychnis*, XVII, pp. 144–155.

Review of Hermann Oldenberg, *Vorwissenschaftliche wissenschaft. Die weltanschauung der Brāhmana-texte*, in *Giornale Critico della Filosofia Italiana*, II, fasc. 2, pp. 123–126.
News of books in *Bilychnis*, XVII, pp. 360–361, 425.

1922

Storia della filosofia cinese antica, Bologna: Zanichelli, 1922.
Giuseppe Tucci (ed.), *La Karpūramañjarī. Dramma pracrito volto in italiano*, Città di Castello: Il solco Casa editrice, 1922.
«Confucio e Lao-tse», in *Nuova Rivista Storica*, VI, pp. 262–276.
«Note ed appunti sul Divyāvadāna», in *Atti del Regio Istituto Veneto di Scienze, Lettere ed Arti*, LXXXI, 2, pp. 449–473 (repr. in *Opera Minora*, pp. 27–48).
«Lhasa e il lamaismo», in *La Terra e la Vita*, I, pp. 359–364.
«Lo Çataçastra, tradotto dal sanscrito e commentato. I», in *Alle Fonti delle Religioni*, I, fasc. 3–4, pp. 46–66.
«Śrī Vijaya Dharma Suri», in *Alle Fonti delle Religioni*, I, fasc. 3–4, pp. 78–79.
Giuseppe Tucci and Cesare Mariotti, *Iscrizioni medievali ascolane*, Ascoli Piceno: s.n., 1922.
Review of Louis Finot (ed.), *La marche à la lumière = Bodhicaryā-vatāra: poème sanscrit de Çantideva / traduit avec introduction par Louis Finot; bois dessinés et gravés par H. Tirman*, in *Alle Fonti delle Religioni*, I, fasc. 2, pp. 45–54.
News of books in *Bilychnis*, XIX, pp. 44–52 e XX, pp. 312–318.

1923

«Note sulle fonti di Kālidāsa», in *Rivista degli Studi Orientali*, IX (1921–23), pp. 1–26 (repr. in *Opera Minora*, pp. 1–26).
«La redazione poetica del Kāraṇḍavyūha», in *Atti della Regia Accademia delle Scienze di Torino*, LVIII, 1922–23, pp. 605–630.
«Lo Çataçastra, tradotto dal sanscrito e commentato. II», in *Alle Fonti delle Religioni*, II, fasc.1, pp. 32–43.

«Saptaśatikāprajñāpāramitā», in *Rendiconti della Reale Accademia dei Lincei, Memorie*, s. V, XVII, pp. 116–139.

«Studio comparativo tra le tre versioni cinesi e il testo sanscrito del I e II capitolo del Laṅkāvatāra», in *Rendiconti della Reale Accademia dei Lincei, Memorie*, serie V, XVII, pp. 170–200.

«Di una leggendaria biografia cinese di Nāgārjuna», in *Bilychnis*, XXII, pp. 213–217.

«Linee di una storia del materialismo indiano. I», in *Rendiconti della Reale Accademia dei Lincei, Memorie*, serie V, XVII, pp. 242–310 (repr. after editing chapt. III in *Opera Minora*, pp. 49–132).

Review of Heinrich Günther, *Buddha in der abendländischen Legende?*, in *Rivista degli Studi Orientali*, IX, 1921–23, pp. 610–614.

Review of three works by Johannes Hertel, in *Rivista degli Studi Orientali*, IX, 1921–23, pp. 614–617.

«Un capolavoro della letteratura bengalica in una recente traduzione inglese», in *Rivista di Cultura*, IV, 4–9 (recensione di Sarat Chandra Chatterji, *Śrī Kānta*, tradotto da Kshitis Chandra Sen e Theodosia Thompson).

News of books in *Alle Fonti delle Religioni*, II, fasc. 1, pp. 57–61, and fasc. 2, pp. 54–55; *Rivista di Cultura*, IV, pp. 216.217, pp. 425.

1924

Apologia del Taoismo, Roma: A. F. Formiggini editore, 1924.

Apologie du taoisme, par Giuseppe Tucci. Traduction française de Maxime Formont, Paris: Nilsson, 1926 (French ed. of *Apologia del Taoismo*).*

News of books in *Alle Fonti delle Religioni*, II, pp. 3–4, 56–57, 59–60, 74–80; *Rivista di Cultura*, V, pp. 99–101, 112; *Bilychnis*, XXIV, pp. 229–235.

1925

*Apologia del confucianesimo / Su Sung Ku; tradotta dall'originale mano-
scritto cinese da G. Tucci*, Roma: A. F. Formiggini editore, 1925.

*In cammino verso la luce; Çantideva; tradotto dal sanscrito in italiano
da G. Tucci*, Torino: G. B. Paravia, VII 1925 (Libretti di vita).

«Note sul Saundarananda kāvya di Açvaghosa», in *Rivista degli
Studi Orientali*, X, 1923–25, pp. 145–149 (repr. in *Opera Minora*,
pp. 157–161).

«Studi mahāyanici (I: La versione cinese del Catuhçataka di
Āryadeva confrontata con il testo sanscrito e la traduzione
tibetana; II: Una nuova edizione del Laṅkāvatāra)», in *Rivista
degli Studi Orientali*, X, 1923–25, pp. 521–590.

«Le cento strofe (Çataçastra), testo buddhistico mahāyana tradotto dal cinese, con introduzione e note», in *Studi e Materiali di
Storia delle Religioni*, I, pp. 66–128, pp. 161–189.

«La preghiera nella Cina», in *Bilychnis*, XXV, pp. 11–27.

«A Sketch of Indian Materialism», in *Acts of the First Indian Philosophical Congress*, Calcutta: 1925, pp. 34–44 [lecture given at
the first Indian Philosophical Congress].

«A Sketch of Indian Materialism», in Debiprasad Chattopadhyaya
(ed.) in collaboration with Mrinal Kanti Gangopadhyaya,
*Cārvāka / Lokāyata: An Anthology of Source Materials and Some
Recent Studies*, New Delhi: Indian Council of Philosophical
Research in association with Ṛddhi-India; Calcutta, 1990, pp.
384–393 [repr. of the previous title].*

«Un traité d'Āryadeva sur le nirvāṇa des hérétiques», in T'oung
Pao, XXIV, pp. 16–31.

«La scienza nella Cina antica», in Aldo Mieli, *Manuale di storia della
scienza. I*, Roma: Casa editrice Leonardo da Vinci [1925], pp.
546–554.

Review of Vasudev Shastri Abhyankar (ed.), *Sarva-darśana-saṁ-
graha of Sāyaṇa-Mādhava*, in *Studi e Materiali di Storia delle Religioni*, I, pp. 236–239.

News of books in *Rivista degli Studi Orientali*, X, 1923–25, pp. 156–159, 168, 711–725; *Bilychnis*, XXV, pp. 261–262; *Studi e Materiali di Storia delle Religioni*, I, pp. 144–145.

1926

Il Buddhismo, Foligno: Campitelli, 1926.

Giuseppe Tucci (ed.), *Saggezza cinese. Scelta di massime. Parabole - leggende. Da Confucio, Mencio, Mo-Ti, Lao-Tze, Yang-Chu, Lieh-Tze, Chuang-Tze, Wang-Ch'ung*, Torino: G. B. Paravia & C., 1926 (Libretti di vita).*

«The idealistic school in Buddhism», in Rabindranath Tagore (ed.), *The Meaning of Art*, Calcutta: The University, 1926 (Dacca University Bulletin; 12), pp. 1–16.

1927

«Tradizionalismo e innovatori nella letteratura dell'India», in *Bilychnis*, XXIX, pp. 162–169 (repr. with light editing as the second part of the chapter «Caratteri generali del pensiero indiano», in *Forme dello spirito asiatico*, pp. 54–60).

1928

«Un epicedio per la morte del Buddha», in *Giornale della Società Asiatica Italiana*, n. s., I, pp. 240–249.

«Is the Nyāyapraveśa by Diṅnāga?», in *Journal of the Royal Asiatic Society of Great Britain and Ireland*, 7–13 (repr. in *Opera Minora*, pp. 169–174).

«La religiosità dell'India», in *Nuova Antologia*, vol. 339, pp. 204–210.

«Notes on the Laṅkāvatāra », in *Indian Historical Quarterly*, IV, pp. 545–556.

«The Vādavidhi», in *Indian Historical Quarterly*, IV, pp. 630–636 (repr. in *Opera Minora*, pp. 163–167).

«On the fragments from Diṅnāga», in *Journal of the Royal Asiatic Society of Great Britain and Ireland*, pp. 377–390, 905–906.

«I conventi del Tibet», in *Bollettino della Reale Società Geografica Italiana*, Serie VI, Vol. V, LXIV, Fasc. 11–12, Nov.-Dic. 1928, pp. 583–588.

Bangla transl. of the Italian titile by Paolo Orano, *Mussolini da vicino*, Roma: Pinciana, 1928.*

Bangla transl. of the Italian Speeches of Benito Mussolini.*

News of books in *Rivista degli Studi Orientali*, XI, 1926–28, pp. 318–322; *Bilychnis*, XXXI, pp. 368–374.

1929

Pre-Diṅnāga Buddhist texts on logic from Chinese sources, Baroda Oriental Institute (Gaekwad's Oriental Series, 49).

«Linee di una storia del materialismo indiano. II», in *Rendiconti della Reale Accademia dei Lincei, Memorie*, s. VI, II, p. 667–713 (repr. without Appendix in *Opera Minora*, pp. 132–155).

«A visit to an 'astronomical' temple in India», in *Journal of the Royal Asiatic Society of Great Britain and Ireland*, pp. 247–258 (repr. in *Opera Minora*, pp. 175–184).

«Buddhist Logic before Diṅnāga (Asaṅga, Vasubandhu, Tarkaśāstras)», in *Journal of the Royal Asiatic Society of Great Britain and Ireland*, pp. 451–488, 870–871.

«Caitanya», in *Bilychnis*, XXXIII, pp. 97–125 (repr. with slight changes with the title «La via dell'amore divino» in *Forme dello spirito asiatico*, pp. 79–123).

«In un paese sconosciuto: il Nepal», in *Nuova Antologia*, vol. 345, pp. 347–358.

1930

On some aspects of the doctrines of Maitreya[nātha] and Asaṅga, Calcutta: Calcutta University (Calcutta University Readership Lectures).

The Nyāyamukha of Diṅnāga, being the Oldest Buddhist Text on Logic after Chinese and Tibetan Materials, Heidelberg: Otto Harrassowitz, 1930 (Materialien zur Kunde des Buddhismus, XV).

«Note indologiche (I: A proposito del Purāṇapañcalakṣaṇa. II: Tracce di culto lunare in India)», in *Rivista degli Studi Orientali*, XII, 1929-30, pp. 408-427 (repr. in *Opera Minora*, pp. 255-275).

«Bhāmaha and Diṅnāga», in *Indian Antiquary*, LIX, pp. 142-147 (repr. in *Opera Minora*, pp. 185-193).

«Animadversiones Indicae. I-VII», in *Journal and Proceedings of the Asiatic Society of Bengal*, XXVI, pp. 125-160 (repr. in *Opera Minora*, pp. 195-229).

«Del supposto architetto del Taj e di altri italiani alla corte dei Moghul», in *Nuova Antologia*, vol. 349, pp. 77-90.

«Italian Literature», in *Calcutta Review*, 35, 5, pp. 182-192.

«The Jātinirākṛti of Jitāri», in *Annals of the Bhandarkar Oriental Research Institute*, XI, pp. 54-58 (repr. in *Opera Minora*, pp. 249-254).

«A fragment from the Pratītya-samutpāda-vyākhyā of Vasubandhu», in *Journal of the Royal Asiatic Society of Great Britain and Ireland*, pp. 611-623 (repr. in *Opera Minora*, pp. 239-248).

«The spirit of Italian literature», in *Calcutta Review*, 37, 2-3, pp. 165-177.

1931

«Influssi stranieri sul pensiero cinese», in *Annali del Regio Istituto Orientale di Napoli*, IV, pp. 3-19.

«Notes on the Nyāyapravésa by Saṅkarasvāmin», in *Journal of the Royal Asiatic Society of Great Britain and Ireland*, pp. 381-413 (repr. in *Opera Minora*, pp. 277-304).

Teorie ed esperienze dei mistici tibetani, Città di Castello: s.n., s.d. (Il Pensiero Religioso, n. 4).

«Teorie ed esperienze dei mistici tibetani», in *Il Progresso Religioso*, XI, pp. 145-156 (reprint of the previous title with slight changes as first part of the chapter «Teorie ed esperienze degli asceti tibetani», in *Forme dello spirito asiatico*, pp. 170–182).

«Note ed appunti di viaggio nel Nepal», in *Bollettino della Reale Società Geografica Italiana*, Serie VI, Vol. VIII, N. 7, Luglio 1931 – IX, pp. 515–531 e Vol. VIII, N. 8–9, Ago.-Sett. 1931– IX, pp. 634–645.

«The sea and land travels of a Buddhist Sadhu in the sixteenth century», in *Indian Historical Quarterly*, VII, pp. 683–702 (repr. with slight changes in *Opera Minora*, pp. 305–319).

«La spedizione scientifica Tucci nell'India, nel Nepal e nel Tibet», in *L'Illustrazione Italiana*, LVIII, 40, pp. 506–510.

1932

Vidhushekhara Bhattacharya and Giuseppe Tucci (eds.), *Madhyāntavibhāgasūtrabhāṣyaṭīkā* of Sthiramati, London: Luzac and Co., 1932 (Calcutta Oriental Series, XXIV).

Prajñāparamitās: Commentaries on the Prajñāparamitā, a Buddhist Philosophical Work, I: Abhisamayālaṅkārāloka of Haribhadra, Baroda Oriental Institute, 1932 (Gaekwad's Oriental Series, 62).

Indo-Tibetica, I: mC'od-rten e ts'a-ts'a nel Tibet indiano ed occidentale, Roma: Reale Accademia d'Italia, 1932.

«Two hymns of the Catuḥstava of Nāgārjuna», in *Journal of the Royal Asiatic Society of Great Britain and Ireland*, pp. 309–325.

Review of Filippo De Filippi, *An account of Tibet; the Travels of Ippolito Desideri of Pistoia, S.J., 1712-1727*, in *Nuova Antologia*, vol. 363, pp. 413–415.

1933

Indo-Tibetica, II: Rin-c'en-bzan-po e la rinascita del buddhismo nel Tibet intorno al mille, Roma: Reale Accademia d'Italia, 1933.

«Carovanieri ed asceti sul Tetto del Mondo», in *L'Illustrazione italiana*, LV, 29, pp. 98–99.

«Oriente ed Occidente», in *Atti dei Convegni della Fondazione A. Volta*, II bis, pp. 424–430 (repr. in *Forme dello spirito asiatico*, pp. 3–11).

«L'ultima mia spedizione sull'Imalaya», in *Nuova Antologia*, vol. 365, pp. 245–258.

«Animadversiones Indicae, VIII», in Otto Stein and Wilhelm Gambert (eds.), *Festschrift Moriz Winternitz. 1863-23. dezember-1933. Hrsg. von Otto Stein und Wilhelm Gampert*, Leipzig: Otto Harrassowitz, 1933, pp. 243–246 (repr. in *Opera Minora*, pp. 230–233).

Entry «Lamaismo», in *Enciclopedia italiana*, XX, pp. 398–400.

Review of Filippo De Filippi, *An account of Tibet; the Travels of Ippolito Desideri of Pistoia, S.J., 1712-1727, in Journal of the Royal Asiatic Society of Great Britain and Ireland*, Part II, April, pp. 353–358.

«Di alcune opere recenti sui vernacoli indiani», in *Rivista degli Studi Orientali*, XIV, pp. 191–192.

News of books in *Rivista degli Studi Orientali*, XIV, pp. 214–215; *Nuova Antologia*, vol. 368, pp. 632–636.

1934

Giuseppe Tucci and Eugenio Ghersi, *Cronaca della missione scientifica Tucci nel Tibet occidentale (1933)*, Roma: Reale Accademia d'Italia, 1934.

Giuseppe Tucci and Eugenio Ghersi, *Secrets of Tibet*, London-Glasgow: Blackie and Son Ltd., 1935 (English ed. of *Cronaca della missione scientifica Tucci nel Tibet occidentale (1933)*.

Giuseppe Tucci and Eugenio Ghersi, Shrines of a thousand Buddhas, New York: Robert M. McBride, 1936 (American ed. of *Cronaca della missione scientifica Tucci nel Tibet occidentale (1933)*).

L'Oriente nella cultura contemporanea, Roma: Istituto Italiano per il Medio ed Estremo Oriente, 1934.

«Unknown monasteries of mysterious Tibet visited during a recent journey of exploration», in *Illustrated London News*, pp. 246–247.

«The Ratnāvalī of Nāgārjuna», part 1, in *Journal of the Royal Asiatic Society of Great Britain and Ireland*, pp. 307–325 (repr. in Opera Minora, pp. 321–336).

«La spedizione Tucci nel Tibet occidentale», in *L'Illustrazione Italiana*, LXI, 3–4, pp. 81–84, 118–121.

News of books in *Journal of the Royal Asiatic Society of Great Britain and Ireland*, pp. 212–214, 409–410.

1935

Indo-Tibetica, III: I templi del Tibet occidentale e il loro simbolismo artistico; Parte I: Spiti e Kunavar, Roma: Reale Accademia d'Italia, 1935.

«Nel Paese dei Lama (Costumi e riti del Tibet occidentale)», in *Le Vie d'Italia e del Mondo*, III, pp. 261–288.

«I segni di Roma nell'India e nell'Estremo Oriente», in *Nuova Antologia*, vol. 378, pp. 3–14 (repr. with the title «I rapporti di Roma con l'India e con l'Estremo Oriente», in *Forme dello spirito asiatico*, pp. 12–19).

«Indirizzi filosofici nell'India contemporanea», in *Bollettino dell'Istituto Italiano per il Medio ed Estremo Oriente*, I, pp. 183–190 (repr. with slight changes in *Forme dello spirito asiatico*, pp. 124–141).

«Some glosses upon the Guhyasamāja», in *Mélanges Chinois et Bouddhiques*, III, pp. 338–353 (rep. in *Opera Minora*, pp. 337–348).

«Splendori di un mondo che scompare: nel Tibet occidentale», in *Le Vie d'Italia e del Mondo*, III, pp. 911–937.

«On some bronze objects discovered in Western Tibet», in *Artibus Asiae*, V, pp. 105–116 (repr. in *Opera Minora*, pp. 349–356).

«La mia ultima spedizione tibetana», in *L'Illustrazione Italiana*, LXII, 50, pp.1124ff.*

«Cina e Giappone secondo un critico cinese», in *Bollettino dell'Istituto Italiano per il Medio ed Estremo Oriente*, I, pp. 1–5 (review of Shih Hu, *The Chinese Renaissance*; repr. in *Forme dello spirito asiatico*, pp. 225–232).

«A propos the legend of Nāropa», in *Journal of the Royal Asiatic Society of Great Britain and Ireland*, pp. 677-688 (review of Albert Grünwedel, *Die Legenden des Nāropa: des Hauptvertreters des Nekromanten-und Hexentums*).

Review of Th. Stcherbatsky, «Buddhist Logic», in *Bulletin of the School of Oriental Studies*, London Institution, VII, 4, pp. 969-971.*

1936

Indo-Tibetica, III: I templi del Tibet occidentale e il loro simbolismo artistico; Parte II: Tsaparang, Roma: Reale Accademia d'Italia, 1936.

Ramakrishna Paramahamsa, Roma: Istituto Italiano per il Medio ed Estremo Oriente, 1936.

«Ramakrishna Paramahamsa», in *East and West*, I (1950-51), pp. 65-72 (English ed. of the previous title).

«Hitherto unknown in Tibet: paintings recalling the art of Ajanta», in *Illustrated London News*, p. 81.

«The Ratnāvalī of Nāgārjuna», part 2, in *Journal of the Royal Asiatic Society of Great Britain and Ireland*, pp. 237-252, 423-435.

«Pionieri italiani in India», in *Asiatica*, II, pp. 3-11 (reworked version of «Del supposto architetto del Taj e di altri italiani alla corte dei Moghul», 1930, repr. in *Forme dello spirito asiatico*, pp. 37-49).

«Il Manasarovar, lago sacro del Tibet», in *Le Vie d'Italia e del Mondo*, IV, pp. 253-270.

«Un libro dell'antica saggezza cinese», in *Asiatica*, II, pp. 167-173 (ripr. in *Forme dello spirito asiatico*, pp. 216-224).

Entry «Roma: L'idea di Roma, Medio ed Estremo Oriente», in *Enciclopedia Italiana*, XXIX, pp. 927-928.

«Il Kailasa, montagna sacra del Tibet», in *Le Vie d'Italia e del Mondo*, IV, pp. 753-772.

«Nel paese delle donne dai molti mariti», in *La Lettura*, XXXVI, pp. 102-107.

Review of Heinrich August Jäschke, *A Tibetan-English dictionary, with special reference to the prevailing dialects. [To which is added an English-Tibetan vocabulary]*, in *Journal of the Royal Asiatic Society of Great Britain and Ireland*, pp. 509–510.

1937

Santi e briganti nel Tibet ignoto, Milano: Hoepli, 1937 (repr. under the title Tibet *ignoto. Una spedizione fra santi e briganti nella millenaria terra del Dalai Lama*, Roma: Newton Compton, 1978; 2nd repr. 1985).

Sadhus et brigands du Kailash: Mon voyage au Tibet occidental, Paris: R. Chabaud; Peuples du Monde, 1989 (Domaine tibétain) (French ed. of the previous titile).*

«Indian paintings in Western Tibetan temples», in *Artibus Asiae*, VII, pp. 191–204 (repr. in *Opera Minora*, pp. 357–362).

«Poesia giapponese», in *Asiatica*, III, pp. 328–336 (repr. in *Forme dello spirito asiatico*, pp. 260–270).

«Umanesimo indiano», in *Asiatica*, III, pp. 416–420 (partly repr. as first part of the chapter «Caratteri generali del pensiero indiano», in *Forme dello spirito asiatico*, pp. 50–54).

«Vecchie razze del Giappone: gli Ainu», in *Le Vie d'Italia e del Mondo*, V, pp. 835–847.

«I Giapponesi fanno sul serio anche a proposito di teatro», in *La Lettura*, XXXVII, pp. 655–659.

Entry «Tibet: Storia, Etnografia, Arte», in *Enciclopedia Italiana*, XXXIII, pp. 805–807, 807–810.

Review of Gustave-Charles Toussaint, *Le dict de Padma. Padma thang yig. Ms. de Lithang; traduit du thibétain par Gustave-Charles Toussaint*, in *Journal of the Royal Asiatic Society of Great Britain and Ireland*, pp. 514–516.

1938

«Cinema indiano», in *La Lettura*, XXXVIII, pp. 350–357 (repr. in *Forme dello spirito Asiatico*, pp. 159–169).

«Poeti e asceti nell'India medievale», in *Asiatica*, IV, pp. 89–96 (enlarged and repr. under the title «Il Dio senza attributi dei poeti medievali» in *Forme dello spirito asiatico*, pp. 66–78).

«Berretti rossi e berretti gialli», in *Asiatica*, IV, pp. 255–262.

«L'Italia e l'esplorazione del Tibet», in *Asiatica*, IV, pp. 435–446.

«La capitale del Tibet centrale: Ghianzé e il suo tempio terrificante», in *Le Vie del Mondo*, VI, pp. 741–758.

Entry «Letterature neo-indiane», in *Enciclopedia Italiana*, Appendice I, pp. 725–727 (repr. in Appendix in Ambrogio Ballini and Mauro Vallauri, *Lineamenti di una storia delle lingue e della letteratura antica e medievale dell'India*, Roma: Istituto della Enciclopedia Italiana, 1943, pp. 136–146).

«Lamaism», in *The Renascence of Religion; Being the Proceedings of the Third Meeting of the World Congress of Faiths; Preface by Sir Francis Younghusband*, London: Pub. for the World Congress of Faiths by A. Probsthain, 1938.*

Review of Walter Eugene Clark, Two Lamaistic pantheons, in *Journal of the Royal Asiatic Society of Great Britain and Ireland*, pp. 591–593.

1939

«Lo Zen e il carattere del popolo giapponese», in *Asiatica*, V, pp. 1–9.

«Ajaṇṭā ed Ellora», in *Asiatica*, V, pp. 213–221 (repr. in *India, I* [1952], pp. 3–11).

«Nuove scoperte archeologiche nell'Afghanistan e l'arte del Gandhara», in *Asiatica*, V, pp. 497–503.

«Recent Italian explorations in Tibet», in *The Young East, Italo-Japanese number*, pp. 33–41 (repr. in *New Asia*, I, fasc. 1, pp. 10–15).

1940

Forme dello spirito asiatico, Milano-Messina: Principato, 1940.

Travels of Tibetan Pilgrims in the Swat Valley, Calcutta: The Greater India Society, 1940 (rev. and repr. without the Appendix in *Opera Minora*, pp. 369–418).

La crisi spirituale dell'India moderna, Roma: Reale Accademia d'Italia, 1940 (Reale Accademia d'Italia, Conferenze, n. 5).

«Il Tibet e l'Italia», in *Il Libro italiano nel mondo*, n. 3, pp. 24–26.

«La mia spedizione nel Tibet», in *Asiatica*, VI, pp. 1–13.

«Antichi ambasciatori giapponesi patrizi romani», in *Asiatica*, VI, pp. 157–165 (repr. in *Società Amici del Giappone*, Roma-Tokyo, Single issue, pp. 23–29).

«Japanese ambassadors as Roman patricians», in *East and West*, II (1951–52), pp. 65–71 (English ed. of the previous title).

«Nel Tibet centrale: relazione preliminare della spedizione 1939», in *Bollettino della Società Geografica Italiana*, LXXVII, pp. 81–85 (repr. in *Opera Minora*, pp. 363–368).

«Itinerari indiani: Benares», in *Asiatica*, VI, pp. 277–283.

«Un principato indipendente nel cuore del Tibet: Sachia», in *Asiatica*, VI, pp. 353–360.

«Bardo Tödöl. Il libro dei morti nel Tibet», in *Sapere*, XI, pp. 189–191.

«Il Dalai Lama è sceso di nuovo sulla terra», in *La Lettura*, XL, pp. 443–448.

«L'arte di far rivivere i cadaveri secondo la tradizione tibetana», in *Sapere*, XII, pp. 105–107.

«Lo Zen», in *Sapere*, XII, pp. 333–334.

1941

Indo-Tibetica, IV: Gyantse e i suoi monasteri, 3 vols., Roma: Reale Accademia d'Italia, 1941.

«Una scuola di pittura tibetana a Nagasaki nel XVII secolo», in *Asiatica*, VII, pp. 9–13.

«Lo Yoga», in *Asiatica*, VII, pp. 171–178.
«Antiche rivalità nei deserti del Lop», in *Asiatica*, VII, pp. 355–363.
«Matteo Ricci», in *Annali della Regia Università di Macerata*, XV, pp. v-xvi.
«India», in *La Lettura*, XLI, pp. 19–24.
«I misteri dei templi tibetani», in *La Lettura*, XLI, pp. 442–447.

1942

Il Buscido, Firenze: Le Monnier, 1942.
«Il cinema indiano», in *Bianco e Nero*, gennaio, pp. 3–11.
«Il teatro indiano», in *Rivista Italiana del Teatro*, VI, n. 5, pp. 1–8.
«Le Marche e il Tibet», in *Atti e Memorie della Regia Deputazione di Storia Patria per le Marche*, serie V, vol. 5, pp. 91–95.
Italy and the Tibetan Studies, s.l., s.n.
«Alessandro Csoma de Körös», in *Universitas Francisco-Iosephina, Kolozsvár, Acta Philosophica*, I, pp. 3–20 (repr. in *Opera Minora*, pp. 419–427).
«La sensibilità artistica giapponese», in *La Lettura*, XLII, pp. 17–23.
«La teoria umorale della medicina indiana», in *Sapere*, XV, pp. 103–105.
«Le maschere del teatro classico giapponese», in *La Lettura*, XLII, pp. 457–463.

1943

Il Giappone, tradizione storica e tradizione artistica, Milano: Fratelli Bocca, 1943.
«Le missioni cattoliche e il Tibet», in Istituto Italiano per il Medio ed Estremo Oriente, *Le missioni cattoliche e la culture dell'Oriente*, conferenze "Massimo Piccinini", a cura di Celso Costantini, Pasquale d'Elia, Georg Schurhammer [e altri], Roma [Tipi della poliglotta "Cuore di Maria"] 1943, pp. 215–231.
«Umanesimo dell'India», in *Asiatica*, IX, pp. 5–10.

«Leopardi e l'India», in *Asiatica*, IX, pp. 161–170 (repr. in *Atti e Memorie della Regia Deputazione di Storia Patria per le Marche*, serie VII, vol. II, 1948).

«Pittori dell'India moderna», in *La Lettura*, XLIII, pp. 33–39.

«Gli dei di burro», in *La Lettura*, XLIII, pp. 397–402.

«Paolo Emilio Pavolini; commemorazione tenuta il 26 novembre 1942», in *Annuario della Reale Accademia d'Italia*, XV, 13 pp. (the paper was published in advance; the volume was never published).

1945

«L'estetica indiana e il concetto del bello», in *Poesia, quaderni internazionali*, I, pp. 227–231.

1946

Asia religiosa, Roma: Partenia, 1946.

«Teoria e pratica del Tummò», in *Scienze del Mistero*, I, *30 marzo*, pp. 47.

1947

«Tibetan book-covers», in K. Bharatha Iyer, *Art and thought, issued in honour of Dr. Ananda K. Coomaraswamy on the occasion of his 70th birthday*, London: Luzac, 1947, pp. 63–68.

«The validity of Tibetan historical tradition», in Instituut Kern (Rijksuniversiteit Leiden), *India antiqua: a volume of oriental studies presented by his friends and pupils to Jean Philippe Vogel, C.I.E., on the occasion of the fiftieth anniversary of his doctorate*, Leiden: E. J. Brill, 1947, pp. 309–322 (repr. in *Opera Minora*, pp. 453–466).

«Minor Sanskrit Texts on the Prajñāpāramitā: the Prajñāpāramitāpiṇḍārtha of Diṅnāga», in *Journal of the Royal Asiatic Society of Great Britain and Ireland*, pp. 53–75 (repr. in *Opera Minora*, pp. 429–452).

«I miei itinerari tibetani», in *Ulisse*, 1, fasc. 1, maggio 1947, pp. 63–68.

News of books in *Artibus Asiae*, X, pp. 248–249.

1948

«Preistoria tibetana», in *Rivista di Antropologia*, XXXVI, pp. 265–268 (repr. in *Opera Minora*, pp. 467–470).

News of books in *Rivista degli Studi Orientali*, XXIII, pp. 100–106.

1949

Il libro tibetano dei morti, Milano: Fratelli Bocca, 1949 (*Il libro tibetano dei morti*, 2nd rev. edition, Torino: Utet, 1972).

Tibetan Painted Scrolls, 2 vols. and portfolio, Roma: Libreria dello Stato, 1949); rep. with microfiche tables, Kyoto: Rinsen Book Co., 1981; rep., 1999; Italian translation with a CD-ROM including all the original scanned tables, *La pittura sacra del Tibet*, 2 vols., Rimini: Il Cerchio, 2015).

Teoria e pratica del Mandala: con particolare riguardo alla moderna psicologia del profondo, Roma: Astrolabio, 1949; 2nd ed., Roma: Ubaldini, 1969.

The theory and practice of the Mandala, with special reference to the modern psychology of the subconscious, London: Rider and Co., 1961 (English ed. of the previous title; repr. in 1969 and in 1973, New York: Weiser).

Théorie et pratique du Mandala, Paris: Fayard, 1974 (French ed. of the previous title).

Teoria e prática da mandala, Sâo Paulo: Editora Pensamento, 1974 (Portoguese ed. of the previous title).

Giuseppe Tucci and Namkhai Norbu (eds.), *Tibetan folk songs from Gyantse and Western Tibet. Collected and translated by Giuseppe*

Tucci, with two appendices by Namkhai Norbu, Ascona: Artibus Asiae, 1949 (Artibus Asiae Supplementum, VII).

Tibetan folk songs from Gyantse and Western Tibet, Ascona: Artibus Asiae, 1966 (Artibus Asiae Supplementum, XXII) (2nd rev. ed. of the previous title).

Italia e Oriente, Milano: Garzanti, 1949.

«Il Nepal», in *Sapere*, XXX, pp. 321–323.

«Medicina lamaista», in *L'Illustrazione del Medico*, 96, settembre, pp. 13–17.

«Un'anima antica», in Eugenio Giovannetti, *Una pittrice incantevole: Ofelia Duranti Maroi*, Bergamo: Istituto Italiano d'Arti Grafiche, pp. 5–11.*

«Tibetan notes (I: The Tibetan Tripiṭaka, II: The diffusion of the Yellow Church in Western Tibet and the kings of Guge)», in *Harvard Journal of Asiatic Studies*, vol. 12, no. 1–2, pp. 477–496 (repr. in *Opera Minora*, pp. 471–488).

1950

A Lhasa e oltre. Diario della spedizione nel Tibet, MCMXLVIII. Con un'appendice sulla medicina e l'igiene nel Tibet, Roma: Libreria dello Stato, 1950 (2nd ed., Roma: Libreria dello Stato, 1952; repr. with the title A*Lhasa e oltre. L'ultima esplorazione italiana alla scoperta dei segreti del Tibet*, Roma: Newton Compton, 1980).

To Lhasa and beyond; diary of the expedition to Tibet in the year MCMXLVIII. With an appendix on Tibetan medicine and hygiene, by R. Moise. [Translated by Mario Carelli], Roma: Istituto poligrafico dello Stato, 1956 (English ed. of the previous title).

The tombs of the Tibetan kings, Roma: Istituto Italiano per il Medio ed Estremo Oriente, 1950 (Serie Orientale Roma, I).

«Esplorazione del Tibet», in *I giorni della creazione*, [Torino] Edizioni Radio italiana [1950] (Quaderni della radio, 4), pp. 115–123.

«To Lhasa and beyond», in *Art and Letters*, XXIV, pp. 35–41.

«La città santa e le tombe dei re del Tibet», in *Le Vie del Mondo*, XII, pp. 157–166.

«Ambrogio Ballini», in *Rivista degli Studi Orientali*, XXV, pp. 156–160.

«In memoria di Schiff-Giorgini», in *Nuova Antologia*, vol. 450, pp. 79–83.

Introduction to Madanjeet Singh, *La scultura indiana nel bronzo e nella pietra. Con una introduzione di Giuseppe Tucci. 20 fotografie di Madanjeet, pubblicate sotto gli auspici del Ministero dell'istruzione del governo dell'India ed a cura dell'Istituto italiano per il Medio ed Estremo Oriente*, Roma, Milano: Amilcare Pizzi [ca. 1950] (La serie delle opere d'arte Indiana, vol. 1).*

Introduction to Madanjeet Singh, *Indian Sculpture in Bronze and Stone: 20 Madanjeet pictures. With an Introduction by Giuseppe Tucci*, Milan: Amilcare Pizzi Art Reproduction, [1951] (Indian works of art series; v. 1) (English ed. of the previous title).*

Introduction to Madanjeet Singh, *Die indische Skulptur in Bronze und Stein. Einführung von Giuseppe Tucci. 20 Aufnahmen der Sammlung Madanjeet, hrsg. unter dem Schutz des Unterrichtsminister der indischen Regierung und auf Veranlassung des Istituto italiano per il Medio ed Estremo Oriente in Rom*, Zürich: Fretz & Wasmuth [1953], (Die Reihe indischer Kunstwerke, 1.Bd) (German ed. of the previous title).*

Review of P. D'Elia, *Fonti Ricciane*, in *Rivista degli Studi Orientali*, XXV, pp. 156–160.

Review of Siegbert Hummel, *Geheimnisse tibetischer Malereien*, in *Artibus Asiae*, XIII, 4, pp. 312–313.*

Review of Siegbert Hummel, *Namenkarte von Tibet*, in *Artibus Asiae*, XIII, 4, p. 312.*

Preface to Alberto Giuganino and Jean-Pierre Dubosc (eds.), *Mostra di pitture cinesi delle dinastie Ming e Ch'ing: [Premessa di Giuseppe Tucci. La Pittura cinese, orientamenti, di Alberto Giuganino. I Pittori della mostra, di Jean-Pierre Dubosc]*, Roma: Istituto Italiano per il Medio ed Estremo Oriente, 1950.*

News of books in *Rivista degli Studi Orientali*, XXV, pp. 135–136.

1951

«Greetings to Pakistan and Hindustan», in *East and West*, I (1950–51), pp. 149–150.

«Il Tibet nel momento attuale», in *Rassegna Italiana di Politica e di Cultura*, XXVIII, pp. 99–108.

«Magia indiana», in *L'Illustrazione del Medico*, 104, gennaio, pp. 15–18.

«Dell'arte di risuscitare i morti», in *L'Economia Umana*, marzo-a-prile, pp. 23–27.

«L'arte di diventare immortali», in *Sapere*, XXXIII, pp. 59–61.

«Buddhist notes (I: A propos Avalokiteśvara; II: On the Tibetan cycle of arhats)», in *Mélanges Chinois et Bouddhiques*, IX, pp. 173–220 (repr. in *Opera Minora*, pp. 489–527).

«La rivolta nel Nepal», in *Le Vie del Mondo*, XIII, pp. 753–760.

News of books in *Rivista degli Studi Orientali*, XXVI, pp. 185–186.

1952

«Shri Aurobindo», in *East and West*, II (1951–52), pp. 1–2.

«Italy and New Asia», in *East and West*, II (1951–52), pp. 129–131.

«On Philosophical Synthesis», in *Philosophy East and West*, aprile, II, 1, p. 3.*

«Il Kashmir, oggi», in *Le Vie del Mondo*, XIV, pp. 537–552.

«The tombs of the Tibetan kings», in *Journal of the Royal Central Asian Society*, XXXIX, pp. 42–44.

«Il demoniaco in Oriente», in *Quaderni dell'Associazione Culturale Italiana*, 8, pp. 7–18.

Contribution of Giuseppe Tucci to *Wim Swaan photograph collection, 1951-1995*, [pictures from all over the world].

News of books in *East and West*, II (1951–52), pp. 31–36, 90–93, 151–155, 224–230.

1953

Tra giungle e pagode, Roma: La Libreria dello Stato, 1953 (repr. under the title *Le grandi civiltà imalaiane nella sacra terra del Buddha*, Roma: Newton Compton editori, 1979).

News of books in *East and West*, III (1952–53), pp. 36–41, 112–116; *Artibus Asiae*, XVI, p. 137.

1954

Marco Polo, Roma: Istituto Italiano per il Medio ed Estremo Oriente, 1954.

«Marco Polo», in *East and West*, V, (1954–55), pp. 5–14 (English ed. of the previous title).

«The demoniacal in the Far East», in *East and West*, IV (1953–54), pp. 3–11.

«My approach to Gandhi», in *East and West*, IV (1953–54), pp. 147–150.

«Earth in India and Tibet», in *Eranos Jahrbuch*, XXII, pp. 323–364; published as a monography, Zürich: Rhein-Verlag, 1954 (repr. in *Opera Minora*, pp. 533–567).

«Marco Polo», in *Italia che scrive*, XXVIII, n.10, pp. 107–112.

«Ratnākaraśānti on Āsraya-parāvṛtti», in Friedrich Weller; Johannes Schubert; Ulrich Schneider, *Asiatica. Festschrift Friedrich Weller: zum 65. Geburtstag gewidmet von seinen Freunden, Kollegen und Schülern. [Hrsg. von Johannes Schubert und Ulrich Schneider]*, Leipzig: Otto Harrassowitz, 1954, pp. 765–767 (repr. in *Opera Minora*, pp. 529–532).

«Alfonsa Ferrari», in *Rivista degli Studi Orientali*, XXIX, pp. 158–159.

«China-Religionsgeschichte», in Alexander von Randa (ed.), *Handbuch der Weltgeschichte*, Olten: O. Walter [1954–56], pp. 287–292.

«Tibet-Religionsgeschichte», in Alexander von Randa (ed.), *Handbuch der Weltgeschichte*, Olten: O. Walter [1954–56], pp. 663–672.

«An Interview with Prof. William MacKenzie, Para-normal and
Super-normal Phenomena in Biology», in *East and West*, V, 4,
pp. 314–317.

News of books in *East and West*, IV (1953–54), pp. 41–46, 117–122,
204–205, 295–299.

1955

«Fifty years of study of Oriental art», in *East and West*, V (1954–55),
pp. 73–85.

«Il popolo della giungla fumante», in *L'Illustrazione del Medico*, 131,
maggio, pp. 18–22.

*Fulvio Maroi: commemorazione tenuta all'Is.M.E.O. il giorno 10 giugno
1955* / *Giuseppe Tucci*, Roma: s.n., 1955 (Roma: Stamperia ro-
mana) (ed. by the Italian Institute for the Middle and Far
East).

«Incontro di religioni nel centro del Himalaya», in *Rivista Shell-
Italia*, V, agosto, pp. 12–16.

«Sur les traces d'une ancienne réligion: l'expédition Tucci 1954»,
in *Alpe, Neige, Roc: Revue alpine internationale*, IX, pp. 35–42.

Introduction to P'u Sung-ling, *I racconti fantastici di Liao*, Milano:
Mondadori, 1955, pp. 13–15.

Review of Cyrill von Korvin-Krasinski, *Die tibetische Medizinphiloso-
phie; der Mensch als Mikrokosmos*, in *Artibus Asiae*, XVIII, 1, p.
106. *

News of books in *East and West*, V (1954–55), pp. 140–142, 227–231.

1956

Minor Buddhist Texts, I, Roma: Istituto Italiano per il Medio ed
Estremo Oriente, 1956 (Serie Orientale Roma, IX, 1).

Preliminary report on two scientific expeditions in Nepal, Roma: Istituto per il Medio ed Estremo Oriente, 1956 (Serie Orientale
Roma, X, 1).

Vita nomade, Roma: Club Campeggiatori Romani, 1956.

«The sacred character of the kings of ancient Tibet», in *East and West*, VI (1955-56), pp. 197-205 (repr. in Opera Minora, pp. 569-583).

«Kodai Chibetto o no shinpiteki seikaku», in *Kodaigaku*, V (1957), pp. 245-259 (Japanese ed. of the previous title).

«La regalità sacra nell'antico Tibet», in *La Regalità sacra. Contributi al tema dell'VIII Congresso internazionale di storia delle religioni (Roma, Aprile 1955), pubblicati con concorso della Giunta etc. (= Studies on the history of religions: the sacral kingship)*, Leiden: E. J. Brill, 1959 (*Supplements to Numen*, vol. IV), pp. 189-203 (original text of the previous title).

«Chibetto no rekishi bunken», in *Tohogaku*, XII, pp. 100-114.

«The simbolism of the temples of bSam yas», in *East and West*, VI (1955-56), pp. 279-281 (repr. in *Opera Minora*, 585-588).

«Il tempio di bSam yas», in *Le Symbolisme cosmique des monuments religieux: actes de la conférence internationle qui a eu lieu sous les auspices de l'Is.M.E.O., à Rome, avril-mai 1955 / conférences par R. Bloch ... [et al.]*, Roma: Istituto Italiano per il Medio ed Estremo Oriente; New York, N.Y.: Sole distributors in the USA & Canada, Paragon Book Gallery, 1957 (Serie Orientale Roma, XIV), pp. 118-123 (original text of the previous title).

«I Taru del Nepal», in *Le Vie del Mondo*, XVIII, pp. 399-418.

Preface to Umberto Dorini and Tommaso Bertelè (eds.), *Il libro dei conti di Giacomo Badoer (Costantinopoli, 1436-1440)*, Roma: Istituto poligrafico dello Stato, Libreria dello Stato, 1956 (Il nuovo Ramusio: raccolta di viaggi, testi e documenti relativi ai rapporti fra l'Europa e l'Oriente; 3), pp. ix-xi.

Preface to Mario Bussagli, *Mostra d'arte iranica. Exhibition of Iranian art: Roma. Palazzo Brancaccio. Giugno–Agosto 1956. Catalogo. Catalogue [A cura di Mario Bussagli. Presentazione di Giuseppe Tucci]*, Milano: "Silvana" editoriale d'arte [1956].*

Preface to *Cina, I*, Roma: Istituto Italiano per il Medio ed Estremo Oriente, pp. 7-8.

Le civiltà dell'Oriente: storia, letteratura, religioni, filosofia, scienze e arte / Sotto la direzione di Giuseppe Tucci, 4 vols., Roma: G. Casini [1956–1962].*
News of books in *East and West*, VI (1955–56), pp. 54–58, 163–167, 256–261.

1957

Storia della filosofia indiana, Bari: Laterza, 1957 (2nd ed., 2 vols., Roma-Bari: Laterza, 1977; repr. 1981).
«Buddha Jayanti», in *East and West*, VII (1956–57), pp. 297–305.
«Buddha Jayanti», in René de Berval (ed.), *Présence du bouddhisme, sous la direction de René de Berval, I-II (1959)*, pp. 203–214 (French ed. of the previous title).
«The Fifth Dalai Lama as a Sanskrit scholar», in *Sino-Indian Studies*, V, pp. 235–240 (repr. in *Opera Minora*, pp. 589–594).
«Letteratura tibetana», in *Le Civiltà dell'Oriente: storia, letteratura, religioni, filosofia, scienze e arte / Sotto la direzione di Giuseppe Tucci*, 4 vols., Roma: G. Casini [1956–1962], pp. 779–790.
«Gli scavi nello Svat», in *L'Illustrazione del Medico*, 153, novembre, pp. 13–17.
News of books in *East and West*, VII (1956–57), pp. 99–102, 178–183, 271–273; *Artibus Asiae*, XX, p. 218.

1958

Minor Buddhist Texts, II, Roma: Istituto Italiano per il Medio ed Estremo Oriente, 1958 (Serie Orientale Roma, IX, 2).
Le grandi vie di comunicazione Europa-Asia, Torino: Edizioni Radio Italiana, 1958.
Collaborazione con l'Oriente, Roma: Istituto Italiano per il Medio ed Estremo Oriente, 1958.
«A propos East and West; considerations of an historian», in *East and West*, VIII (1957–58), pp. 343–349.

«On the path of Alexander the Great: Italian excavations in Swat, Northern Pakistan», in *Illustrated London*, 12 April, pp. 603–605.

«On a sculpture of Gandhara», in *East and West*, IX, pp. 227–230 (repr. in *Opera Minora*, pp. 595–598).

«Preliminary report on an archaeological survey in Swat», in *East and West*, IX, pp. 279–328.

«Impressioni sulla musica giapponese», in *Giappone*, II, pp. 5–8.

«Induismo», in *Le Civiltà dell'Oriente: storia, letteratura, religioni, filosofia, scienze, e arte / Sotto la direzione di Giuseppe Tucci*, vols. 4, Roma: G. Casini [1956–1962], pp. 563–632.

Preface to Giovanni Pugliese Carratelli (ed.), *Un editto bilingue greco-aramaico di Aśoka: la prima iscrizione greca scoperta in Afghanistan / testo, traduzione e note a cura di G. Pugliese Carratelli e di G. Levi della Vida, con prefazione di G. Tucci e introduzione di U. Scerrato*, Roma: Istituto italiano per il Medio ed Estremo Oriente, 1958, pp. v-vii.

Review of René de Nebesky-Wojkowitz, *Oracles and demons of Tibet*, in *Orientalistische Literaturzeitung*, LIII, pp. 270–272.

News of books in *East and West*, VIII (1957-58), pp. 104–110, 217–222, 321–330; IX, pp. 95, 102–104, 105–107, 110–111, 238–244, 246–248, 256–262, 270–272, 358, 377–378.

1959

«Le Marche e l'Oriente», in *Rivista d'Ancona*, II, pp. 2–5.

«Gerardo Rasetti, uomo ed umanista», in *Comitato nazionale promotore delle onoranze a G. Rasetti (a cura di), Gerardo Rasetti: l'uomo e l'opera*, Roma: F.lli Palombi, 1959, pp. 9–13.

«Animadversiones Indicae, [IX–X]», in Claus Vogel (ed.), *Jñana-muktāvalī; commemoration volume in honour of Johannes Nobel, on the occasion of his 70th birthday. Edited by Claus Vogel*, New Delhi: International Academy of Indian Culture (Sarasvati-vihara series, v. 38), pp. 221–227 (repr. in *Opera Minora*, pp. 233–238).

«Nello Swat sulle orme di Alessandro Magno e Buddha», in *Le Vie del Mondo*, XXI, pp. 481–492.

«A Hindu image in the Himalayas», in *Asia Major*, n.s., VII, pp. 170–175 (repr. in *Opera Minora*, pp. 599–604).

«A Tibetan classification of Buddhist images according to their style», in Artibus Asiae, XXII, pp. 179–187.

«Gli asceti itineranti», in *L'Illustrazione del Medico*, 164, febbraio, pp. 17–21.

Contribution to Rome — New York Art Foundation, *Omaggio a Rabindranath Tagore: souvenir catalogue*, [Roma: Istituto grafico tiberino, 1959].*

Preface to Sum-pa Mkhan-po Ye-śes-dpal-'byor, *Phags-yul Rgya-nag-chen-po, Bod, daṅ Sog-yul du dam pa'i chos byuṅ tshul dpag bsam ljon bzaṅ = Dpag-bsam-ljon-bzaṅ of Sum-pa-mkhan-po Ye-śes-dpal-hbyor : part III, containing a history of Buddhism in China and Mongolia, preceded by the reḥu-mig or chronological tables / edited by Lokesh Chandra; with a foreword by G. Tucci and a preface by L. Petech*, New Delhi, India: International Academy of Indian Culture, pp. ix-xii.

Orientalisti Marchigiani, conferenza tenuta ad Ancona il 4 marzo 1959, Ancona: Camera di Commercio, 1959.

News of books in *East and West*, X, pp. 111–112, 115–116, 122–123, 125, 136, 289–292, 306, 308.

1960

Nepal. Alla scoperta dei Malla, Bari: Leonardo da Vinci, 1960 (2nd ed., Bari: Leonardo da Vinci 1960 (repr. under the title *Nepal: alla scoperta del regno dei Malla*, Roma: Newton Compton, 1977).

The discovery of the Mallas, London: George Allen and Unwin, 1962 (English ed. of the previous title).

«A Tibetan history of Buddhism in China», in *Wissenschaftliche Zeitschrift der Karl Marx-Universität. Gesellschafts- und sprachwissenschaftliche Reihe. Sonderband, IX* (the abstract was published, after adding at the bottom the page number 230, in Eduard Erkes and Johannes Schubert (eds.), *Eduard Erkes in memoriam, 1891-1958*, [Leipzig]: [s.n.], [c. 1961]),

«Commemorazione di Tagore», in *Centenario di Tagore, 1861-1961*, Roma: Istituto Italiano per il Medio ed Estremo Oriente, 1962.*

Preface to Giorgio Gullini (ed.), *Attività archeologica italiana in Asia; mostra dei risultati delle missioni in Pakistan e in Afghanistan, 1958-1959. Torino, Galleria civica d'arte moderna, aprile 1960; Roma, Palazzo Brancaccio, 25 maggio-giugno 1960*, Torino: Centro scavi e ricerche archeologiche in Asia del'Is.M.E.O. e di Torino, 1960.*

News of books in *East and West*, XI, pp. 42, 50-51, 189-191, 201, 212-215, 277-278, 287-290, 294-297, 304-305.

1961

«La Sposa del Cielo», in *Storia Illustrata*, luglio, pp. 56-63.

«Recollection of Tagore», in *East and West*, XII, pp. 111-117.

«Recollections of Tagore», in *Sahitya Akademi, A centenary volume, Rabindranath Tagore. 1861-1891*, New Delhi: Sahitya Akademi, [1961], pp. 59-60.

«L'arte del Gandhara», in *L'Illustrazione del Medico*, 186, novembre, pp. 13-17.

Preface to dBaṅ p'yug rghal-po, *The Samye monastery. Tibetan text edited by Lokesh Chandra, with a foreword by Giuseppe Tucci*, New Delhi: International Academy of Indian Culture, 1961, pp. 9-11 (International Academy of Indian Culture).

Introduction to the second volume of Raghu Vira and Lokesh Chandra (eds.); Blo-bzaṅ-bstan-pa'i-ñi-ma, Paṇ-chen Bla-ma IV, Institute for Advanced Studies of World Religions, *A new Tibeto-mongol pantheon*, 20 vols., New Delhi: International Academy of Indian Culture, 1961-1972 (Sata-piṭaka series. Indo-Asian literatures, v. 21. Bhoṭa-piṭaka, v. 8).*

Giuseppe Tucci with the collaboration of Mario Bussagli and Hermann Goetz, *Cinquemila Anni di Arte dell'India. Catalogo della*

Mostra. Organizzata dall'Istituto Italiano per il Medio ed Estremo Oriente, Roma: Palazzo Venezia, 1961.*

News of books in *East and West*, XII, pp. 180–183, 190–191, 195–196, 207–209, 217, 219–221.

1962

««The Wives of Sroṅ-btsan-sgam-po», in *Oriens Extremus*, IX, pp. 121–126 (repr. in *Opera Minora*, pp. 605–611).

«Un paese senza laici», in *Il Milione*, VIII, pp. 205–208.

«Remarkable discoveries in Swat», in *Tourist World*, II, 12, pp. 5–7.

Preface to Bla-ma Btsan-po, dit aussi Smin-grol No- mon-han, and Turrell Verl Wylie (eds.), *The Geography of Tibet according to the Dzamgling — rgyas-bshad: [By the Lama called Bla-ma Btsan-po, also know as Smin-grol No-mon-han. Foreword by Giuseppe Tucci]. Text and English translation*, Roma, 1962 (Serie Orientale Roma, XXV).*

Preface to Edward Conze (ed.), *The Gilgit manuscript of the Aṣṭā-daśasāhasrikāprajñāpāramitā: chapters 55 to 70 corresponding to the 5th Abhisamaya / edited and translated by Edward Conze*, Roma: Istituto Italiano per il Medio ed Estremo Oriente, 1962 (Literary and historical documents from Pakistan, 1. Serie Orientale Roma , XXVI).*

«Arte del Tibet», in *Le civiltà dell'Oriente: storia, letteratura, religioni, filosofia, scienze e arte / Sotto la direzione di Giuseppe Tucci*, 4 vols., Roma: G. Casini [1956–1962], pp. 905–924.

Entry «Buddhismo», in *Enciclopedia Universale dell'Arte*, Roma, III, pp. 1–41.

Entry «Demoniche, figurazioni: Giappone», in *Enciclopedia Universale dell'Arte*, Roma, IV, pp. 273–274.

Introduction to Domenico Faccenna and Giorgio Gullini, *Reports on the campaigns 1956-1958 in Swāt (Pakistan)*, Roma: Libreria dello Stato, 1962, pp. vii-xiii.

News of books in *East and West*, XIII, pp. 59–60, 61–65, 66–67, 72–73, 80–81, 363–365, 368–373, 390, 395–397, 399–401.

1963

La via dello Svat, Bari: Leonardo da Vinci, 1963 (Piccolo orizzonte) (repr. Roma: Newton Compton editori, 1978).

«The tombs of the Asvakayana-Assakenoi», in *East and West*, XIV, pp. 27–28.

«Oriental notes, I: The Tibetan 'White-sun-moon' and cognate deities», in *East and West*, XIV, pp. 133–145.

«Oriental notes, II: An image of Devi discovered in Swāt and some connected problems», in *East and West*, XIV, pp. 146–182.

Preface to Centro studi e scavi archeologici in Asia (Istituto Italiano per il Medio ed Estremo Oriente), *Mostra delle sculture buddiste dello Swāt. Sculture rinvenute a Mingora dalla missione archeologica in Pakistan del Centro scavi dell'Ismeo e di Torino, assegnate agli enti torinesi e da questi donate al Museo civico. Torino, Galleria civica d'arte moderna, aprile-maggio 1963*, [Torino, 1963].*

Introduction to Leonida Macciotta and Tullia Gasparrini Leporace, *Usi e costumi dell'India dalla «Storia del Mogol» di Nicolò Manucci veneziano*, Milano: Dalmine, 1964, pp. 11–27.

News of books in *East and West*, XIV, pp. 95–97, 105, 107–108, 119–121, 242–244, 248–258, 273–277, 280–283.

1964

«In the footsteps of Alexander and the land of the Assakenoi; excavations in faraway Swat, Northern Pakistan», in *Illustrated London News*, vol. 244, pp. 856–861.

Preface to Giovanni Pugliese Carratelli and Giovanni Garbini, *A bilingual Graeco-Aramaic edict by Aśoka: the First rst Greek inscription discovered in Afghanistan / Text, translation and notes by G. Pugliese Carratelli and G. Garbini. Foreword by G. Tucci. Introd. by U. Scerrato*, Roma: Istituto Italiano per il Medio ed Estremo Oriente (Serie Orientale Roma, XXIX), 1964, pp. ix-xi.

1965

«The creative individual», in Jawaharlal Nehru Souvenir Volumes
    Committee (India), *The emerging world: Jawaharlal Nehru memo-
    rial volume*, Bombay: Asia Publishing House, pp. 248-252.
Entry «Tibetane, Scuole», in *Enciclopedia Universale dell'Arte*, XIII,
    pp. 889-906.

1966

«Explorations récentes dans le Swat», in *Muséon*, LXXIX, pp.
    42-58.
Review of Giorgio Gullini, *Architettura iranica dagli Achemenidi ai
    Sasanidi*, in *East and West*, XVI, pp. 143-147.
«Lettera aperta», in *Rivista degli Studi Orientali*, XLI, fasc. 1, p. 93.*
News of books in *East and West*, XVI, pp. 153, 162, 174-175.

1967

Tibet, paese delle nevi, Novara: Istituto Geografico De Agostini,
    1967.
*Tibet, Land of Snows. Photogr. by Wim Swaan, Edwin Smith and oth-
    ers. Transl. by J. E. Stapleton Driver*, London: Elek Books, 1967
    (English ed. of the previous title).
*Tibet, pays des neiges: par Giuseppe Tucci. Texte francais de Robert
    Latour. Photos de Wim Swaan, Edwin Smith et autres*, Paris: Albin
    Michel, 1967 (French ed. of the previous title).
Il trono di diamante, Bari: De Donato, 1967.
Preface to Paolo Daffinà, *L'immigrazione dei Sakā nella Drangiana*,
    Roma: Istituto Italiano per il Medio ed Estremo Oriente, 1967
    (Istituto Italiano per il Medio ed Estremo Oriente. Centro
    studi e scavi archeologici in Asia. Reports and memoirs, 9),
    pp- xi-xii.
Notizie di libri in *East and West*, XVII, pp. 135-136, 141, 155-156,
    164, 168-169.

1968

«Oriental notes, III: A peculiar image from Gandhāra», in *East and West*, XVIII, pp. 289–292.

«Oriental notes, IV: The syncretistic image of Mazar-i-Sharif», in *East and West*, XVIII, pp. 293–294.

News of books in *East and West*, XVIII, pp. 209–212, 220–223, 228–232, 235–236, 248–252.

1969

Rati-līlā: an interpretation of Tantric imagery of the temples of Nepal, Geneva: Nagel, 1969.

Rati-līlā: Essai d'interprétation des représentations tantriques des temples du Népal, Genève: Nagel, 1969 (French ed. of the previous title).

Rati-līlā: Studie über die erotischen Darstellungen in der nepalesischen Kunst, Genf: Nagel, 1969 (German ed. of the previous title).

«Nomina Numina», in Joseph M. Kitagawa and Charles H. Long, *Myths and Symbols: Studies in Honour of Mircea Eliade*, Chicago: Univ. of Chicago Pr., <1969>, pp. 3–7.

Speech for the centenary of Gandhi's birth (published posthumously), *Nel Centenario della nascita di Gandhi. Testo italiano e traduzione inglese*, Roma: Istituto Italiano per l'Africa e l'Oriente, 1998 (Conferenze Istituto Italiano per il Medio ed Estremo Oriente, 12).*

Notizie di libri in *East and West*, XIX, pp. 242, 248–251, 256, 260, 268–269.

1970

«Die Religionen Tibets», in Giuseppe Tucci and Walther Heissig, *Die Religionen Tibets und der Mongolei, Stuttgart: W. Kohlhammer*, 1970 (Die Religionen der Menschheit, Bd. 20).

«Les religions du Tibet», in Giuseppe Tucci and Walther Heissig, *Les religions du Tibet et de la Mongolie*, Paris: Payot, 1973 (French ed. of the previous title).

Le religioni del Tibet, Roma: Edizioni Mediterranee, 1976 (revised Italian ed. of the previous title).

The religions of Tibet, London: Routledge and Kegan Paul, 1980 (revised English ed. of the previous title).

«La letteratura del Tibet», in Vittore Pisani and Laxman Prasad Mishra, *Le letterature dell'India*, [Firenze] Sansoni; [Milano] Accademia, 1970, pp. 531–544.

«Oriental notes, V: Preliminary account of an inscription from North-Western Pakistan», in *East and West*, XX, pp. 103–104.

«Commemoration of Ambassador Auriti», in *East and West*, XX, pp. 231–232.

«Le relazioni italo-iraniane», in *Il Veltro*, XIV, febbraio–aprile, pp. 5–8.

Preface (in arabic) to al-Idrīsī, *Opus geographicum; sive, Liber ad eorum delectationem qui terras peragrare studeant. Consilio et auctoritate E. Cerulli [et al.] Una cum aliis ediderunt A. Bombaci [et al.]*, Neapoli: prostat apud E.J. Brill, Lugduni Batavorum, 1970–1984.*

Notizie di libri in *East and West*, XX, pp. 473–474, 485, 487–490, 492, 502, 505–506.

1971

Opera Minora, 2 voll., Roma: G. Bardi, 1971.

Ciro il Grande. Discorso commemorativo tenuto in Campidoglio il 25 maggio 1971, Testo italiano e traduzione inglese, Roma: Istituto Italiano per il Medio ed Estremo Oriente.

«Himalayan Cīna; Padmasambhava in Swāt», in Ariane MacDonald; Rolf Alfred Stein; Centre national de la recherche scientifique (eds.), *Etudes tibétaines dédiées à la mémoire de Marcelle Lalou*, Paris: A. Maisonneuve: Librairie d'Amérique et d'Orient, 1971, pp. 548–552.

«Iran e Tibet», in Accademia nazionale dei Lincei, *Atti del Convegno Internazionale sul tema: La Persia nel Medioevo (Roma, 31 marzo - 5 aprile 1970)*, Roma: Accademia Nazionale dei Lincei (Problemi attuali di scienza e di cultura, quaderno n. 160), pp. 355-360.

«Iran et Tibet», in *Commémoration Cyrus: actes du Congrès de Shiraz 1971 et autres études rédigées à l'occasion du 2500e anniversaire de la fondation de l'Empire perse. Hommage universel*, Téhéran: Bibliothèque Pahlavi; Leiden: diffusion, E. J. Brill, 1974 (Acta Iranica; 1-3.1. sér.; v. 1), pp. 299-305 (French ed. of the previous title).

Giuseppe Tucci with the collaboration of Namkhai Norbu, Jampel Senghe e Chhimed Rigdzin, *Deb t'er dmar po gsar ma. Tibetan chronicles by bSod nams grags pa, vol. I. Tibetan text, emendations to the text, English Translation and an Appendix containing two Minor Chronicles*, Roma: Istituto Italiano per il Medio ed Estremo Oriente, 1971.

Minor Buddhist Texts, III, Roma: Istituto Italiano per il Medio ed Estremo Oriente, 1971 (Serie Orientale Roma, XLIII).

Preface to Gabriele Paresce, *Russia e Cina. Quattro secoli tra guerra e pace. Prefazione di Giuseppe Tucci*, Milano: V. Bompiani, 1971.*

1972

Introduction to Ann Britt Tilia, *Studies and restorations at Persepolis and other sites of Fārs*, Rome: Istituto Italiano per il Medio ed Estremo Oriente, 1972 (Istituto Italiano par il Medio ed Estremo Oriente. Centro studi e scavi archeologici in Asia. Reports and memoirs, v. 16), pp. xi-xiii.

Addressing speech in Maurizio Tosi, *Iran, l'alba della civiltà*, [Milano?]: Provinciali Spotorno [1972], pp. 11-13.

Review of Étienne Lamotte, *Le traité de la grande vertu de sagesse de Nagarjuna avec une nouvelle introduction*, in *East and West*, XXII, pp. 366-367.

Preface to Metamorph and Istituto Italiano per il Medio ed Estremo Oriente, *Italian Architecture in the Sixties*, Roma: S. De Luca, 1972.*

Preface to Blanche Christine Olschak with the collaboration of geshe Thupten Wangyal, *Mystik und Kunst Alttibets. In Zusammenarbeit mit Geshé Thupten Wangyal*, Bern; Stuttgart: Hallwag, 1972.*

Preface to the English edition of the previous text, published with the title of *Mystic art of ancient Tibet*, New York: McGraw-Hill [1973].*

Preface to Gina Labriola, *Istanti d'amore ibernato*, Bari: G. Laterza, 1972.*

News of books in *East and West*, XXII, pp. 338–345, 348–349, 365–366, 367–369, 372–373.

1973

Tibet, Genève: Nagel, 1973 (Archaeologia Mundi).

The ancient civilization of Transhimalaya, London: Barrie and Jenkins, 1973 (English ed. of the previous title).

Tibet, Genf: Nagel, 1973 (Archaeologia Mundi) (German ed. of the previous title).

Tibet, Ginevra: Nagel, 1975 (Archaeologia Mundi) (Italian ed. of the previous title).

Xizang kaogu, edited by G. Degi, Lhasa: Xizang renmin, 2004 (Chinese ed. of the previous title).*

«Archaeologia Mundi, Tibet – Author's Note», in *East and West*, XXIII, p. 371.*

«Sir Aurel Stein», in *East and West*, XXIII, pp. 11–12.

Introduction to Giuseppe Tucci; Alessandro Bausani; Corrado Pensa; Lionello Lanciotti; Adolfo Tamburello, *Uomo e società nelle religioni asiatiche*, Roma: Ubaldini Editore, 1973 (Civiltà dell'Oriente), pp. 7–14.

Preface to Marco Dezzi Bardeschi (ed.), *Italian Architecture 1965-70. Second Itinerant Triennial Exhibition of Contemporary Italian Architecture. Promoted by IsMEO, Istituto italiano per il Medio ed Estremo Oriente*, Firenze: Arti grafiche Giorgi & Gambi, 1973.*

1974

Introduction to Rosa Maria Cimino and Fabio Scialpi, *India and Italy, Catalogo della Mostra*, Roma: Istituto Italiano per il Medio ed Estremo Oriente, 1974, pp. ix-xiii.

Introduction to Bianca Maria Alfieri [et al.], *Armi e armature asiatiche*, Milano: Bramante, [1974] (Arte e tecnica).*

«L'"incompiuta" divinità Khmer di Ca' Pesaro», in *L'Illustrazione italiana*, Autunno 1974, pp. 4-5.*

1975

«Afghanistan, da Alessandro a Daud», in *Storia Illustrata*, 206, gennaio, pp. 68-79.

Enciclopedia archeologica, ed. by Jean Marcadé, Roma; Ginevra: Nagel, [1975]. Italian translation edited by Giuseppe Tucci.*

1976

Entry «Buddhismo», in *Enciclopedia del Novecento*, I, Roma: Istituto dell'Enciclopedia Italiana, pp. 557-574.

Preface to Brijendra Nath, *Iconography of Sadāśiva*, New Delhi: Abhinav Publications, 1976, pp. ix-x.

Preface to Calambur Sivaramamurti, *Śatarudrīya: Vibhūti of Śiva's iconography*, New Delhi: Abhinav Publications, 1976.*

1977

«On Swāt. The Dards and connected problems», in *East and West*, XXVII, pp. 9-85, 94-103.

Addressing speech in Piero Basaglia et al., *La città bruciata del deserto salato [= The burnt city in the salt desert]*, Mestre / Venezia: Erizzo, 1977, pp. 9–17 (English translation, pp. 17–22).

«New Areas of Research for Archaeologists and Buddhologists», in *Journal of the International Association of Buddhist Studies*, I, pp. 71–74.

1978

Premio Jawaharlal Nehru per la Comprensione Internazionale. Ringraziamento di G. T. in occasione della cerimonia per il conferimento del Premio che ha avuto luogo all'Istituto Accademico di Roma il 3 ottobre 1978, Roma: Istituto Italiano per il Medio ed Estremo Oriente, 1978.

Preface to Ann Britt Tilia, *Studies and restorations at Persepolis and other sites of Fārs, Part 2*, Rome: Istituto Italiano per il Medio ed Estremo Oriente (Istituto Italiano per il Medio ed Estremo Oriente. Centro studi e scavi archeologici in Asia. Reports and memoirs, v. 18), pp. xi-xii.

«E Ganga scese dal cielo...», in *Il Gange*, Novara: Istituto Geografico De Agostini, pp. 6–8.

1979

Presentazione su Giorgio Monaco (a cura di), *Medicina tibetana*, Mestre / Venezia: Erizzo, 1979 (Studi e documenti, 2), pp. 9–17.

1980

Chapters «Cerimonies and festivals» (pp. 299–301) and «Prospects for the future» (pp. 312–313) of the entry «The Buddha and Buddhism», in *The New Encyclopaedia Britannica*, 15th ed., vol. 3, pp. 374–403.

Preface to Puspa Niyogi, *Buddhism in ancient Bengal*, Calcutta: Jijnasa: distributors, Best Books, 1980, pp. vii-viii.

Preface to *Studi e restauri di architettura. Italia-Iran*, Roma: Istituto italiano per il Medio ed Estremo Oriente, Centro Restauri: Istituto italiano di cultura di Teheran, 1980, pp. vii-viii.

1981

Preface to Giuseppe M. Toscano (ed.), *Opere tibetane di Ippolito Desideri / 1, Il T'o-raṅs = L'aurora*, Roma: Istituto Italiano per il Medio ed Estremo Oriente, pp. 7–9.

Review of Maria Teresa Lucidi, *Riflessioni sulla natura e funzioni di alcune proposizioni del pensiero cinese, per lo studio della concezione spaziale*; Maria Teresa Lucidi, *La fisionomia dell'urbanizzazione e dei suoi modelli, nella Cina antica*, in *East and West*, XXXI, pp. 148–150.

1982

Preface to *Italian Archaeological Mission (Istituto Italiano per il Medio ed Estremo Oriente). Pakistan, Swāt, 1956-1981*, Catalog of the documentary exhibition, Roma, pp. xi-xii.

1983

Premessa a Maurizio Tosi (a cura di), *Prehistoric Sistan, I*, Rome: Istituto Italiano per il Medio ed Estremo Oriente (Reports and Memoirs, XIX), pp. xi-xii.

BIBLIOGRAPHY

This is a selected bibliography including only the main works quoted and consulted in the previous chapters. A selected bibliography of all the works quoted in *Il Duce's Explorer: The Adventures of Giuseppe Tucci and Italian Policy in the Orient from Mussolini to Andreotti: With the Correspondence of Giulio Andreotti* will be published in volume 9.

Bibliographic Abbreviations

ACS Archivio Centrale dello Stato (Central Archives of the State), Rome

AP Serie affari politici (Ministry of Foreign Affairs, Historic-Diplomatic Archive, Series Political Affairs), Rome

ASMAE Archivio Storico-diplomatico del Ministero degli Affari Esteri (Historic-Diplomatic Archive of the Ministry of Foreign Affairs), Rome

FGG Fondazione Giovanni Gentile (Giovanni Gentile Foundation, Villa Mirafiori, Faculty of Philosophy of the Sapienza University of Rome), Rome

MPI Ministero della Pubblica Istruzione (Ministry of Public Education), Rome

Archival Documents

ACS, MPI, Direzione Generale Istruzione Superiore, Div. I-III, b. 48, 1929–1945, fasc. Formichi Carlo.

ACS, Segreteria Particolare del Duce, Carteggio ordinario 1922–43, «Reale Accademia d'Italia», Relazione della R. Accademia d'Italia (1940).

ASMAE, AP, India, folder 1 (1931–1932), misc. 1927–1931, fasc. 5, Rabindranath Tagore.

British intelligence on China in Tibet, 1903–1950 [microform]: [formerly classified British intelligence and policy files], Leiden: IDC, 2002. It includes 576 microfiches accompanied by a printed guide containing the following information for each file: fiche number, subject description (or bibliographical details for print items), covering dates, OIOC reference number, original India Office registry reference, and number of folios/page (Contents: CIT-1. From Younghusband to the revolution, 1903 — CIT-2. Revolution in China, 1911 — CIT-3. Simla Conference and the 1914 Convention, 1912 — CIT-4. Internal affairs and boundaries, 1912 — 5. Travellers and entry control, 1905 — CIT-6. Trade, 1904 — CIT-7. Education for modernisation, 1912 — CIT-8. 14th Dalai Lama, World War II and Communist China, 1933. Title from printed guide includes 303 intelligence files on China in Tibet (43,200 pages) collected at the India Office in London during the first half of the twentieth century (1903–1950). Collection illustrates how the three players on the British side (the government of India, the India Office, and the Foreign Office) grappled with different imperatives. It also deals with the diplomatic friction and outright competition between the three main powers in the area (Russia, Britain, and China). Contains details for the history of what is generally referred to as "The Great Game")

FGG, Corrispondenza (Terzi a Gentile), fasc. G. Tucci.

FGG, Corrispondenza (Terzi a Gentile), fasc. M. Carelli.

FGG, Enti vari, s.d. – 1944.

Letters, Correspondence, and Diaries (in chronological order)

Letter by Carlo Formichi to the President of the University of Pisa, December 1902.

Letter by Carlo Formichi to the Minister of Public Education, December 18, 1902.

Letter by Carlo Formichi to the Minister of Public Education, June 27, 1904.

Letter by Carlo Formichi to Uberto Pestalozza, February 12, 1910.

Correspondence Giuseppe Tucci – Giovanni Gentile (1916–1944).

Letter by Carlo Formichi to Pietro Fedele, October 3, 1925.

Letter by Benito Mussolini to Rabindranath Tagore, October 21, 1925.

Letter by Rabindranath Tagore to Benito Mussolini, November 21, 1930.

Letter by Carlo Formichi to Hem Raj Sharma, December 8, 1933 (in Sanskrit).

Correspondence Mario Carelli – Adriana Capocci di Belmonte (c. 1938–1940).

Fondo Silvana de Luca (private).

Yearbooks, Atlases, Dictionaries, Encyclopedias

Ansaldo, Giovanni e Marcello Staglieno, *Dizionario degli italiani illustri e meschini dal 1870 a oggi*, Milano: Longanesi, 1980 (Il Cammeo, 7).

Archivio biografico italiano sino al 2001 [microform], a cura di Tommaso Nappo, München: K. G. Saur, [c2002?–2005].

Chi è? Dizionario degli italiani d'oggi, Roma: A. F. Formiggini, 1928; 2nd ed.; Roma: A. F. Formiggini, 1931; 3rd ed., Roma: A. F. Formiggini, 1936; 4th ed., Roma: Cenacolo, 1940; 7th ed., Roma: Filippo Scarano editore [1961].

Enciclopedia del Novecento, Roma: Istituto della enciclopedia italiana, c1975–c2004.

Enciclopedia italiana di Scienze, Lettere ed Arti, 36 vols., [Roma]: Istituto Giovanni Treccani, 1929–1939.

Enciclopedia Universale dell'Arte, Venezia, Roma: Istituto per la Collaborazione Culturale, [1958–67].

«Italy under Fascism», in *Encyclopaedia of the Social Sciences*, Editor-in Chief Edwin R. A. Seligman, Associate Editor, Alvin Johnson, 15 vols., New York: The Macmillan company, c1930-, vol. 1, pp. 277–279.

The New Encyclopaedia Britannica, 32 Vols., 15th ed. Chicago: Encyclopædia Britannica, c1980.

Congresses and Newspapers Articles

1898-1998: Julius Evola: Un pensiero di fine millennio, November 27–28, 1998, Congress Center "Le Stelline", Milano (sponsored and patronized by the Department of Culture of the Lombardy region, the Julius Evola Foundation in Rome, and the publisher Edizioni Mediterranee).

Anonymous, article on the new teaching of Italian culture at the University of California, Berkeley, in *L'Italia*, San Francisco, October 6, 1928.

Carelli, Mario, articles on *Casa dei Fasci* and on the *Corporazioni*, s.n. [c. 1938–40].

Cardelli, Claudio, «Ritrovato il dizionario italo-tibetano di Padre Orazio. Era in una cassa polverosa a Calcutta», in *Il Resto del Carlino*, 2 gennaio 1999.

Cavallera, Hervé A., «Giuseppe Tucci: l'uomo che visitò la terra degli dei», in *Problemi Pedagocici e Didattici*, n. 8, 2014, pp. 31–33.

Chanakya (pseud. of Jawaharlal Nehru), «The Rashtrapati», in *The Modern Review*, October 5, 1937.

Chitarin, Federico, «Le imprese di Giuseppe Tucci, l'Indiana Jones di Mussolini», in *Memori Mese*, 24 ottobre 2012.[1]

Dar, A. N., «A Love Affair with India», in *Indian Express*, April 13, 1984 (unnumbered pages).

Garzilli, Enrica, «Giuseppe Tucci: l'Indiana Jones italiano», in *L'Illustrazione italiana*, anno 3, numero 1, pp. 84–86.

Gualdana, Claudia, «Tibet ultima frontiera: i viaggi di un pioniere. Una monumentale biografia in due volumi ricostruisce imprese, studi ed eredità del maggiore orientalista del 900», in *Libero*, 27 ottobre 2012, p. 3.

Restelli, Marco, «Una leggenda italiana. In un libro, le gesta di un esploratore dell'Oriente riscoperto ai giorni nostri», in *Yoga Journal*, giugno–luglio 2013, pp. 41–42.

Interviews (in chronological order)

Garzilli, Enrica, interviews with Pio Filippani-Ronconi, Milan, November 27–28, 1998, personal archive.

Garzilli, Enrica, oral and email interviews with Prakash A. Raj, Kathmandu, January 20-February 25, 1999, and February 2000-January 2007, personal archive.

Garzilli, Enrica, interviews with Kesari Raj Pandey, Kathmandu, January 20-February 25, 1999, and February 1–15, 2000, personal archive.

Garzilli, Enrica, interviews with Kiran Pandey, Kathmandu, January 20-February 25, 1999, personal archive.

Garzilli, Enrica, interviews with Paolo Daffinà, Rome, May 1999–January 2002, personal archive.

Garzilli, Enrica, video interview with Fosco Maraini, Florence, May 23, 2003, personal archive.

Garzilli, Enrica, phone interview with Fosco Maraini, June 2003, personal archive.

Garzilli, Enrica, interview with Pio Filippani-Ronconi, Rome, October 2003, personal archive.

Garzilli, Enrica, interview (recorded) with Gilda Tucci, Rome, December 13, 2009, and December 11, 2010, personal archive.

Sources, Scientific Articles, Monographies, Translations, Films, Photos, Websites

American League for Peace and Democracy, The *Fascist Road to Ruin*, pamphlet, New York: American League for Peace and Democracy [c. 1935].

American League for Peace and Democracy and Seldes, George, *Young People Against War and Fascism*, pamphlet, New York: American League for Peace and Democracy [c. 1935].

Āryaśūra, *Jātakamālā*, I. Critical edition in *The Jātaka-mālā; or, Bodhisattvāvadāna-mālā, by Ārya-Çūra; ed. by Dr. Hendrik Kern*, Boston: Published for Harvard University by Ginn, 1891 (Harvard Oriental Series; 1)

Amorosino, Vito, *Tra giungle e pagode*, Roma: Istituto Italiano per il Medio ed Estremo Oriente, 1954 (film).

Andreotti, Giulio, *Un gesuita in Cina (1552-1610): Matteo Ricci dall'Italia a Pechino*, Milano: Rizzoli, 2001.

Asiatica Association Onlus.[2]

Barocelli, Piero; Boccassino, Renato; Carelli Mario (eds.), *Il Regio museo preistorico-etnografico "Luigi Pigorini" di Roma; [a cura di] Piero Barocelli, Renato Boccassino [e] Mario Carelli*, Roma: Libreria dello Stato, [1937].

Bartoli, Daniello, *Dell'huomo di lettere difeso et emendato: parti due / del P. Daniello Bartoli*, Roma: per gli Heredi di Francesco Corbelletti, 1645.

Belloni-Filippi, Ferdinando, *I maggiori sistemi filosofici indiani*, Milano: Sandron, [1914].

Cardini, Franco, «Introduzione», in *La pittura sacra del Tibet*, 2 vols., Rimini: Il Cerchio, 2015, vol. 1, pp. 13–16.

Carelli, Mario, articles on the Fascist municipal building, Casa dei Fasci, and on the Corporazioni (s.n.).

Carelli, Mario, «Esplorazioni tibetane», in *Asiatica*, III, 1 (1937), a detailed presentation of Giuseppe Tucci, *Santi e Briganti nel Tibet ignoto*, Milano: Hoepli, 1937.

Carelli, Mario E. (ed.), *Sekoddeśaṭīkā of Naḍapāda (Nāropā): being a commentary of the Sekoddeśa Section of the Kālacakra tantra. The Sanskrit text edited for the first time with an introduction in English by Mario E. Carelli*, Baroda Oriental Institute, 1941 (Gaekwad's Oriental Series, 90).

Carelli, Mario E. (tr.), *To Lhasa and beyond; diary of the expedition to Tibet in the year MCMXLVIII by Giuseppe Tucci. With an appendix on Tibetan medicine and hygiene, by Regolo Moise* [Translated by Mario Carelli], [Roma] Istituto poligrafico dello Stato [1956].

Cavallera, Hervé A. (ed.), *Politica e cultura. Opere complete di Giovanni Gentile*, ed. by the Fondazione Giovanni Gentile per gli studi filosofici, Firenze: Le Lettere, 1990–1991.

Chandra, Lokesh (ed.), *Indo-Tibetica. English*, [By Giuseppe Tucci; edited by Lokesh Chandra], 7 vols., New Delhi: Aditya Prakashan, 1988- (Śata-piṭaka series; v. 347-353).

Conze, Edward, *The Memoirs of a Modern Gnostic. Part II: Politics, People and Places*, Sherborne, England: The Samizdat Publishing Company, [c. 1979-].

D'Elia, Pasquale M., S.I., *Fonti Ricciane: documenti originali concernenti Matteo Ricci e la storia delle prime relazioni tra l'Europa e la Cina (1579-1615) editi e commentati da Pasquale M. D'Elia; sotto il patrocinio della Reale Accademia d'Italia*, 3 vols., Roma: Libreria dello Stato, 1942–1949.

De Felice, Renzo, *Il fascismo e l'Oriente. Arabi, ebrei e indiani nella politica di Mussolini*, Bologna: Il Mulino, 1988.

De Felice, Renzo, «L'india nella strategia politica di Mussolini», in *Storia Contemporanea*, XVIII, 6, 1987, pp. 1309–1363.

De Rossi Filibeck, Elena, *Catalogue of the Tucci Tibetan Fund in the Library of IsMEO*, vol. I, Roma: Istituto Italiano per il Medio ed Estremo Oriente, 1994; vol. II, Roma: Istituto Italiano per l'Africa e l'Oriente, 2003.

Del Ponte, Renato, *Evola e il magico "Gruppo di Ur". Studi e documenti per servire alla storia di "Ur-Krur"*, Borzano: Sear Edizioni, 1994 (Il Cinabro),

Evans-Wentz, Walter Yeeling, *The Tibetan book of the great liber-ation: Or, The Method of Realizing Nirvāṇa through Knowing the Mind: Preceded by an Epitome of Padma-Sambhava's Biography / [by YesheyTshogyal] and Followed by Guru Phadampa Sangay's Teachings, According to English Renderings by Sardar Bahādur S. W. Laden La and by the Lāmas Karma Sumdhon Paul, Lobzang Mingyur Dorje, and Kazi Dawa-Samdup; Introductions, Annotations and Edit-ing by W. Y. Evans-Wentz, with Psychological Commentary by C. G. Jung*, New York: Oxford University Press, 1954.

Filippani-Ronconi, Pio, «La formulazione liturgica della dottrina del Bodhicitta nel capitolo 2 del Guhyasamājatantra», *in Annali dell'Istituto Universitario Orientale di Napoli, XXXII (nuova serie XXII)*, 1972.

Flora, Giuseppe, «Tagore and Italy: Facing History and Politics», in *University of Toronto Quarterly*, Vol. 77, No. 4, Fall 2008, pp. 1025–1057.

Formichi, Carlo, *Apologia del Buddhismo*, Roma: Formiggini edi-tore, 1923.

Formichi, Carlo, *Aśvaghoṣa poeta del Buddhismo*, Bari: Editore Laterza e Figli, 1912.

Formichi, Carlo, *Il Nepal. Conferenza tenuta all' «Augusteo» di Roma il 26 febbraio 1934-XII*, Roma: Reale Accademia d'Italia, 1934-XII (Conferenze).

Formichi, Carlo, «Il simbolismo nella Vita Nuova e nel Can-zoniere di Dante Alighieri», in *Italica, The Quarterly Bulletin of the American Association of Teachers of Italian*, V, December (1928).

Formichi, Carlo, *Il tarlo delle università italiane*, Pisa: Tipografia editrice F. Mariotti, 1908.

Formichi, Carlo, *India e Indiani*, Milano: Edizioni Alpes, 1929.

Formichi, Carlo, *India: pensiero e azione*, ed. by G. Tucci and A. Ballini, Milano: Fratelli Bocca Editori, 1944 (Biblioteca di scienze moderne, n. 135),

Formichi, Carlo, *Kālidāsa: La stirpe di Raghu. Gl'Immortali*, Milano: Istituto Editoriale Italiano, 1917.

Garzilli, Enrica, «A Sanskrit Letter Written by Sylvain Lévi in 1923 to Hemarāja Śarmā Along With Some Hitherto Unknown Biographical Notes (Cultural Nationalism and Internationalism in the First Half of the 21st Cent.: Famous Indologists Write to the Raj Guru of Nepal — no. 1)», in *Commemorative Volume for 30 Years of the Nepal-German Manuscript Preservation Project, Journal of the Nepal Research Centre*, vol. 12 (Kathmandu, 2001), ed. by A. Wezler et al., pp. 115–149.

Garzilli, Enrica, «A Sanskrit Letter Written by Sylvain Lévi in 1924 to Hemarāja Śarmā (Cultural Nationalism and Internationalism in the First Half of the 20th Century: Famous Indologists Write to the Raj Guru of Nepal - no. 2)», in K. Karttunen (ed.), *History of Indological Literature*, Delhi: Motilal Banarsidass, (Papers of the 12th World Sanskrit Conference 11-2), pp. 17–52.

Garzilli, Enrica, «A Sanskrit Letter Written by Carlo Formichi in 1933 to Hemarāja Śarmā along with Hitherto Unkown Biographical Notes (Cultural Nationalism and Internationalism in the First Half of the 20th Century: Famous Indologists Write to the Raj Guru of Nepal no. 3)» (under editorial revision).

Garzilli, Enrica, «First Greek and Latin Documents on Sahagamana and Some Connected Problems», part 1, in *Indo-Iranian Journal*, vol. 40, no. 3 (July 1997); part 2, in *Indo-Iranian Journal*, vol. 40, no. 4 (November 1997).

Garzilli, Enrica, *Il Duce's Explorer. The Adventures of Giuseppe Tucci*, English blog.[3]

Garzilli, Enrica, *L'esploratore del Duce. Le avventure di Giuseppe Tucci e la politica italiana in Oriente da Mussolini a Andreotti. Con il carteggio di Giulio Andreotti*, 2. Vols., 1st ed. Milano: Asiatica; Roma: Memori, 2012, pp. 479–512 (2nd ed. 2012; 3rd ed. Milano: Asiatica, 2014).

Garzilli, Enrica, *L'esploratore del Duce. Le avventure di Giuseppe Tucci*, Italian blog.[4]

Garzilli, Enrica, «Strage a palazzo, movimento dei Maoisti e crisi di governabilità in Nepal», in *Asia Major 2002: l'Asia prima e dopo l'11 settembre*, in C. Molteni, F. Montessoro, M. Torri (eds.), Bologna: Il Mulino, 2003 (Centro Studi per i Popoli Extraeuropei Cesare Bonacossa - Università di Pavia), pp. 143–160.

Garzilli, Enrica, «Un grande maceratese che andò lontano: Giuseppe Tucci, le Marche e l'Oriente / A Great Citizen of Macerata Who Went Far: Giuseppe Tucci, Marche, and the East», in *Identità sibillina: Arte cultura e ambiente tra Marche e Umbria*, n. 2, Novembre 2006, pp. 32–41.[5]

Gentile, Giovanni, «L'Italia e l'Oriente», in *Nuova Antologia*, 72, fasc.1564, 16 maggio 1937, pp. 146–157; reprinted in Hervé A. Cavallera (ed.), *Politica e cultura, Opere complete di Giovanni Gentile*, edited by the Fondazione Giovanni Gentile per gli Studi filosofici, vol. XLVI, Firenze: Le Lettere, 1990–1991.

Ghersi, Eugenio, *Il Nepal. La spedizione di Carlo Formichi in Nepal per conto della Reale Accademia d'Italia*, Roma: Istituto Luce, 1933 (film).

Ghersi, Eugenio, *Nel Tibet occidentale*, Roma: Istituto Luce, 1933 (film).

Gnoli, Gherardo, and Lanciotti, Lionello (eds.), *Orientalia. Iosephi Tucci Memoriae Dicata*, 3 vols., Roma: Istituto Italiano per il Medio ed Estremo Oriente, 1985–1988 (Serie Orientale Roma, LVI), vol. 1 (1985).

Gnoli, Raniero, «La Scuola di Studi Orientali», in *Le grandi scuole della Facoltà*, Roma: Università degli Studi "La Sapienza" - Facoltà di Lettere e Filosofia, 1994.[6]

Gnoli, Raniero (ed.), *Testi buddhisti in sanscrito*, Torino: Unione tipografico-editrice torinese, 1983 (Classici delle religioni, Sezione prima, Le religioni orientali; 42).

Gnoli, Raniero, *Ricordo di Giuseppe Tucci. Con contributi di Luciano Petech, Fabio Scialpi, Giovanna Galluppi Vallauri*, Roma: Istituto Italiano per il Medio ed Estremo Oriente, 1985 (Serie Orientale Roma, LV).

Hakl, Hans Thomas, «L'esploratore del Duce. Le avventure di Giuseppe Tucci e la politica italiana in Oriente da Mussolini a Andreotti. Con il carteggio di Giulio Andreotti», review, in *Gnostika*, Mai 2013, pp. 26-28.

Han, Suyin (pseud. of Rosalie Elizabeth Kuanghu Chow), *The Mountain is Young*, New York: Putnam [1958].

Jung, Carl Gustav, *Erinnerungen, Träume, Gedanken. Aufgezeichnet und hrsg. von Aniela Jaffé*, Zürich [etc.]: Rascher Verlag, 1962.

Kerbaker, Michele, *Il Mahābhārata: tradotto in ottava rima nei suoi principali episodi, a cura di C. Formichi e V. Pisani*, Roma: Reale Accademia d'Italia, 1933 (Collezione Varia, 2).

Kipling, Rudyard, *The Jungle Book. By Rudyard Kipling; with illustrations by J. L. Kipling, W. H. Drake, and P. Frenzeny*, London; New York: Macmillan & Co., 1894.

Kishlansky Mark A. (ed.), *Sources of World History: Readings for World Civilization*, 2 Vols., New York: HarperCollins College Publishers, 1995.

Kundu, Kalyan, «Mussolini and Tagore», in K. Kundu, *Parabaas*, May 7, 2009.[7]

Kuppuswami Sastri, S., *A primer of Indian logic according to Annambhaṭṭa's Tarkasaṁgraha*, Madras: P. Varadachary & Co., 1932.

Mele, Pietro Francesco, *Tibet proibito*, Italia, 1949 (film).

Laufer, Berthold, *Das Citralakshaṇa nach dem tibetischen Tanjur / hrsg. und übers. von Berthold Laufer. Mit einer subvention der Königlich bayerischen akademie der wissenschaften aus der Hardystiftung*, Leipzig: O. Harrassowitz, 1913 (Dokumente der indischen Kunst, 1. hft. Malerei).

Maraini, Fosco, *Segreto Tibet. Presentazione di Bernardo Berenson. 60 tavole fuori testo da fotografie dell'autore*, Bari: Edizioni Leonardo da Vinci, 1951.

Massone, Consolata, *Epistolario Uberto Pestalozza (1872-1966)*, 2000 (typed Index).

Nāḍapāda or Nāropā, *Paramārthasaṁgrahanāmasekoddeśaṭīkā* (transl. by Gnoli, Raniero and Orofino, Giacomella, *Iniziazione:*

Kālacakra, Milano: Adelphi, 1994; a critical edition of the Tibetan translations by G. Orofino, *Sekoddeśa: a critical edition of the Tibetan translations, with an appendix by Raniero Gnoli on the Sanskrit Text*, Roma: Istituto Italiano per il Medio ed Estremo Oriente, 1994 (Serie Orientale Roma, LXXII).

Naḍapāda or Nāropā, *Sekoddeśaṭīkā* (ed. by Carelli, Mario E., *Sekoddeśaṭīkā of Naḍapāda (Nāropā): being a commentary of the Sekoddeśa Section of the Kālacakra tantra. The Sanskrit text edited for the first time with an introduction in English by Mario E. Carelli*, Baroda Oriental Institute, 1941 (Gaekwad's Oriental Series, 90).

Nehru, Jawaharlal, *Selected Works of Jawaharlal Nehru*: [Advisory board: M. Chalapathi Rau, H. Y. Sharada Prasad, and B. R. Nanda; general editor: S. Gopal,] 10 Vols., Series One, New Delhi: Orient Longman, 1972-.

Petech, Luciano, and Scialpi, Fabio, «Bibliografia degli scritti», in R. Gnoli, *Ricordo di Giuseppe Tucci. Con contributi di Luciano Petech, Fabio Scialpi, Giovanna Galluppi Vallauri*, Roma: Istituto Italiano per il Medio ed Estremo Oriente, 1985 (Serie Orientale Roma, LV), pp. 56–79.

Petech, Luciano, and Scialpi, Fabio, «The Works of Giuseppe Tucci (1894–1984)», in *East and West*, XXXIV, 1–3 (1984), pp. 23–42.

Porru, Giulia, *Studi d'indianistica in Italia dal 1911 al 1938*, Firenze: Felice Le Monnier editore, 1940.

Renouvin, Pierre, *Histoire des relations internationales*, 8 vols., Paris: Hachette, 1953–1958.

Said, Edward W., *Orientalism*, New York: Pantheon Books, 1978.

Sistema Statistico Nazionale / Istituto Nazionale di Statistica, *Il valore della moneta in Italia dal 1861 al 2004, Informazioni*, n. 24, 2005.

Sferra, Francesco, «Sanskrit Manuscripts and Photos of Sanskrit Manuscripts in Giuseppe Tucci's Collection. A Preliminary Report», in *Studia Indologiczne*, VII, 2000.

Sferra, Francesco (ed.), *Sanskrit Texts from Giuseppe Tucci's Collection. Part I*, Roma: Istituto Italiano per l'Africa e l'Oriente, 2008 (Manuscripta Buddhica. 1).

Tacchi Venturi, Pietro, *Opere storiche del P. Matteo Ricci, S. I.; edite a cura del Comitato per le onoranze nazionali, con prolegomeni, note e tavole dal P. Pietro Tacchi Venturi*, Macerata: Premiato stab. tip. F. Giorgetti, 1911–1913.

Taddei, Maurizio, «Giuseppe Tucci (1984–1894)», in *Annali dell'Istituto Universitario Orientale di Napoli*, vol. 44 (1984).

Tagore, Rabindranath; Dutta, Krishna; Robinson, Andrew, *Selected Letters of Rabindranath Tagore*, Cambridge: Cambridge UP, 1997.

Tagore, Rabindranath, *All'Italia*, 1925.

Tagore, Rabindranath, «23. Farewell Address to Carlo Formichi», in *The English writings of Rabindranath Tagore / edited by Sisir Kumar Das*, vol. 2, New Delhi: Sahitya Akademi, 1996, p. 770.

Tagore, Rabindranath, *Ghare-bāire*. Engl. ed., *The home and the world / Rabindranath Tagore; translated by Surendranath Tagore; introduction by Anita Desai*, Harmondsworth, Middlesex, England: Penguin; New York, N.Y., U.S.A.: Viking Penguin, 1985.

Tagore, Rabindranath, *The English writings of Rabindranath Tagore / edited by Sisir Kumar Das*, 4 Vols., New Delhi: Sahitya Akademi, 1994-.

Tucci, Giuseppe, Istituto Universitario Orientale, *Gururājamañjarikā: studi in onore di Giuseppe Tucci*, Napoli: Istituto Universitario Orientale, 1974 (Istituto Universitario Orientale, Seminario di Studi asiatici, Series minor, 1).

Von Staël-Holstein, Freiherr A. (ed.), *Kien-ch'ui-fan-tsan: (Gandīstotragāthā)*, St. Petersburg: Imperatorskaja Akademija Nauk, 1913.

Wilson, Epiphanius, *Sacred books of the East; including selections from the Vedic hymns, Zend-Avesta, Dhammapada, Upanishads, the Koran, and the life of Buddha; with critical and biographical sketches by Epiphanius Wilson*, rev. ed., New York: Colonial Press, 1900.

Repr. in Mark A. Kishlansky (ed.), *Sources of World History*, Volume I, New York: HarperCollins College Publishers, 1995, pp. 67–71.

NOTES

Preface to the English Edition

1. http://giuseppetucciexplorer.com/

Introduction

1. De Felice's paper was published in *Storia Contemporanea*, XVIII, 6, 1987, pp. 1309–1363. This is likely the first Italian essay on the topic. It was republished as part of the volume of Renzo De Felice, *Il fascismo e l'Oriente. Arabi, ebrei e indiani nella politica di Mussolini*, Bologna: Il Mulino, 1988. De Felice talks of Mussolini's deep-rooted interest in India (his «radici profonde») at p. 187. Pierre Renouvin speaks many times of the "deep-seated forces" that sway the history of international relations in his masterful work *Histoire des relations internationales*, 8 vols., Paris: Hachette, 1953–1958.

2. Carlo Formichi, *Il Nepal. Conferenza tenuta all' «Augusteo» di Roma il 26 febbraio 1934-XII*, Roma: Reale Accademia d'Italia, 1934-XII, p. 5.

3. Giuseppe Tucci, «Note ed appunti di viaggio nel Nepal», in *Bollettino della Società Geografica Italiana*, vol. VIII, n. 7, luglio 1931, p. 515.

4. Giuseppe Tucci, *Tra giungle e pagode. Le grandi civiltà imalaiane nella sacra terra del Buddha*, Roma: Newton Compton editori, 1979 (1st ed. Roma: Libreria dello Stato, 1953), p. 12.

5. Luciano Petech and Fabio Scialpi, «Bibliografia degli scritti», in R. Gnoli, *Ricordo di Giuseppe Tucci. Con contributi di Luciano Petech, Fabio Scialpi, Giovanna Galluppi Vallauri*, Roma: Istituto Italiano per il Medio ed Estremo Oriente, 1985 (Serie Orientale Roma, LV), pp. 56–79; cf. Idem, «The Works of Giuseppe Tucci (1894–1984)», in *East and West*, XXXIV, 1–3 (1984), pp. 23–42; Enrica Garzilli, *L'esploratore del Duce. Le avventure di Giuseppe Tucci e la politica italiana in Oriente da Mussolini a Andreotti. Con il carteggio di Giulio Andreotti*, 2. Vols., 1st ed. Milano: Asiatica; Roma: Memori, 2012, pp. 479–512 (2nd ed. 2012; 3rd ed. Milano: Asiatica, 2014).

6. Enrica Garzilli, «A Sanskrit Letter Written by Sylvain Lévi in 1923 to Hemarāja Śarmā Along With Some Hitherto Unknown Biographical Notes (Cultural Nationalism and Internationalism in the First Half of the 21st Cent.:

Famous Indologists Write to the Raj Guru of Nepal — no. 1)», in *Commemorative Volume for 30 Years of the Nepal-German Manuscript Preservation Project, Journal of the Nepal Research Centre*, vol. 12 (Kathmandu, 2001), ed. by A. Wezler et al., pp. 115-149. A second paper on the topic, «A Sanskrit Letter Written by Sylvain Lévi in 1924 to Hemarāja Śarmā (Cultural Nationalism and Internationalism in the First Half of the 20th Century: Famous Indologists Write to the Raj Guru of Nepal - no. 2)», in K. Karttunen (ed.), *History of Indological Literature*, Delhi: Motilal Banarsidass, (Papers of the 12th World Sanskrit Conference 11-2), pp. 17-52.

7. Maurizio Taddei, «Giuseppe Tucci (1984-1894)», in *Annali dell'Istituto Universitario Orientale di Napoli*, vol. 44 (1984), p. 700.

8. Eugenio Ghersi, *Nel Tibet occidentale*, Roma: Istituto Luce, 1933; Idem, *Il Nepal. La spedizione di Carlo Formichi in Nepal per conto della Reale Accademia d'Italia*, Roma: Istituto Luce, 1933; Pietro Francesco Mele, *Tibet proibito*, Italia, 1949; Vito Amorosino, *Tra giungle e pagode*, Roma: Istituto Italiano per il Medio ed Estremo Oriente, 1954.

Acknowledgements

1. Asiatica Association Onlus: http://asiatica.org/.
2. *L'esploratore del Duce. Le avventure di Giuseppe Tucci*: http://esploratoredelduce.it/.

Note on the Text

1. https://www.globalfinancialdata.com/index.html.

Chapter I

1. Introduction by Lionello Lanciotti to the volume by G. Gnoli and L. Lanciotti (eds.), *Orientalia. Iosephi Tucci Memoriae Dicata*, 3 vols., Roma: Istituto Italiano per il Medio ed Estremo Oriente, 1985-1988 (Serie Orientale Roma, LVI), vol. 1 (1985), p. XI.
2. Giulio Andreotti, *Un gesuita in Cina (1552-1610): Matteo Ricci dall'Italia a Pechino*, Milano: Rizzoli, 2001.
3. Claudio Cardelli, «Ritrovato il dizionario italo-tibetano di Padre Orazio. Era in una cassa polverosa a Calcutta», in *Il Resto del Carlino*, 2 gennaio 1999.
4. The two quotes are taken from Pasquale M. D'Elia, S.I., *Fonti Ricciane: documenti originali concernenti Matteo Ricci e la storia delle prime relazioni tra l'Europa e la Cina (1579-1615) editi e commentati da Pasquale M. D'Elia; sotto il patrocinio della*

Reale Accademia d'Italia, 3 vols., Roma: Libreria dello Stato, 1942–1949, 3 vols., Roma: Libreria dello Stato, 1942–1949, vol. 1, n. 171, pp. 110 ff.

5. Giuseppe Tucci, «Inscriptiones in agro Maceratensi nuper repertae neque iam vulgatae», in *Mitteilungen des Deutschen Archäologischen Instituts, Römische Abteilung*, XXVI (1911).

6. Giuseppe Tucci, «Ricerche sul nome personale romano nel Piceno», in *Atti e Memorie della Regia Deputazione di Storia Patria per le Marche*, n.s., VII (1911–12).

7. Edward Conze, *The Memoirs of a Modern Gnostic. Part II: Politics, People and Places*, Sherborne, England: The Samizdat Publishing Company, [c. 1979-], p. 48.

8. Giuseppe Tucci, «Le Marche e l'Oriente», in *Rivista d'Ancona*, II, (1959), p. 5.

9. Cit. in Enrica Garzilli, «Un grande maceratese che andò lontano: Giuseppe Tucci, le Marche e l'Oriente / A Great Citizen of Macerata Who Went Far: Giuseppe Tucci, Marche, and the East», in *Identità sibillina: Arte cultura e ambiente tra Marche e Umbria*, n. 2, Novembre 2006, p. 36.

10. Giuseppe Tucci and C. Mariotti, *Iscrizioni medievali ascolane*, Ascoli Piceno: s.n., 1922.

11. Giovanni Gentile, «L'Italia e l'Oriente», in *Nuova Antologia*, 72, fasc. 1564, 16 maggio 1937, pp. 146–157; reprinted in Hervé A. Cavallera (ed.), *Politica e cultura. Opere complete di Giovanni Gentile*, edited by the Fondazione Giovanni Gentile per gli Studi filosofici, vol. XLVI, Firenze: Le Lettere, 1990–1991, p. 433.

12. Giuseppe Tucci, «Totemismo ed esogamia», in *Rivista Italiana di Sociologia*, XVII (1912); Idem, «Note sull'Asia preistorica», in *Rivista di antropologia*, XIX (1914); Idem, «Osservazioni su Fargard II del Vendidad», in *Giornale della Società Asiatica Italiana*, XXVI (1914); Idem, «Nota sul rito di seppellimento degli antichi persiani», in *Rivista di Antropologia*, XIX (1914).

13. Giuseppe Tucci, «Il Tao e il Wu-wei di Lao-tzu», in *Coenobium*, VIII, fasc. 10; Idem, «Dispute filosofiche nella Cina antica», in *Rivista Italiana di Sociologia*, XIX.

14. In *Rivista di Filosofia*, VII.

15. Pietro Tacchi Venturi, *Opere storiche del P. Matteo Ricci, S. I.; edite a cura del Comitato per le onoranze nazionali, con prolegomeni, note e tavole dal P. Pietro Tacchi Venturi*, Macerata: Premiato stab. tip. F. Giorgetti, 1911–1913. Tucci's review was published in *Atti e Memorie della R. Deputazione di Storia Patria per le Marche*, n.s., X.

16. Both published in *Rivista Italiana di Sociologia*, XX. Ferdinando Belloni-Filippi, *I maggiori sistemi filosofici indiani*, Milano: Sandron, [1914].

17. Giuseppe Tucci, «Note cinesi, I (I: Come Sse-ma Ts'ien concepì la storia; II: Han-fei-tzu e le sue critiche al confucianesimo)», in *Giornale della Società Asiatica Italiana*, XXVIII (1916–17); Idem, review of F. A. von Staël-Holstein,

«Gaṇḍīstotragāthā» in *Giornale della Società Asiatica Italiana*, XXVIII (1916–17); Idem, «Aspirazioni di pace e necessità di guerra nell'Estremo Oriente», in *La rassegna Nazionale*, XXXIX, fasc. 2 (1917). The book by Alexander Freiherr von Staël-Holstein (ed.), *Kien-ch'ui-fan-tsan: (Gaṇḍīstotragāthā)*, St. Petersburg: Imperatorskaja Akademija Nauk, 1913.

18. *Indo-Tibetica* I, 1932; II, 1933; III (2 vols.), 1935 e 1936; IV (3 vols.), 1941. After Tucci's death it was republished in English by Lokesh Chandra et al. In 2009 it was republished in Chinese by IsIAO and Shangai Classics Publishing House.

19. Giuseppe Tucci, *Tibetan Painted Scrolls*, 2 vols. and 1 portfolio of 256 plates, Roma: Libreria dello Stato, 1949.

20. Giuseppe Tucci, *Teoria e pratica del Mandala, con particolare riguardo alla moderna psicologia del profondo*, Roma: Astrolabio, 1949 (Psiche e coscienza, collana di testi e documenti per lo studio della psicologia del profondo); 2nd ed., Roma: Ubaldini, 1969. In 1949 the book was translated into French, English, and Portuguese.

21. Giuseppe Tucci, *Il libro tibetano dei morti*, Milano: Fratelli Bocca, 1949. The 2nd rev. and enl. ed., including plates and illustrations, was published in Turin by Utet in 1972.

22. Carl Gustav Jung, *Erinnerungen, Träume, Gedanken. Aufgezeichnet und hrsg. von Aniela Jaffé*, Zürich [etc.]: Rascher Verlag, 1962.

23. Walter Yeeling Evans-Wentz, *The Tibetan book of the great liberation: Or, The Method of Realizing Nirvāṇa through Knowing the Mind: Preceded by an Epitome of Padma-Sambhava's Biography / [by YesheyTshogyal] and Followed by Guru Phadampa Sangay's Teachings, According to English Renderings by Sardar Bahādur S. W. Laden La and by the Lāmas Karma Sumdhon Paul, Lobzang Mingyur Dorje, and Kazi Dawa-Samdup; Introductions, Annotations and Editing by W. Y. Evans-Wentz, with Psychological Commentary by C. G. Jung*, New York: Oxford University Press, 1954.

24. Carlo Formichi, *Apologia del Buddhismo*, Roma: Formiggini editore, 1923.

25. The first article was published in *East and West*, XXVII, the second in the inaugural issue of the *Journal of the International Association of Buddhist Studies*.

26. *The New Encyclopaedia Britannica*, 15th ed., vol. 3. Tucci wrote the chapters «Cerimonies and festivals» (pp. 299–301) e «Prospects for the future» (pp. 312–313). I do not know with certainty the names of all the other scholars, since in this edition the list of contributors to the entry is lacking.

27. Luciano Petech and Fabio Scialpi, «Bibliografia degli scritti», in R. Gnoli, *Ricordo di Giuseppe Tucci. Con contributi di Luciano Petech, Fabio Scialpi, Giovanna Galluppi Vallauri*, Roma: Istituto Italiano per il Medio ed Estremo Oriente, 1985 (Serie Orientale Roma, LV), pp. 56–79.

28. Edward W. Said, *Orientalism*, New York: Pantheon Books, 1978.

29. Epiphanius Wilson, *Sacred books of the East; including selections from the Vedic hymns, Zend-Avesta, Dhammapada, Upanishads, the Koran, and the life of Buddha; with critical and biographical sketches by Epiphanius Wilson*, rev. ed., New York: Colonial Press, 1900. Repr. in Mark A. Kishlansky (ed.), *Sources of World History: Readings for World Civilization*, Volume I, New York: HarperCollins College Publishers, 1995, pp. 67–71.

30. In *Indian Express*, April 13, 1984 (unnumbered pages).

31. Carlo Formichi, *India e Indiani*, Milano: Edizioni Alpes, 1929, passim.

32. Giuseppe Tucci, *Tra giungle e pagode. Le grandi civiltà imalaiane nella sacra terra del Buddha*, Roma: Newton Compton editori, 1979, pp. 155–156 (1st ed., Roma: Libreria dello Stato, 1953).

33. Giuseppe Tucci, «La spedizione Tucci nel Tibet Occidentale», in *L'Illustrazione Italiana*, LXI, 3–4, 1934, p. 84.

34. Venerable U. Lokanatha Thera (Salvatore Cioffi, 1897–1966), of the World's Buddhist Mission in Myanmar, was an Italian monk naturalized US citizen, living most of his life in Myanmar. He was very famous in Thailand, Sri Lanka, and Myanmar.

35. Raniero Gnoli, *Ricordo di Giuseppe Tucci. Con contributi di Luciano Petech, Fabio Scialpi, Giovanna Galluppi Vallauri*, Roma: Istituto Italiano per il Medio ed Estremo Oriente, 1985 (Serie Orientale Roma, LV), p. 10.

36. Giuseppe Tucci, Istituto Universitario Orientale, *Gururājamañjarikā: studi in onore di Giuseppe Tucci*, Napoli: Istituto Universitario Orientale, 1974 (Istituto Universitario Orientale, Seminario di Studi asiatici, Series minor, 1).

37. Raniero Gnoli, *Ricordo di Giuseppe Tucci*, cit., p. 10.

38. Giuseppe Tucci, *La via dello Swat. Una civiltà di grandi confluenze, un'arte dal fascino segreto nel cuore dell'Asia*, Roma: Newton Compton editori, 1978 (1st ed., *La via dello Svat*, Bari: Leonardo da Vinci, 1963 – Piccolo orizzonte), pp. 17–18.

39. Giuseppe Tucci, «Alessandro Csoma De Körös», in *Acta Philosophica Universitas Francisco-Josephina, Kolozsvár*, I (1942) (rep. in *Opera Minora*), pp. 3–4.

40. In Raniero Gnoli, *Ricordo di Giuseppe Tucci. Con contributi di Luciano Petech, Fabio Scialpi, Giovanna Galluppi Vallauri*, cit., pp. 12–13.

41. Carlo Formichi, *Il tarlo delle università italiane*, Pisa: Tipografia editrice F. Mariotti, 1908.

42. I took inspiration from the poetic version of the tale, often quoted in Buddhist sources, told by Āryaśūra, *Jātakamālā*, I. Critical edition in *The Jātakamālā; or, Bodhisattvāvadāna-mālā, by Ārya-Çūra; ed. by Dr. Hendrik Kern*, Boston: Published for Harvard University by Ginn, 1891 (Harvard Oriental Series; 1), pp. 1–6.

43. Giuseppe Tucci, «Linee di una storia del materialismo indiano. I», in *Rendiconti della Reale Accademia dei Lincei, Memorie*, serie V, XVII (rep. with review of chapter III in *Opera Minora*); Idem, «Linee di una storia del materialismo indiano. II», in *Rendiconti della [Reale] Accademia dei Lincei, Memorie*, serie VI, II (rep. omitting the Appendix in *Opera Minora*).

44. Giuseppe Tucci, *Pre-Diṅnāga Buddhist Texts on Logic from Chinese Sources*, Baroda Oriental Institute, 1929 (Gaekwad's Oriental Series, 49).

45. In *Journal of the Royal Asiatic Society of Great Britain and Ireland*.

46. Cf. S. Kuppuswami Sastri, *A primer of Indian logic according to Annambhaṭṭa's Tarkasaṁgraha*, Madras: P. Varadachary & Co., 1932.

47. Giuseppe Tucci, «Dei rapporti tra la filosofia greca e l'orientale», in *Giornale Critico della Filosofia Italiana*, I (1920); Idem, «Note cinesi, II (I: Le biografie 2–7 di Sse-ma Ts'ien; II: Kuan Chung)», in *Giornale della Società Asiatica Italiana*, XXIX (1919–1920); Idem, review of Berthold Laufer, *Das Citralakṣaṇa nach dem tibetischen Tanjur / hrsg. und übers. von Berthold Laufer. Mit einer subvention der Königlich bayerischen akademie der wissenschaften aus der Hardy-stiftung* (Leipzig: O. Harrassowitz, 1913 - Dokumente der indischen Kunst, 1. hft. Malerei), in *Rivista degli Studi Orientali*, VIII.

48. Giuseppe Tucci, «A proposito dei rapporti tra cristianesimo e buddhismo», in *Bilychnis*, XV, pp. 332–341. The journal was published in 1912–31 by the Baptist Theological Seminary at Rome.

49. Giuseppe Tucci, *Tibet ignoto. Una spedizione fra santi e briganti nella millenaria terra del Dalai Lama*, Roma: Newton Compton, 1978, p. 145 (1st ed., *Santi e briganti nel Tibet ignoto*, Milano: Hoepli, 1937).

50. Giuseppe Tucci, *La crisi spirituale dell'India moderna. Conferenza: tenuta alla Reale Accademia d'Italia: il 26 Febbraio 1940-XVIII*, Roma: Reale Accademia d'Italia, 1940–XVIII, pp. 12–13.

51. Giuseppe Tucci, *La via dello Swat. Una civiltà di grandi confluenze, un'arte dal fascino segreto nel cuore dell'Asia*, cit., pp. 91–92 (1978 ed., *La via dello Svat*, cit.).

52. As we will see in the following chapters, sometimes Tucci talked of six explorations in Nepal, sometimes of five. In the following chapters, and particularly in chapter 10, I will try to clear up this point.

53. The Tibetan catalogue was published by Elena De Rossi Filibeck, *Catalogue of the Tucci Tibetan Fund in the Library of IsMEO*, vol. I, Roma: Istituto Italiano per il Medio ed Estremo Oriente, 1994, vol. II, Roma: Istituto Italiano per l'Africa e l'Oriente, 2003. A first report of Sanskrit manuscripts was published by Francesco Sferra, «Sanskrit Manuscripts and Photos of Sanskrit Manuscripts in Giuseppe Tucci's Collection. A Preliminary Report», in *Studia Indologiczne*, VII, 2000. A small part of the Sanskrit manuscripts from the Tucci collection has been published, together with their photografic reproduction

and philological studies, in Francesco Sferra (ed.), *Sanskrit Texts from Giuseppe Tucci's Collection. Part I*, Roma: Istituto Italiano per l'Africa e l'Oriente, 2008 (Manuscripta Buddhica. 1).

54. Raniero Gnoli, *Ricordo di Giuseppe Tucci. Con contributi di Luciano Petech, Fabio Scialpi, Giovanna Galluppi Vallauri*, cit., p. 36.

55. Giuseppe Tucci, entry «Tibet» in *Enciclopedia Italiana di scienze, lettere ed arti*, XXXIII (1937).

56. This evaluation and all those given in the book are based on Sistema Statistico Nazionale / Istituto Nazionale di Statistica, *Il valore della moneta in Italia dal 1861 al 2004, Informazioni*, n. 24, 2005.

57. Suyin Han, *The Mountain is Young*, New York: Putnam [1958], p. 144.

58. Cf. Enrica Garzilli, «First Greek and Latin Documents on Sahagamana and Some Connected Problems» part 1, in *Indo-Iranian Journal*, vol. 40, no. 3 (July 1997); part 2, in *Indo-Iranian Journal*, vol. 40, no. 4 (November 1997).

59. See Enrica Garzilli, «A Sanskrit Letter Written by Sylvain Lévi in 1923 to Hemarāja Śarmā Along With Some Hitherto Unknown Biographical Notes (Cultural Nationalism and Internationalism in the First Half of the 21st Cent.: Famous Indologists Write to the Raj Guru of Nepal — no. 1)», *Commemorative Volume for 30 Years of the Nepal-German Manuscript Preservation Project, Journal of the Nepal Research Centre*, vol. 12 (Kathmandu, 2001), ed. by A. Wezler et al., pp. 115–133; idem, «Strage a palazzo, movimento dei Maoisti e crisi di governabilità in Nepal», in C. Molteni, F. Montessoro, M. Torri (eds.), *Asia Major 2002: l'Asia prima e dopo l'11 settembre*, Bologna: Il Mulino, 2003 (Centro Studi per i Popoli Extraeuropei Cesare Bonacossa - Università di Pavia), pp. 143–160.

60. Giuseppe Tucci, *La crisi spirituale dell'India moderna. Conferenza: tenuta alla Reale Accademia d'Italia: il 26 Febbraio 1940–XVIII*, cit., p. 22.

Chapter II

1. Carlo Formichi, *India: pensiero e azione*, ed. by G. Tucci and A. Ballini, Milano: Fratelli Bocca Editori, 1944 (Biblioteca di scienze moderne, n. 135), p. V.

2. Giuseppe Tucci, *Italia e Oriente*, Milano: Garzanti, 1949, p. 256.

3. Carlo Formichi, *Aśvaghoṣa poeta del Buddhismo*, Bari: Editore Laterza e Figli, 1912; Idem, *Kālidāsa: La stirpe di Raghu. Gl'Immortali*, Milano: Istituto Editoriale Italiano, 1917 [footnote by E. Garzilli].

4. Giuseppe Tucci, *Italia e Oriente*, cit., pp. 256–257.

5. ACS, MPI, Direzione Generale Istruzione Superiore, Div. I-III, b. 48, 1929–1945, fasc. Formichi Carlo.

6. Formichi had to support five natural children born to his relationship with Luisa Aloisi, his two sisters, living with him in Rome, and a widowed mother.

7. It was in 1913 not in 1931, as Raniero Gnoli wrote in «La Scuola di Studi Orientali», in *Le grandi scuole della Facoltà*, Roma: Università degli Studi "La Sapienza" - Facoltà di Lettere e Filosofia, 1994 (http://w3.uniroma1.it/oriente/archivio/sc_orientale.htm. Accessed in February 1996, May 1998 and May 2000).

8. ACS, MPI, Direzione Generale Istruzione Superiore, Div. I-III, b. 48, 1929–1945, fasc. Formichi Carlo.

9. ACS, MPI, Direzione Generale Istruzione Superiore, Div. I-III, 1929–1945, b. 48, fasc. Formichi Carlo.

10. Carlo Formichi, *India e Indiani*, Milano: Edizioni Alpes, 1929, pp. 118–120. Formichi mentions Tucci on a number of occasions in this book, though only briefly.

11. See e.g. Luciano Petech and Fabio Scialpi, «Bibliografia degli scritti», in *R. Gnoli, Ricordo di Giuseppe Tucci. Con contributi di Luciano Petech, Fabio Scialpi, Giovanna Galluppi Vallauri*, Roma: Istituto Italiano per il Medio ed Estremo Oriente, 1985 (Serie Orientale Roma, LV), p. 45.

12. It should be the 1916 novel *Ghare-bāire*, translated into English as *The Home and the World*. I thank Mario Prayer for this information. See Rabindranath Tagore, *Ghare-bāire*. Engl. ed., *The home and the world / Rabindranath Tagore; translated by Surendranath Tagore; introduction by Anita Desai*, Harmondsworth, Middlesex, England: Penguin; New York, N.Y., U.S.A.: Viking Penguin, 1985.

13. Carlo Formichi, *India e Indiani*, cit., p. 163.

14. Ivi, p. 199.

15. Giuseppe Tucci, «La religiosità dell'India», in *Nuova Antologia*, vol. 339 (1928), p. 204.

16. Giuseppe Tucci, «A Sketch of Indian Materialism», in *Acts of the First Indian Philosophical Congress*, Calcutta, 1925.

17. Carlo Formichi, *India e Indiani*, cit., p. 183.

18. See *British intelligence on China in Tibet, 1903–1950* [microform]: [formerly classified British intelligence and policy files], Leiden: IDC, 2002. Travellers and entry control, 1905-.

19. Giuseppe Tucci, «La spedizione scientifica Tucci nell'India, nel Nepal e nel Tibet», in *L'Illustrazione Italiana*, LVIII, 40, pp. 507–508.

20. Ivi, pp. 509–510.

21. Giuseppe Tucci and Eugenio Ghersi, *Cronaca della Missione scientifica Tucci nel Tibet Occidentale (1933)*, Roma: Reale Accademia d'Italia, 1934, pp. 11–12.

22. Carlo Formichi, *India e Indiani*, cit., pp. 183–184.

23. Ivi, p. 177.

24. Ivi, pp. 194–195.

25. Ivi, pp. 195–196.

26. Rudyard Kipling's tales were published in journals and newspapers in 1893; in 1894 they were published together in the volume *The Jungle Book. By Rudyard Kipling; with illustrations by J. L. Kipling, W. H. Drake, and P. Frenzeny*, London; New York: Macmillan & Co., 1894. *Rikki-tikki-tavi* is the tale of a heroic mongoose, who is able to rid all snakes from the garden of a British family settling in India who has saved its life.

27. Carlo Formichi, *India e Indiani*, cit., p.138.

28. Fosco Maraini, *Segreto Tibet. Presentazione di Bernardo Berenson. 60 tavole fuori testo da fotografie dell'autore*, Bari: Edizioni Leonardo da Vinci, 1951.

29. Carlo Formichi, *India e indiani*, cit., p. 224.

30. Ivi, p. 228.

31. Rabindranath Tagore, «23. Farewell Address to Carlo Formichi», in *The English writings of Rabindranath Tagore / edited by Sisir Kumar Das*, vol. 2, New Delhi: Sahitya Akademi, 1996, p. 770.

32. E.g., on October 5, 1937 Jawaharlal Nehru published in *The Modern Review*, under the pen name of Chanakya, his famous self-criticism titled «The Rashtrapati», where he wrote of himself: «His conceit is already formidable. It must be checked. We want no Caesars» (p. IV). Nehru later appended the following note to this article: "This article was written by Jawaharlal Nehru but It was published anonymously in The Modern Review of Calcutta, November 1937. Rashtrapati is a Sanskrit word meaning Head of the State. The title is popularly used for President of the Indian National Congress. Chanakya was a famous Minister of Chandragupta, who built an empire in north India in the fourth century B.C , soon after Alexander's raid on India Chanakya is the prototype of Machiavelli. (Fn. 1, Copy of Nehru's «Rashtrapati» article, 5 October 1937 reprinted in *Selected Works of Jawaharlal Nehru*: [Advisory board: M. Chalapathi Rau, H. Y. Sharada Prasad, and B. R. Nanda; general editor: S. Gopal] Series One, Volume 8, New Delhi: Orient Longman, 1972, pp. 520–522).

33. Carlo Formichi, *India e indiani*, cit., pp. 241–242.

34. Ivi, pp. 234–235.

35. Ivi, p. 7.

36. Rabindranath Tagore, «23. Farewell Address to Carlo Formichi», cit., pp. 522–523.

37. Carlo Formichi, *India e indiani*, cit., pp. 22–24.

38. Ivi, p. 21.

39. Ivi, p. 29.

40. Ivi, p. 32.

41. Ivi, p. 260. In *Italica, The Quarterly Bulletin of the American Association of Teachers of Italian*, V, December (1928).

42.   ASMAE, AP, India, folder 1 (1931–1932), misc. 1927–1931, fasc. 5, Rabindranath Tagore. Copy of the letter in Giuseppe Flora, «Tagore and Italy: Facing History and Politics», in *University of Toronto Quarterly*, Vol. 77, No. 4, Fall 2008, p. 1046. Cf. Rabindranath Tagore, Krishna Dutta, and Andrew Robinson. *Selected Letters of Rabindranath Tagore*, Cambridge: Cambridge UP, 1997, p. 394. This way is solved the question whether the letter, sent first by Tagore to his son to know his point of view, was received by Mussolini (cf. Kalyan Kundu, «Mussolini and Tagore», in K. Kundu, *Parabaas*, May 7, 2009, http://www.parabaas.com/rabindranath/articles/pKalyan.html. Accessed Sept. 5, 2014).

43.   American League for Peace and Democracy, *The Fascist Road to Ruin*, pamphlet, New York: American League for Peace and Democracy [ca. 1935]; American League for Peace and Democracy and George Seldes, *Young People Against War and Fascism*, pamphlet, New York: American League for Peace and Democracy [ca. 1935].

44.   On Formichi and his stay in Nepal, cf. E. Garzilli, «A Sanskrit Letter Written by Carlo Formichi in 1933 to Hemarāja Śarmā along with Hitherto Unkown Biographical Notes (Cultural Nationalism and Internationalism in the First Half of the 20th Century: Famous Indologists Write to the Raj Guru of Nepal no. 3)», under editorial revision.

45.   Michele Kerbaker, *Il Mahābhārata: tradotto in ottava rima nei suoi principali episodi, a cura di C. Formichi e V. Pisani*, Roma: Reale Accademia d'Italia, 1933 (Collezione Varia, 2).

46.   Carlo Formichi, *Il Nepal. Conferenza tenuta all'«Augusteo» di Roma il 26 febbraio 1934-XII*, Roma: Reale Accademia d'Italia, 1934-XII (Conferenze).

47.   Ivi, p. 5.

48.   Ivi, p. 6.

49.   Ivi, pp. 6–7. Formichi goes on to write that Brian Houghton Hodgson, acting not as an Indologist but as a British resident, sent a collection of Buddhist manuscripts to London in the 1930s. In Formichi's time the collection was still kept in the India Office. Between Nepal, which was not included in the British Raj, and the United Kingdom, the relationship was excellent: only the British legation was present in Kathmandu, and according to Formichi the few Europeans called by the Prime Minister to serve the court as «physicians, engineers, military consultants» were English.

50.   Ivi, p. 8.

51.   Ivi, p. 9. The bungalow belonged to the Rana family, who owned vast estates in the Terai region, along the Indian border, partly rented, and partly used as game preserve.

52.   The Sal tree is the medicinal plant *Couroupita guianensis.*

53. Carlo Formichi, *Il Nepal. Conferenza tenuta all' «Augusteo» di Roma il 26 febbraio 1934-XII*, Roma: Reale Accademia d'Italia, 1934-XII, p. 11.

54. Ivi, p. 11.

55. Ivi, p. 12.

56. Ivi, p. 13.

57. Ivi, p. 31.

58. ACS, Segreteria Particolare del Duce, Carteggio ordinario 1922–43, «Reale Accademia d'Italia», Relazione della R. Accademia d'Italia (1940), p. 4.

59. Carlo Formichi, *India e indiani*, cit., p. 16.

60. Cf. the typed Index by Consolata Massone, *Epistolario Uberto Pestalozza (1872-1966)*, 2000.

61. *1898-1998: Julius Evola: Un pensiero di fine millennio*, November 27–28, 1998, Congress Center "Le Stelline", Milano (sponsored and patronized by the Department of Culture of the Lombardy region, the Julius Evola Foundation in Rome, and the publisher Edizioni Mediterranee).

62. Renato Del Ponte, *Evola e il magico "Gruppo di Ur". Studi e documenti per servire alla storia di "Ur-Krur"*, Borzano: Sear Edizioni, 1994 (Il Cinabro), p. 52.

63. I transcribed the interview and was allowed by Pio Filippani-Ronconi to publish it during our meeting of November 28, 1998.

64. *Paramārthasaṃgrahanāmasekoddeśaṭīkā* of Nāḍapāda, also known as Nāropā, translated by Raniero Gnoli and Giacomella Orofino, *Iniziazione: Kālacakra*, Milano: Adelphi, 1994; a critical edition of the Tibetan translations by G. Orofino, *Sekoddeśa: a critical edition of the Tibetan translations, with an appendix by Raniero Gnoli on the Sanskrit Text*, Roma: Istituto Italiano per il Medio ed Estremo Oriente, 1994 (Serie Orientale Roma, LXXII).

65. Mario E. Carelli (ed.), *Sekoddeśaṭīkā of Naḍapāda (Nāropā): being a commentary of the Sekoddeśa Section of the Kālacakra tantra. The Sanskrit text edited for the first time with an introduction in English by Mario E. Carelli*, Baroda Oriental Institute, 1941 (Gaekwad's Oriental Series, 90). This critical edition has been defined by R. Gnoli «very faulty and with many omissions» (in G. Orofino, *Sekoddeśa: a critical edition of the Tibetan translations, with an appendix by Raniero Gnoli on the Sanskrit Text*, cit., p. 128).

66. Both Tucci and Filippani-Ronconi published on the text: Giuseppe Tucci, «Some glosses upon the Guhyasamāja», in *Mélanges Chinois et Bouddhiques*, III (1935), pp. 338–353 (repr. in *Opera Minora*, pp. 337–348); Pio Filippani-Ronconi, «La formulazione liturgica della dottrina del Bodhicitta nel capitolo 2 del Guhyasamājatantra», *in Annali dell'Istituto Universitario Orientale di Napoli, XXXII (nuova serie XXII)*, 1972. Raniero Gnoli, too, published chapters 1, 2 and 5 of the *Guhyasamājatantra* in *Testi buddhisti in sanscrito*, Torino: Unione tipografico-editrice torinese, 1983 (Classici delle religioni, Sezione prima, Le religioni

orientali; 42).

67.   Piero Barocelli; Renato Boccassino; Mario Carelli (eds.), *Il Regio museo preistorico-etnografico "Luigi Pigorini" di Roma; [a cura di] Piero Barocelli, Renato Boccassino [e] Mario Carelli*, Roma: Libreria dello Stato [1937Mario Carelli, «Esplorazioni tibetane», in *Asiatica*, III, 1 (1937); Giuseppe Tucci, *Santi e Briganti nel Tibet ignoto*, Milano: Hoepli, 1937. Tucci's book is referred to by Giulia Porru in *Studi d'indianistica in Italia dal 1911 al 1938* (Firenze: Felice Le Monnier editore, 1940, p. 218) as *Santi e Briganti nel Tibet inesplorato*.

68.   The documents on Carelli's mission in Bombay in *Corrispondenza (Terzi a Gentile), fasc. M. Carelli*, Fondazione Giovanni Gentile, Villa Mirafiori, Facoltà di Filosofia of the Sapienza University of Rome. See also Correspondence Mario Carelli - Adriana Capocci di Belmonte (Fondo Silvana de Luca).

69.   Letter of March, 3, 1940, Correspondence Mario Carelli - Adriana Capocci di Belmonte (Fondo Silvana de Luca).

70.   Giuseppe Tucci, *A Lhasa e oltre. Diario della spedizione nel Tibet, MCMXLVIII. Con un'appendice sulla medicina e l'igiene nel Tibet*, Roma: Libreria dello Stato, 1950. English translation, *To Lhasa and beyond; diary of the expedition to Tibet in the year MCMXLVIII. With an appendix on Tibetan medicine and hygiene, by R. Moise. [Translated by Mario Carelli]*, Roma: Istituto poligrafico dello Stato, 1956. In a later edition Carelli's name was left out in the title and the XIV Dalai Lama wrote the preface (Ithaca, N.Y. USA: Snow Lion Publications, 1987). 1

Bibliography of Giuseppe Tucci

1.   With the exception of the article «Fame, malattia endemica della Cina» («Hunger, Endemic Illness of China»), in *Epoca*, 21 maggio 1951, pp. 31–34.

2.   Giuseppe Tucci, «L'ateismo del prof. Tucci» («Prof. Tucci's Atheism»). It was followed by an untitled answer of Rospigliosi, in *Il Tempo*, 8 ottobre 1973, p. 3 (column *Copialettere*).

Bibliography

1.   http://goo.gl/dz4WOU accessed on May 20, 2015.

2.   http://asiatica.org/

3.   http://giuseppetucciexplorer.com/

4.   http://esploratoredelduce.it/

5.   Also online at http://www.identitasibillina.com/rivista_n2/ ita/8.html. Accessed on May 19, 2015.

6.   http://w3.uniroma1.it/oriente/archivio/sc_orientale.htm. Accessed in February 1996, May 1998 and May 2000.

7. http://www.parabaas.com/rabindranath/articles/pKalyan.html. Accessed Sept. 5, 2014.

THE TRANSLATOR

Todd Portnowitz (1986) was born in Melbourne, FL and lives and works in New York City. He is translator of two novels with the Italian publisher Mondadori, and his poetry translations from and into Italian — including poets Pierluigi Cappello, Emilio Rentocchini, Donald Justice, Amy Clampitt, and W.S. Merwin — have appeared widely in literary reviews and journals.

A poetry editor with the Sheep Meadow Press and co-founder and co-editor of the Italian poetry blog, *Formavera*, he holds a Master's in Italian Literature from the University of Wisconsin-Madison and was a fellow of the 2015 Bread Loaf Translator's Conference.

Figure 38: The Author in front of Tucci's home in Macerata.

THE AUTHOR

Enrica Garzilli is a specialist of Indology and modern Asian studies, editor-in-chief of the *International Journal of Tantric Studies* and the *Journal of South Asia Women Studies*, a former professor at the universities of Delhi, Perugia, Harvard, and Turin, and author of the first official biography of Giuseppe Tucci. She graduated in Sanskrit (Doctor, 110/110) from the University of Rome *La Sapienza* with Raniero Gnoli, Giuseppe Tucci's most beloved pupil, and studied with other of his renowned students as well, including the art historian Mario Bussagli, and the famed Tibetologist Luciano Petech.

In 1989 she published her thesis, *The Spandasaṃdoha of Kṣemarāja*, a critical edition and translation of the 12th-century philosophical text in Sanskrit. Following graduation, she went on to take a post-doc Master in Computer Science for the Humanities at the University of Rome *La Sapienza*, and later received a post-doc Master in History from the University for Foreigners of Perugia. Among her professors were the great historians Giovanni Pugliese Carratelli and Jacques Le Goff. She was also the recipient of a fellowship from the Cultural Exchange Program between the Italian Ministry of Foreign Affairs and the Government of India, as Research Affiliate at the University of Delhi.

During her fifteen-year teaching career, she has been a professor at various Italian and foreign universities, teaching principally Sanskrit, Indian Studies, Hinduism, Buddhism, Zen, History of Indian Law, Human Rights, and the History of Asia. From her initial studies of ancient South Asia—India and Nepal—she has since broadened her geopolitical and temporal horizons to cover contemporary times and countries such as Pakistan, Afghanistan,

Tibet (or what is now the Tibet Autonomous Region or Xizang, a region of the People's Republic of China).

While teaching, she persisted in her studies and was admitted to the Graduate Program at Harvard Law School as a Visiting Researcher (y. 1994–1996), attending courses on International Law and Human Rights. Thanks to her years spent in Asia, she has become increasingly interested in contemporary politics, its institutions and its relations with the West. From 2002 she began researching and publishing on contemporary India, Nepal, Afghanistan and Pakistan. Since 2006 she has been publishing on Asia in leading Italian newspapers and magazines such as *Limes*, *ISPI - Institute for International Policy Studies*, *Il Sole 24 Ore*, and *Il Fatto quotidiano*.

Her curriculum, including a list of publications, can be viewed on her blog *Il Duce's Explorer: The Adventures of Giuseppe Tucci* (http://giuseppetucciexplorer.com/). A number of her books can be viewed on her Amazon Author page (http://www.amazon.com/Enrica-Garzilli/e/B009ACBIWI), along with a few photographs. Follow the adventures of Tucci on Facebook at https://www.facebook.com/pages/Il-Duces-Explorer-The-Adventures-of-Giuseppe-Tucci/1515786141972130, and the author's Twitter feed at @Boh. Email Enrica at: info@asiatica.org.

And last but not least, she is a passionate — yet tentative — gardener.